The Handbook of Global Outsourcing and Offshoring

The Handbook of Global Outsourcing and Offshoring

Second Edition

Ilan Oshri
Professor of Technology and Globalization
Loughborough School of Business and Economics,
Loughborough University, UK

Julia Kotlarsky
Associate Professor, Operations Research and
Information Systems Group, Warwick Business School, UK

Leslie P. Willcocks
Professor of Information Systems,
London School of Economics, UK

First published 2011 by
PALGRAVE MACMILLAN

Palgrave Macmillan in the UK is an imprint of Macmillan Publishers Limited, registered in England, company number 785998, of Houndmills, Basingstoke, Hampshire RG21 6XS.

Palgrave Macmillan in the US is a division of St Martin's Press LLC, 175 Fifth Avenue, New York, NY 10010.

Palgrave Macmillan is the global academic imprint of the above companies and has companies and representatives throughout the world.

Palgrave® and Macmillan® are registered trademarks in the United States, the United Kingdom, Europe and other countries.

ISBN: 978–0–230–29352–6

This book is printed on paper suitable for recycling and made from fully managed and sustained forest sources. Logging, pulping and manufacturing processes are expected to conform to the environmental regulations of the country of origin.

A catalogue record for this book is available from the British Library.

A catalog record for this book is available from the Library of Congress.

10 9 8 7 6 5 4 3 2 1
20 19 18 17 16 15 14 13 12 11

Printed and bound in Great Britain by
CPI Antony Rowe, Chippenham and Eastbourne

CONTENTS

List of Tables

List of Figures

Acknowledgments

We were inspired by the insights and learning we gained from being a part of a group of passionate individuals whom we met in several events, conferences and while doing work together.

One event that in particular inspired us to start working on this book is our annual Global Sourcing Workshop (www.globalsourcing.org.uk). This annual gathering of researchers and practitioners is now in its sixth year and has created a small community that discusses social, technical, and managerial aspects of global sourcing. We have learned a lot from each participant and will ever be grateful to them for sharing with us their experience and research. Special thanks go to Accenture, particularly to Dr. John Hindle, for partially sponsoring some of the workshops.

Another stimulating event has been the NYU-IBM global sourcing workshop organized by Prof. Natalia Levina which we attended in May 2008. One of the tracks was devoted to teaching Global Sourcing. This track helped us think about the outsourcing profession and the future needs of outsourcing professionals.

We thank Drs. Eleni Lioliou, Yingqin Zheng, and Maha Shaikh who helped in various ways to bring this project into conclusion. Our thanks go also to Erran Carmel, David Feeny, Rudy Hirschheim, Evgeny Kaganer, Rajiv Kishore, Onook Oh, Sandra Sieber, and Mark Skilton for contributing case studies to this book.

Our great thanks to colleagues and students at our universities– Rotterdam School of Management, Warwick Business School, and London School of Economics and Political Science. We thank you for your support, insights, and sometimes patience over the years we have undertaken this research. Ilan and Julia thank their children Dari and Eden for quickly falling asleep, giving them a bit of time in the evenings to work on this book. Leslie thanks Damaris for her amused encouragement on this one (what? another book?) and Rosemary O'Hanlon for her priceless description of the first edition as "sobering." He thinks she meant this in the positive sense, but , if not, he has to apologize that there are no more lighter moments in this edition than the last. Last but not least, we thank all the practitioners and academics with whom we have held fascinating discussions about outsourcing and offshoring. The practitioners who have actively supported our research now number in the thousands, and without them our work would have been possible. A massive thanks to you all. Many of them are good friends with whom we hope to continue exploring this topic.

Ilan, Julia and Leslie

Notes on Case Study Contributors

Erran Carmel is a tenured full Professor at the Kogod School of Business, American University, Washington D.C. His area of expertise is globalization of technology work and his 1999 book *Global Software Teams* was a pioneering book on the topic. His second book *Offshoring Information Technology* (2005) is used in many global sourcing courses. He has written over 80 articles, reports, and manuscripts. In 2008–2009 he was the Orkand Chaired Professor at the University of Maryland University College. He has been a Visiting Professor at Haifa University (Israel) and University College Dublin (Ireland).

David Feeny is Professor of Information Management, and Fellow at Templeton-Green College, University of Oxford. He has published widely on CIO and retained capability, strategy, and the management of Information Technology, especially in *Harvard Business Review* and *Sloan Management Review* as well as in many highly ranked IS journals. His current research interests are in the evaluation of executive education and innovation. Previously he was a senior executive for over 20 years at IBM.

Rudy Hirschheim is the Ourso Family Distinguished Professor of Information Systems at Louisiana State University. He was on the faculties of the University of Houston, the London School of Economics (University of London), and Templeton College (University of Oxford). His PhD is in Information Systems from the University of London. He was the founding Editor of the John Wiley Series in Information Systems in 1985. He is Senior Editor for the journal *Information & Organization*, and is on the editorial boards of the following journals: *Information Systems Journal*; *Journal of Strategic Information Systems*; *Journal of Management Information Systems*; *Journal of Information Technology*; *Wirtschaftsinformatik/ Business & Information Systems Engineering*; and *Strategic Outsourcing*.

Evgeny Kaganer is Assistant Professor at IESE Business School where he teaches MBA and executive courses in IT strategy, online business, and Enterprise 2.0. His research focuses on online social technologies and their impact on individuals, organizations, and business models. He has published in the *Journal of the Association for Information Systems*, *European Journal of Information Systems*, and the *Academy of Management Best Papers*

Proceedings. His work has also been featured in international press, including *Financial Times*, *BusinessWeek*, and *CIO Magazine* among others.

Rajiv Kishore is Associate Professor in the School of Management at the State University of New York at Buffalo. His interests are in improving organizational and IT performance through the effective management of global outsourcing projects, new forms of IT outsourcing including crowdsourcing, technology and innovation management, and strategic IT management. His papers have been accepted or published in *MIS Quarterly*, *Journal of Management Information Systems*, *IEEE Transactions on Engineering Management*, *Communications of the ACM*, *Decision Support Systems*, *Information & Management*, among others. Kishore has consulted with a number of large companies, some of which include BellSouth, Blue Cross Blue Shield of Minnesota, IBM, and Pioneer Standard Electronics.

Onook Oh is a doctoral candidate in the School of Management at the State University of New York at Buffalo. His research interests are in the areas of new modalities of information exchange and social media, crowdsourcing, and use of social media in information assurance and extreme events. His papers have been published in leading IS journals. He has also presented papers at ICIS and other international and national conferences.

Sandra Sieber is Associate Professor and Chair of the Information Systems Department at IESE Business School. She is also the Academic Director of the IESE Global Executive MBA. She has done extensive work looking at the impact of information and communication technologies on organizational and individual work practices. Her recent research focuses on the impact of social media and crowdsourcing on organizations. Sieber has published scholarly and general articles in national and international journals, magazines, and newspapers. Her research has also been presented at leading international conferences in the field.

Mark Skilton is Global Director, strategy group, infrastructure services, at Capgemini where his responsibilities include global standards and interoperability. Skilton is currently Co-chair of The Open Group Cloud Computing Work Group and Project Co-chair for Cloud Business Artifacts project. He has spoken internationally on Cloud Computing as part of The Open Group Standards Body in America, India, and Europe and has published papers on the subject of Cloud Computing ROI, monetization strategies and metrics and is an editor of a cloud computing book. He is a graduate of Sheffield University and Cambridge University and holds an MBA from Warwick Business School.

Introduction

In 2010 the market for information technology outsourcing (ITO) world-wide was reported as $270 billion (US dollars are used throughout the book) and for business process outsourcing (BPO), $165 billion. Recent estimates predict that between 2011 and 2014, ITO growth will be 5 to 8 percent per annum and BPO growth will be 8 to 12 percent per annum. In addition, BPO market size worldwide will soon overtake the ITO market. Brazil, Russia, India, and China (BRIC) are considered the inheritors of global-ization, offering both offshore IT and back office services, and with their vast populations and developing economies, they are huge potential markets. However, offshoring and offshore outsourcing are certainly expanding, with, by our count, some 125 centers developing around the world. Therefore, it has become increasingly important to understand the phenomenon, not least as a basis for suggesting what directions it will take, its impacts, how it has been conducted, and how its management can be better facilitated.

These points are particularly pertinent because recent evidence has suggested that a number of offshore outsourcing relationships and off-shoring projects have failed to live up to some of their promises. The rea-sons for this are many, ranging from poor quality delivered by vendors to rising management costs that result in frustration and disappointment. Collaboration between remote sites and the ability to share and transfer knowledge between dispersed teams have also been mentioned as impera-tive to successful offshore outsourcing projects. In addition, our own research highlights certain capabilities that vendors and clients should develop, the governing structures that they need to put in place, and the bonding activities that they need to promote and make time for. Although offshore outsourcing brings its own distinctive issues, it is the case that the principles for running any ITO or BPO venture also apply to offshoring and offshore outsourcing arrangements. However, offshoring is increas-ingly part of most deals of any significant size, so it becomes necessary to see and manage outsourcing within a global context.

The main objectives of this book

This book offers a broad perspective on various issues relating to the sourc-ing of systems and business processes in a national and global context.

Its key objectives are to:

- Assess the impacts of global sourcing on business
- Assess the risks and benefits for firms engaging in sourcing activities
- Devise a plan to outsource a system or a process from a client viewpoint
- Devise a plan to offer services from a vendor viewpoint
- Ensure sustainability over the life cycle of an outsourcing relationship
- Raise awareness to recent developments in the global sourcing arena such as captive strategies and innovation potential

This book therefore examines both the client's and the vendor's involvement in sourcing relationships by emphasizing not only on the capabilities that each side should develop prior to entering a relationship but also the capabilities that they should develop as a result of their interactions with each other.

Key definition: sourcing

The field of sourcing is replete with jargon and acronyms. For example, the term *bestshoring* has become a recent buzzword, widely used by managers but poorly defined by the professional press and academic publications. Even more worrisome is the inaccurate use of the terms *outsourcing* and *offshoring* by both managers and academics. Although these terms and others are defined in Chapter 1, we offer this explanation of *sourcing* from the outset: Sourcing is the act through which work is contracted or delegated to an external or internal entity that could be physically located anywhere. It encompasses various insourcing and outsourcing arrangements such as offshore outsourcing, captive offshoring, nearshoring, and onshoring.

Clearly, almost all firms are engaged in some way in sourcing activities, and each of them has developed a sourcing arrangement that suits its particular needs.

The structure of the book

The book is organized into 11 chapters in three key parts. Chapters 1 through 3 are about *making a sourcing decision*, Chapters 4 to 6 about *building sourcing competencies*, and Chapters 7 to 11 about *managing sourcing relationships.* Some chapters can be read as a stand-alone body of knowledge (e.g., Chapters 1, 10 and 11), while others are more connected with other chapters.

Chapter 1 provides a historical perspective on outsourcing and offshoring, the marketplace, and the incentives for firms from around the globe to tap into sourcing opportunities. Chapter 2 discusses the various types of IT and business processes that could be sourced globally. It also examines the sourcing arrangements available according to the nature of work outsourced. Chapter 3 considers geographical location in sourcing decisions and the factors that both client and supplier companies should consider when deciding on where a particular activity should be located.

Chapter 4, which begins Part II, provides an overview of the vendor's landscape by examining certain vendor characteristics and the vendor's desired core capabilities. Chapter 5 examines the notions of expertise and knowledge in sourcing relationships from both the vendor and client perspectives and discusses issues related to the knowledge transfer process. Chapter 6 considers the vendor selection strategy from a client's viewpoint. This includes the evaluation of vendors, the outsourcing arrangements, the retained organization capabilities, and legal issues.

Chapter 7, opening Part III, considers the outsourcing life cycle and its key activities from a client's perspective. It also provides an overview of key transition issues. Chapter 8 addresses the key challenges that both client and vendor face regarding governance of various outsourcing projects. Chapter 9 focuses on the management of globally distributed teams from a sourcing relationship perspective. Chapter 10 discusses one of the emerging topics in outsourcing: the potential to achieve innovation through outsourcing engagements. Finally, Chapter 11 explores the role that captive centers play in a firm's global sourcing strategy and, consequently, the strategies a firm can pursue regarding its captive center.

PART I

Making a Sourcing Decision

CHAPTER 1

Overview of the global sourcing marketplace

With the advent of globalization and heightened levels of competition, many organizations are having considerable difficulties in developing and maintaining the range of expertise and skills they need to compete effectively. The emergence of American, European, Japanese, and other Asian multinationals has created a competitive environment requiring the globalization, or at least semiglobalization, of corporate strategy. Moreover with developments in information and communication technologies (ICT), firms do not have to be large multinationals to compete globally. These developments have led many companies to turn to various sourcing strategies, such as outsourcing, offshoring, offshore outsourcing, nearshoring, and onshoring. Therefore, this chapter focuses on:

- The key terminologies used in the sourcing literature
- The background of global sourcing
- The key drivers, benefits, and risks of global sourcing
- Market trends and future developments in global sourcing
- Outsourcing in difficult times

Definitions

Sourcing is the act through which work is contracted or delegated to an external or internal entity that could be physically located anywhere. It encompasses various insourcing (keeping work in-house) and outsourcing arrangements such as offshore outsourcing, captive offshoring, nearshoring, and onshoring.

Outsourcing is defined as contracting with a third-party provider for the management and completion of a certain amount of work, for a specified length of time, cost, and level of service.

Offshoring refers to the relocation of organizational activities (e.g., information technology, finance and accounting, back office, human resources) to a wholly owned subsidiary or an independent service provider in another country. This definition illuminates the importance of distinguishing whether the offshored work is performed by the same organization or by a third party. When the work is offshored to a center owned by the organization, we refer to a *captive* model of service delivery. When the work is offshored to an independent third party, we refer to an *offshore outsourcing* model of service delivery. And when organizational activities are relocated to a neighboring country (e.g., US organizations relocating their work to Canada or Mexico), we use the term *nearshoring*.

These definitions include various sourcing models: for example, staff augmentation, domestic and rural sourcing, crowd sourcing, cloud services, microsourcing, bundled services, out-tasking, and shared services (these terms are explained in Chapter 2). In addition, there are various common buzzwords such as *best-sourcing* (or *best-shoring, right-shoring,* and *far-shoring* (as opposed to nearshoring)), usually coined and used by vendor companies. Finally, there is also backsourcing trend, which implies bringing work back in-house.

Global sourcing background

In 2010 the market for information technology outsourcing (ITO) worldwide was reported to be $270 billion and for business process outsourcing (BPO), $165 billion. Recent estimates predict that between 2011 and 2014, ITO growth will be 5 to 8 percent per annum and BPO growth 8 to 12 percent per annum, with the BPO market size worldwide overtaking the ITO market.

In terms of specific functions outsourced, Figure 1.1 depicts the results of surveys of more than 250 chief information officers (CIOs) and chief financial officers (CFOs) in major European companies with regard to the major functions outsourced. Clearly with ITO growing rapidly, IT and IT-enabled business processes remain the most popular candidates for outsourcing. On the basis of the latest survey results (November 2010), among the vast range of services outsourced, IT infrastructure and data management are at the top of the list, being outsourced by 58 percent of companies, followed by IT and technology consultancy, and enterprise resource planning support (53 percent each). Business processes such as finance and administration, human resources, payroll, and many others that in the past were largely moved offshore to captive facilities (Lewin and Peeters, 2006) are increasingly outsourced to third parties. For example, compared to results from early 2009 (Oshri and Kotlarsky, 2009), in late 2010

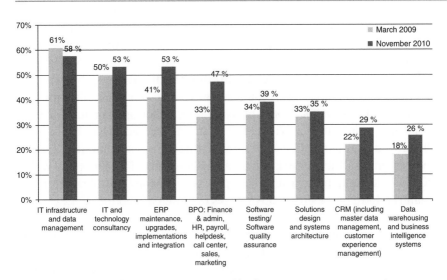

Figure 1.1 Areas of business outsourced by large European companies

Source: Oshri and Kotlarsky (2011)

(Oshri and Kotlarsky, 2011) we observed a significant increase in out-sourcing on BPO (from 33 to 47 percent). However while more knowledge-intensive processes such as customer relationship management (CRM) and business analytics (data warehousing and business intelligence systems) are less popular for outsourcing, there was an increase in outsourcing these processes in late 2010 compared to early 2009.

Offshoring is also growing worldwide. The strategy to offshore appears promising in terms of the reduction of costs as certain organizational activities would be moved to a subsidiary or an independent service provider in a country with favorable conditions. The United States is a major player in the offshoring of IT and business process applications. However, offshoring has appeared to be gaining momentum in Europe and Asia Pacific as well.

Drivers, benefits, and risks of global sourcing

The growth of global sourcing has been attributed to many factors. First, technological advances in the telecommunications industry and the Internet have shrunk space and time and have enabled the coordination of organizational activities at the global level. Other reasons are the supply of skilled yet low-cost labor in countries such as India, and subsequently over

125 further locations; investments in infrastructure; an improved business, economic, and political climate in a number of developing countries; and the standardization of IT processes and communication protocols that contribute to the efficiency of interorganizational activities.

Along these lines, many countries have invested heavily in improving their telecommunications infrastructure, which is essential for electronically transmitted services. For example, Barbados has had a fully digitalized communications system with direct international dialing since the beginning of the 1990s. Jamaica has constructed its Digiport, with a 20,000-telephone-line capacity and speeds of 1.5 Mbps. Furthermore, many countries have provided tax advantages to attract offshoring. For example, Bulgaria offers a 10 percent flat enterprise tax rate that is dropping to 0 percent in areas with high unemployment. In Jamaica, the Digiport BPO free trade zones are tax free. The US tax code also favors offshoring over keeping work domestic. US corporations are allowed to defer taxes on offshore units until the money comes back to the United States. Thus, firms are given an interest-free loan on taxes owed if they offshore their work.

Global sourcing may offer several benefits associated with the advantages of outsourcing in general. Along these lines, a company may reap significant cost advantages through the creation of economies of scale, access to the unique expertise of a third party, and the reduction or stabilization of overhead costs.

Furthermore, a company may benefit from outsourcing by concentrating on core activities, organizational specializations, or focusing on achieving key strategic objectives. More specifically, a strategy of following a core competency through outsourcing may enable a company to focus its resources on a relatively few knowledge-based core competencies where it can develop best-in-the-world capabilities (Quinn and Hilmer, 1994). Concentration on a core business may allow a company to exploit distinctive competencies that will constitute significant competitive tools for it.

Another major benefit of outsourcing is that it can give the organization access to the service provider's capabilities and innovative abilities, which may be expensive or impossible for the company to develop in-house (Quinn and Hilmer, 1994). Some analysts contend that an important source of user value is the firm's access to economies of scale and the unique expertise that a large provider can deliver. Since providers typically have many clients, they often achieve lower unit costs than any single company can (Alexander and Young, 1996).

Even more important, a network of suppliers can provide any organization with the ability to quickly adjust the scale and scope of its production capability upward or downward, at a lower cost, in response to changing demand. In this way, outsourcing can provide greater flexibility (McCarthy and Anagnostou, 2003). Furthermore, outsourcing can decrease the product or process design cycle time if the client uses multiple best-in-class suppliers that work simultaneously on individual components of the system, as each supplier can contribute greater depth and sophisticated knowledge in specialized areas and thus offer higher-quality inputs than any individual supplier or client can (Quinn and Hilmer, 1994). On this basis, having several offshore centers can provide around-the-clock workdays. In other words, development and production can take place constantly by exploiting the time difference between different countries.

Nevertheless, adopting sourcing strategies poses several disadvantages. Loss of critical skills or overdependence on an outside organization for carrying out important business functions may evolve into significant threats to a company's well-being. Furthermore, security and confidentiality of data can be a major issue for many companies. Another concern is losing control over the timing and quality of outputs since these will be undertaken by an outside vendor; the result may be poorer quality of the final product or service, which may sully a company's image.

The following case study illustrates the challenges that companies, such as BSkyB, face when pursuing a sourcing strategy. It highlights the responsibility both client and vendor hold when signing an outsourcing contract and the implications for both parties when things go wrong.

Case Study

BSkyB: THE BUMPY ROAD OF OUTSOURCING

In 1983, Rupert Murdoch purchased Satellite Television (SATV), a company founded in 1981 by Brian Haynes, and renamed it Sky. After years of competition between BSB and Sky, the two companies merged on October 30, 1990, to form BSkyB. By 2007, BSkyB had become the UK's largest independent broadcast operation, supplying a broad range of programs, channels, and services to more than 10 million people around the world.

In 2000, BSkyB was looking for a company that would redesign and implement a new CRM system for it that would be the heart of its business. The system needed to be built around Chordiant Software and run on Sun Microsystems hardware. BSkyB's contact centers in

▶

▶

Livingston and Dunfermline in Scotland would use the new CRM system.

To achieve this objective, BSkyB conducted a competitive tender exercise to find a vendor that would be able to meet its criteria. Several bidders emerged during the tendering process, including PricewaterhouseCoopers and Electronic Data Systems (EDS). In the end, EDS was chosen as the supplier for the CRM system.

EDS was founded in 1962 by H. Ross Perot, a former salesman from IBM who came up with the idea that, besides delivering computer equipment, IBM should also deliver electronic data processing services to its customers. When IBM rejected the idea, Perot resigned and founded his own company: EDS. In 2008, Hewlett-Packard (HP) acquired EDS, which now delivered a broad range of infrastructure technology, applications, and business process outsourcing services. In 2009, EDS changed its name to HP Enterprise Services.

The initial idea was that EDS would provide BSkyB a technically advanced solution that would make a valuable contribution to BSkyB's drive to lead innovation in customer service and maintain Sky Digital's industry-leading levels of customer retention. BSkyB's customers would be able to access account, billing, and other information and services by phone, the Web, or the television service itself.

On November 30, 2000, BSkyB and EDS signed a contract, estimated at a value of £48 million. Due to the uncertainty about the cost of this work, which stemmed from the uncertainty of the amount of work that needed to be done, BSkyB employed EDS on a time-and-materials basis. EDS stated that it would be able to go live in nine months and complete delivery in eighteen months. However, just five months later, in March 2002, BSkyB terminated its relationship with EDS because, according to BSkyB, EDS did not fulfill its contractual obligations. BSkyB switched to in-house development, and the residual work was taken over by BSkyB's subsidiary, Sky Subscribers Services Ltd. (SSSL).

By 2004, BSkyB had invested over £170 million; in addition, its IT department had budgeted £50 million over the next four years to complete the implementation. By March 2006, BSkyB successfully completed the project after spending £265 million.

In 2004, BSkyB initiated legal action against EDS, citing that EDS had not been honest during the competitive tender about its resources, technology, and the methodology it planned to use in order to deliver

▶

▶

the system within the defined time frame and within budget. BSkyB claimed that it would have probably chosen PricewaterhouseCoopers for the work if EDS had not given a false sales pitch in which it over-estimated its capabilities. EDS, for its part, claimed that the most critical element in this project was that BSkyB did not specify the project properly and that it did not know exactly what BSkyB wanted or needed.

In October 2007, the trial started at the High Court in London and was concluded in July 2008. On January 26, 2010, 18 months after the end of the trial, the High Court ruled on the dispute between BSkyB and EDS (now part of HP). It found that EDS had been deceit-ful when it claimed that it had carried out an accurate analysis of the time needed to complete the delivery and go live and that it was able to deliver the system within the agreed-to schedule. According to the court, the CRM manager for EDS had known that it was not possible to finish the project according to schedule and that there had not been an accurate analysis of what needed to be done. In addi-tion, BSkyB proved that EDS had violated the contract. BSkyB was therefore awarded damages up to the liability cap set out in the con-tract. In addition, the court stated that the responsibilities for deceitful misrepresentations that were not described in the contract were not accurately excluded by the same contract.

One major outcome of this trial was that BSkyB was able to prove that EDS had made a deceitful sales pitch, so the liability cap was not applicable. On February 3, 2010, the Technology and Construction Court ordered EDS to pay an interim payment of £200 million of damages by February 17, 2010.

Even more important is the fact that unless the buyer's core compe-tency is a true block to entry into the marketplace, some suppliers, after building up their expertise with the buyer's support, may attempt to bypass the buyer directly in the marketplace (Quinn and Hilmer, 1994). On these grounds, it is critical for companies to manage their sourcing strategy in a way that is not nurturing a future competitor.

Outsourcing arrangements can pose risks. For example, outsourcing is usually followed by changes in organizational structure, with redun-dancies and layoffs. Research and experience indicate that outsourcing effectively signals to employees their employer's intention to initiate a change that may involve deskilling and redundancies (Kakabadse and

Kakabadse, 2000). Such initiatives generate internal fears and employee resistance.

Moreover, as Hendry (1995) highlighted, outsourcing can be associated with problems related to the company's ability to learn because it can increase insecurity among the workforce and decrease its motivation thus reducing employees' willingness to question and experiment. There are fears as well that interactions among skilled people in different functional activities that often lead to unexpected new insights or solutions will become less likely (Quinn and Hilmer, 1994).

With regard to offshore outsourcing, Rottman and Lacity (2006) offered a comprehensive list of risks associated with such ventures. These include different kinds of business, legal, political, workforce, social, and logistical risks (see Table 1.1).

Table 1.1 Offshore outsourcing risks

Risk category	Sample risks
Business	No overall cost savings Poor quality Late deliverables
Legal	Inefficient or ineffective judicial system at offshore locale Intellectual property rights infringement Export restrictions Inflexible labor laws Difficulty obtaining visas Changes in tax laws that could significantly erode savings Inflexible contracts Breach in security or privacy
Political	Backlash from internal IT staff Perceived as unpatriotic Politicians' threats to tax US companies that source offshore Political instability within offshore country Political instability between United States and offshore country
Workforce	Supplier employee turnover Supplier employee burnout Inexperienced supplier employees Poor communication skills of supplier employees
Social	Cultural differences Holiday and religious calendar differences
Logistical	Time zone challenges Managing remote teams Coordination of travel

Source: Adapted from Rottman and Lacity (2006)

A study by Oshri and Kotlarsky (2009) on strategic drivers and risks of offshoring, based on interviews with CIOs and CFOs in 263 major European companies, is particularly revealing. In contrast to the common belief that cost cutting is the key strategic driver for outsourcing (Lewin and Peeters, 2006), the results of this survey show that CIOs and CFOs believe that access to skills not available internally is more important (64 percent). The second driver is a tie between cost reduction and access to innovative processes and practices, both at 41 percent (see Figure 1.2).

Clearly, there is a shift in the way client organizations see the strategic drivers behind outsourcing. CIOs and CFOs are now focusing on the need to access talent and innovative ideas as a source of competitive advantage at the right price. In this regard, vendors with extensive domain knowledge developed through work with multiple client engagements are perceived as knowledge bases of ideas and innovations. Vendors achieve cost advantages through locating some of their support in either nearshore or offshore locations. These results also show that the benefits expected from outsourcing are not the one-off type. Seeking innovation and accessing talent imply that client organizations perceive their vendors as partners in the long-term development of their business strategy through the support and improvement of services and products. In this way, the vendor becomes a true partner in improving the client's competitive advantage through cutting-edge ideas and cost cutting. Another key strategic driver that came out from the interviews is flexibility. CIOs argued that outsourcing has allowed them to quickly scale operations up or down in response to market demand without

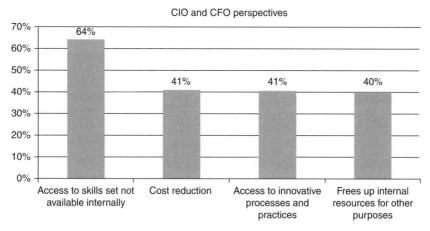

Figure 1.2 Key drivers of outsourcing

Source: Oshri and Kotlarsky (2009)

having to bear the costs involved. This key driver has become critical during global economic downturn as firms need to respond quickly to changes in markets. One CIO stated: "Our vendor is much more able to scale up staff than we do. I would need to think twice before hiring staff. But I can ask my vendor: 'Can you scale up the number staff working for us in the next couple of weeks to 200 because we have a new project?'" That's agility!

Outsourcing in difficult times

As the global economy continues to battle the downturn, CIOs and CFOs are taking some actions to shelter their firms from the storm. CFOs are looking for cost reductions across the board. Also, there are indications that firms are hesitant regarding new outsourcing projects, delaying their decisions to better times, while some CIOs attempt to renegotiate the terms of some of their large-scale ongoing outsourcing projects. One CIO from the survey by Oshri and Kotlarsky (2009) commented: "We would want to increase and improve the delivery of services from outsourcing, but will hold off in the short term"

About 40 percent of the survey respondents (Oshri and Kotlarsky, 2009) indicated that they have pulled work back from outsourcing providers or slowed the growth of outsourcing initiatives. Among those who have pulled work back from outsourcing providers or slowed the growth of outsourcing initiatives (105 respondents), Figure 1.3 shows that the main reasons were unclear value for money (78 percent), high vendor management costs (46 percent), and lack of governance (38 percent). Poor quality

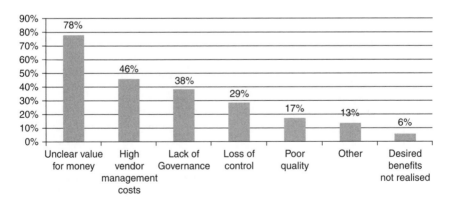

Figure 1.3 Causes of cutback or slowdown of outsourcing

Source: Oshri and Kotlarsky (2009)

(17 percent) was not considered a key factor to backsourcing work or slowing the growth of outsourcing initiatives. Clearly client firms perceive value creation as a critical element in developing long-term relationships with outsourcing partners. To develop such partnerships between vendors and clients, the benefits of outsourcing should be transparent, timely, easy to communicate, and in line with the key success criteria of the business.

The future of outsourcing and offshoring

Willcocks and Lacity (2006, 2009) have identified 12 trends for the future of global sourcing markets:

Trend 1: spending will continue to rise in all global sourcing markets, but BPO will overtake ITO

In 1989, global ITO was only a $9 billion to $12 billion market. In 2007, it was estimated to be between $200 billion and $250 billion (Willcocks and Lacity, 2006). The BPO market in 2007 was much smaller than the ITO market but growing at a faster rate. Global BPO revenues, which were $165 billion in 2010, are likely to rise by 8 to 12 percent annually between 2011 and 2015. BPO expenditures will be in areas such as the human resource function, procurement, back office administration, call centers, legal, finance and accounting, customer-facing operations, and asset management.

BPO is outpacing ITO because many executives recognize that they under-manage their back offices and do not wish to invest in back office innovations. Suppliers are rapidly building capabilities to reap the benefits from improving inefficient processes and functions. IT provides major underpinning for, and payoff from, reformed business processes. Thus, many of the BPO deals will encompass back office IT systems. This is also evidenced by the shift in strategy of traditional IT suppliers such as IBM, HP, and EDS to provide more business process services. Suppliers will increasingly replace clients' disparate back office IT systems with Web-enabled, self-serve portals.

There have been some high-profile backsourcing (i.e., returning services in-house) cases in the past couple of decades: Sears in 1997, the Bank of Scotland in 2002, JPMorgan Chase in 2004, and Sainsbury in 2005, for example. Although these cases have drawn the attention of the media, they have never represented a dominant trend toward backsourcing. Willcocks and Lacity (2009) found that the most common course of action at the end of a contract continues to be contract renewal with the same supplier. They also estimated that a quarter would be retendered and awarded to new suppliers, and only a tenth backsourced. More recently we have seen several backshoring cases when companies (Dell is one of them) brought back in-house the onshore call centers that they had offshored to India, South Africa, and other remote locations.

Trend 2: the ITO and BPO outsourcing markets will continue to grow through multisourcing

Although ITO and BPO spending is increasing, the average size of individual contracts and the duration of contracts is decreasing. For example, the Everest Group found that among the ITO contracts signed in 1998, 24 percent of contracts were worth more than $400 million and 33 percent of contracts were worth between $50 and $100 million. In 2005, only 11 percent of contracts were worth more than $400 million and 57 percent were worth between $50 and $100 million. Concerning contract duration, the Everest Group found that 37 percent of contracts signed in 1998 were more than nine years in duration compared to 18 percent in 2005 (Tisnovsky, 2006). According to a Gartner report from December 2009, in 2009 only six megadeals (contracts with a total reported contract value exceeding $1 billion) were signed, with an average term of seven years, which is lower than the nine-year-average term in 12 megadeals signed in 2008.

All of these figures suggest that client organizations are pursuing multisourcing. In fact, multisourcing has always been the dominant practice, and its overall growth is driven by client organizations that are signing more contracts with more suppliers. Although multisourcing helps clients access the best suppliers and mitigates the risks of relying on a single supplier, it also means increased transaction costs because clients must manage more suppliers. In addition, suppliers themselves incur more transaction costs: they must bid more frequently because their contracts are shorter, they face more competition because smaller deals mean that more suppliers qualify to bid, and they need to attract more customers in order to meet growth targets. (We discuss multisourcing in greater details in Chapter 6.)

Trend 3: Global clients will view India primarily as a destination for excellence rather than a way to lower costs

Many US clients initially engaged Indian suppliers to provide technical services such as programming and platform upgrades. As these relationships matured, US clients assigned more challenging work to Indian suppliers. For example, a US retailer first engaged an Indian supplier to help with Y2K compliance. As the relationship matured, the retailer assigned development and support tasks for critical business applications to the supplier. From this retailer and other satisfied clients we heard: "We went to India for lower costs, but we stayed for quality."

Trend 4: China's investment in ITO and BPO services signals promise, but Western clients will still be wary

China invested \$142.3 billion in ICT in 2006, which it hopes will pay off in terms of its ability to compete globally in the offshore services market. Its long-term ITO and BPO future is expected to be strong (Lacity, Willcocks, and Zheng, 2010). So far, the main ITO or BPO suppliers in China are either large US-based suppliers such as Accenture, Capgemini, Dell, HP, and IBM, or large India-based suppliers such as Genpact, Infosys, and TCS. Like Indian suppliers, many Chinese suppliers do not want to compete solely on low-level technical skills.

Nevertheless, many Western client organizations are wary of China's ITO and BPO services. Language barriers, cultural barriers, and fears over losing intellectual property remain significant obstacles for the executives we talked to in North America and Western Europe. The Chinese government and Chinese business sectors are well aware of these barriers and are seeking ways to address them. For example, the Chinese government is investing \$5 billion in English-language training to target the ITO and BPO markets (Lacity, Willcocks and Zheng, 2010).

Trend 5: developing countries beyond India and China will become important players in the global business and IT services market

Suppliers from six continents will develop centers of excellence. Many US clients already use Central American suppliers for Spanish-speaking business processes such as help desks, patient scheduling, and data entry. Synchronous time zones are another favorable factor for US firms looking to Central or South America for sourcing.

In Western Europe, organizations will increasingly source IT and businesses services to providers located in Eastern Europe. For example, the Visegrad-Four countries (Czech Republic, Hungary, Poland, and Slovakia) offer Western European firms closer proximity, fewer time zone differences, and lower transaction costs than Asian alternatives.

In Africa too, many countries are actively seeking to become players in the global ITO and BPO markets. North Africa already exports IT services to Europe. One interesting study examined five Moroccan IT suppliers that provide services to clients in France (Bruno et al., 2004). The common language, similar time zone, and cultural compatibility make Morocco attractive for French organizations seeking to outsource. South Africa is also exporting IT and BP services, primarily to UK-based clients. South Africa appeals primarily to UK-based clients because of the similar time zone, cultural similarities, English-speaking capabilities, and good infrastructure. Even some sub-Saharan countries are building their future economies on IT (see Willcocks, Griffiths, and Kotlarsky, 2009).

Trend 6: Large companies will give application service provision a second look

Many thought that application service provision (ASP) had died with the dot-com bust. But there are several reasons to believe that large organizations will reconsider the proposition of renting applications software, infrastructure, services, and storage over the Internet. First, large organizations will want Net-native applications (proprietary applications designed and delivered specifically for Internet delivery) that are available only through software as a service (SaaS) delivery (e.g., Salesforce.com). Second, large organizations may finally be ready to abandon their expensive proprietary suites for cheaper SaaS and cloud alternatives. Third, SaaS providers have gotten the message: clients want customized services, even if the products are standardized. The need for customized services actually increases the service providers' viability because they can generate profits by charging for value-added services.

Trend 7: outsourcing will help insourcing

As organizations become smarter at outsourcing, they also become smarter at insourcing. In-house operations are facing tough competition in nearly every area and can no longer assume they will retain their monopoly status with the organization. As a result, in-house operations are adopting the techniques of the market. However, insourcing will be impeded by a supply shortage of talent within developed countries, particularly for IT skills.

The US is not alone in this. Nearly every research report suggests that other developed countries will suffer a shortage of domestic IT workers within the next five to ten years. The shortages in developed countries will be caused by the gap between a strong demand for domestic IT workers and a dwindling supply due to the lingering effects of declining enrolments today and future effects of baby boomers' retiring.

Trend 8: nearshoring will become more prevalent

Compared to offshoring to remote locations, the benefits of nearshoring include lower travel costs, fewer time zone differences, and closer cultural compatibility. Canada, for example, is a significant nearshore destination for US clients. Some analysts argue that US clients can have lower total costs with nearshoring to Canada than with offshoring to India.

The Czech Republic, Poland, and Hungary are significant nearshore destinations for Western Europe. Clients in Western Europe are attracted to Central and Eastern European suppliers for many of the same reasons that the US is attracted to Canadian suppliers: common language, cultural understanding, minimal time zone differences, and low labor costs. However, Central and Eastern Europe may be more attractive for BPO than ITO because these countries provide excellent general education, but do not graduated IT students at near the pace that India has. For that reason, IDC predicts that Western Europe's growth in BPO will increase annually by 14.6 percent compared to 7.2 percent for ITO.

Trend 9: Knowledge process outsourcing will increase

Knowledge process outsourcing (KPO), which is the outsourcing of knowledge-intensive processes such as business, market, and industry research, requires a significant amount of domain knowledge and analytical skills. KPO suppliers design surveys, collect new data, mine existing data, statistically analyze data, and write reports. Although the KPO market was quite small in 2009, industry analysts expected a huge growth in this sector over the next five years. Evalueserve (2007) estimated that the KPO market in 2007 was $3.05 billion and will grow annually by 39 percent. They expected the market to be $16 billion by 2011, employing approximately 350,000 professionals globally.

The increase in KPO is directly related to offshore suppliers' moving up the value chain. As client–supplier relationships mature, suppliers have gained an enormous amount of knowledge about the client's business domain, as well as the expertise to find, analyze, and report on domain knowledge. US, Canadian, and UK clients value this deep knowledge and will pay Indian suppliers $20 to $100 per hour for KPO services compared to onshore rates of $80 to $500 per hour. Offshore suppliers are struggling to find enough workers with advanced degrees to fill the demand. But once they are hired, their turnover will be lower because professionals finally have the client-facing and intellectually challenging work they did not find in programming.

Trend 10: More companies will sell their captive centers or create virtual captive centers

Although it is widely recognized that Western companies are setting up sites offshore, there is an emerging trend that might be called "The GE Effect." General Electric (GE) may not have been the first US footprint in India, but certainly Jack Welch's enthusiasm for India made it acceptable for other CEOs to locate back offices in India. GE established GECIS (GE Capital International Services) as a captive center in India in 1997. In winter 2004, it sold off 60 percent of GECIS to two equity companies, Oak Hill Capital Partners and General Atlantic Partners. A year later, the name was changed to Genpact, and it is now one of the top 10 BPO or ITO suppliers in India. Some have called GE's approach "the virtual captive center" because GE still maintains primary equity holding. With a virtual captive center, the company owns the physical operations, but staff are employed by a third-party supplier. Presumably the virtual captive center offers the best of both worlds: the client investor maintains strategic control while the supplier attracts, develops, and retains local talent.

Among US clients are several examples of organizations selling their captive centers. Beyond the anecdotes, the Black Book of Outsourcing 2007 survey of 18,272 buyers found that selling captive centers may be a significant trend. Respondents from large organizations were more likely than those in midsized businesses to investigate selling. The main reasons for selling captive centers were as follows:

1. The captive center was built to protect data and intellectual property, which is no longer viewed as a threat if provided by a third-party supplier.
2. Senior executives are no longer committed to captive centers.

3. It is no longer necessary to keep decision-making authority in-house.
4. Third parties are now able to handle complex processes.
5. There is a difference between the ITO and BPO captive centers: companies are much more likely to erect a captive center for BPO than ITO.

Trend 11: outsourcing failures and disappointments will continue

Outsourcing will continue to be a high-risk practice with significant hidden costs in organizations where learning is sometimes painfully slow, in deals where suppliers do not make reasonable margins, and when client organizations do not strategize, configure, contract for, monitor, and manage their deals effectively. There will also be suppliers that overpromise and underdeliver.

Extrapolating from past evidence, Willcocks and Lacity (2009) estimated that some 70 percent of selective sourcing deals will be considered relatively successful. Typically clients will be spending between 15 and 58 percent of their operating budgets on outsourcing. In contrast, only 50 percent of large-scale deals involving complex processes that represent more than 80 percent of the operating budgets will be successful. Ironically, the client organizations with the messiest back offices will benefit the most from total outsourcing – if they can successfully manage the outsourcing life cycle.

Trend 12: the global economic downturn will have mixed but deep impacts on these trends

By 2008, many clients were delaying making decisions to commit to new contracts; they were also negotiating lower rates in current contracts, looking for dramatic cost savings in new contracts, seeking to reduce the number of suppliers used, trying to cut down on the use of outsourcing contractors, exploring offshoring destinations for either cheaper captive or outsourced service, examining how to cut the amount of work carried out in existing deals, and negotiating for better and longer-term financing and asset transfer deals as part of their outsourcing arrangements. At the same time, outsourcing is as likely to grow during recession as in a time of economic upturn, even though the terms of trade will be different and the objectives pursued by the client may well have quite different emphases.

In 2007–2008, the global economic downturn deepened, and economic conditions began to pick up only in late 2010. Willcocks, Cullen, and Craig (2011) suggest that it was particularly important not to jettison the learning from the evidence on what works and what does not accumulated over the 20-year history of global outsourcing. Economic conditions and technologies change, but sound management principles tend to be long lasting.

Summary

In this chapter, we explained the key terminology relating to global sourcing and provided an extensive review of past, current, and future trends in global sourcing. It is clear that more and more firms have introduced business solutions relating to global sourcing to access scarce skills and reduce costs. Furthermore, interest is growing in outsourcing business processes.

CHAPTER 2

Sourcing models and sourcing decisions: what and when to outsource or offshore

Clients are facing a large variety of alternatives to choose from when making sourcing decisions, which means that they need to take into account a number of considerations to be able to make the right decision. This chapter focuses on sourcing models for client firms and how to make sourcing decisions. In particular, it covers the following topics:

- Sourcing models
- Factors to consider when making a decision about outsourcing and offshoring
- The most suitable processes for outsourcing and offshoring

Sourcing models

Various types of global sourcing models have begun to emerge. The major distinction among these models lies in whether the function is performed by a subsidiary business unit of the firm or an external vendor (or by both, as a joint effort), and also whether the function is performed on the firm's premises (i.e., on-site) or off-site, which can be onshore (in the country where the organization is located), nearshore (in a neighboring country), or in an offshore location. Figure 2.1 provides overview of the most popular sourcing models, which we explain further here:

- *Insourcing:* Managing the provision of services internally, through buying in skills that are not available in-house, on a temporary basis. This is usually achieved through staff augmentation (also referred to as *bodyshopping*), a sourcing model that implies that staff are supplied to clients on demand, at a preagreed rate. Most large outsourcing vendors and management consultancies offer staff augmentation services.

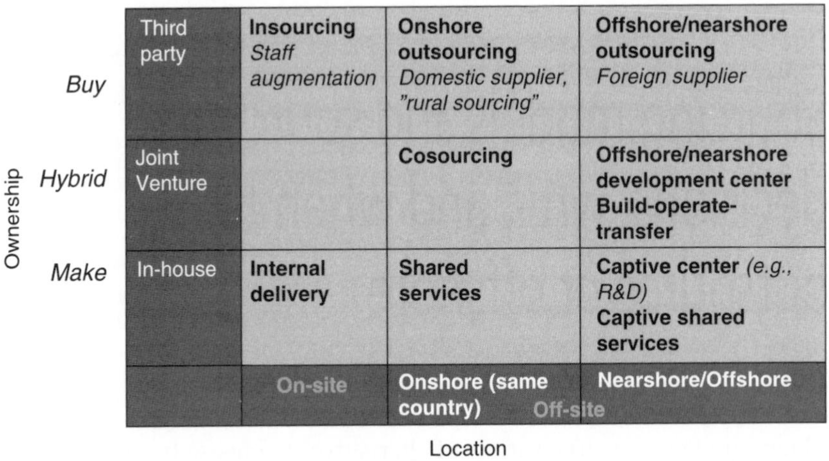

Ownership			Insourcing *Staff augmentation*	Onshore outsourcing *Domestic supplier, "rural sourcing"*	Offshore/nearshore outsourcing *Foreign supplier*
	Buy	Third party			
	Hybrid	Joint Venture		Cosourcing	Offshore/nearshore development center Build-operate-transfer
	Make	In-house	Internal delivery	Shared services	Captive center *(e.g., R&D)* Captive shared services
			On-site	Onshore (same country) *Off-site*	Nearshore/Offshore

Location

Figure 2.1 Overview of sourcing models

- *Domestic outsourcing:* Contracting with a third party situated in the same country as the client organization for the completion of a certain amount of work, for a specified length of time, and at a certain cost and level of service. Domestic outsourcing implies that the vendor is in close proximity to the client. A variant is *homeshoring* or *rural outsourcing,* which involves sending the work to lower-wage, usually rural, regions within the home country. This trend is popular in the US, Israel, India, and several other countries.
- *Offshore* (or *nearshore*) *outsourcing:* Outsourcing arrangements with vendors situated in a different country from the client organization.
- *Out-tasking:* Outsourcing on a small scale. It usually implies ongoing management of and support for selected packaged applications. Out-tasking is popular with local suppliers; however, it can also be provided from offshore locations (in particular if the supplier is a global company, such as IBM).
- *Captive models:* A strategic choice to locate organizational activities within a wholly owned subsidiary in another country. Captive sourcing models offer *basic, shared, hybrid,* and *divested* captive options (they are discussed in detail in Chapter 11).
- *Build-operate-transfer (BOT) models:* The client contacts with an offshore or nearshore vendor to execute an outsourcing arrangement whereby the vendor will build and operate the service center (e.g., a call center or any other business process) for an extended period of time. The client retains the right to take over the operation under certain conditions and certain financial arrangements.

- *Joint venture in the outsourcing or offshoring context:* A partnership between a client firm and an offshore vendor whereby the parties contribute resources to the new venture. Many of the offshoring joint ventures have a BOT component built into the agreement.
- *Shared services:* An operational approach of centralizing administrative and business processes that were once carried out in separate divisions or locations – for example, finance, procurement, human resources, and IT. A shared service center can be a captive center or outsourced to a third party. With the increasing popularity of the shared services model, we believe it deserves a more detailed explanation.

Shared services imply the consolidation of support functions from several departments into a stand-alone organizational entity whose objective is to provide services as efficiently and effectively as possible. When managed well, shared services can reduce costs, improve services, and even generate revenue. Creating successful IT shared services is listed as one of the seven habits of effective technology leaders (Andriole, 2007).

A shared service can take various forms of commercial structure such as unitary, lead department, or joint initiatives. *Unitary* refers to a single organization that consolidates and centralizes a business service, and a *lead department* is an organization that is consolidating and centralizing a business service to share with other organizations. *Joint initiatives* are set up by two or more organizations that have reached an agreement to build and operate shared services. Similar to outsourcing arrangements, shared services can be run onshore, nearshore, or offshore.

Shared services allow companies to analyze the value of a service that is provided to internal customers in order to change or optimize them. The end result should be increased flexibility in institutionalizing business changes to improve the management of cost centers. Compared with outsourcing to a third party, shared services allow companies to retain greater control over provided services. However, some argue that the shared services model still faces the barrier of internal bureaucracy. It has been reported that achieving full benefits from shared services is not easy because of the need for substantial organizational changes, such as the standardization of processes and the consolidation of services (Lacity and Fox, 2008).

Lacity and Fox (2008) propose that shared services require senior managers to manage four programs of change:

- *Business process redesign (BPR; also referred to as business process reengineering):* The standardization of processes around best practices, cost reduction, and improvement of controls.

- *Organizational redesign:* Allocation of staff according to the value of services they provide. Typically, standard services are moved to shared services facilities.
- *Sourcing redesign:* Decision making about which business processes to keep in-house and which ones to outsource to an external partner.
- *Technology enablement:* The implementation of other changes and coordination of work internally across units and externally with sourcing partners.

Models based on Internet delivery

Sourcing models based on Internet delivery of products or services are cloud computing, software as a service, crowdsourcing, and microsourcing.

Cloud computing

Cloud computing provides common business applications online that are accessed from a Web browser, while the software and data are stored on the servers. It describes a system where users can connect to a vast network of computing resources, data, and servers that reside somewhere "out there," usually on the Internet, rather than on a local machine or a local area network or in a data center. The metaphor of the cloud draws on how the Internet is depicted in computer network diagrams and represents an abstraction of the complex infrastructure it conceals. In other words, cloud computing allows users to access technology-enabled services on the Internet without having to know or understand the technology infrastructure that supports them. Nor do they have much control over it. Key properties of cloud services are (Armbrust et al., 2009):

- *Pay-as-you-go usage of the IT service*
- *The service is on-demand, able to scale up and scale down*
- *Access to applications and information from any access point*
- *Abstraction of the infrastructure so applications are not locked into devices or locations*
- *The ability to create the illusion of infinite capacity*

The key benefit of cloud computing is that it provides on-demand access to supercomputer-level power, even from a smartphone or laptop. Enabling massively scalable services characterizes cloud computing. For example, those who log on to Facebook or search for flights online are taking advantage of cloud computing. They are connecting to large volumes of data stored in remote clusters or networks of computers. Google is another example of cloud computing. A company using cloud computing does not have to own any server. It needs only to have key application software on its terminals and pay a service charge for a host company to provide storage and processing capacity.

The downside of cloud computing is that companies have limited control over their basic IT services and databases. They may suffer loss of access to their data when there is a problem in the cloud or with the physical infrastructure of the cloud. Privacy and confidentiality issues have also increasingly become a concern, especially when clients use service providers in a different country, where the local law may allow the government of that country to access certain data stored on hosted servers.

There are four basic types of clouds:

- *Private clouds,* operated solely for the use of a single organization
- *Community clouds,* operated for a specific group that shares infrastructure
- *Public clouds,* which use cloud infrastructure available over a public network
- *Hybrid clouds,* which combine the infrastructure of two or more clouds (public, community and private)

In terms of commercial sourcing models, cloud computing offers IT as utility, providing firms an opportunity to rent applications, computing power, or space from someone else's data center on a pay-per-use basis. Applications, infrastructure, and platforms can be delivered over public or private networks. Commercial sourcing models associated with cloud services are software as a service (SaaS; see the box that follows for more information on this), which is very common for enterprise systems (e.g., ERP, CRM, and collaboration tools by Saleforce.com, NetSuite, and other providers of cloud services); platform as a service (PaaS), which includes platform infrastructure and integration services (e.g., Google apps by Google); and infrastructure as a service (IaaS), which includes computing, storage, and backup services (e.g., a virtual machine by Amazon's Web Services).

According to Gartner Research (2010), in 2009 the worldwide market for cloud services was worth $58.6 billion, with North America being the largest regional market (60 percent of the worldwide total). Gartner predicts cloud services market will grow to $148.8 billion by 2014.

The following case discusses the various challenges faced and approached applied by Global Pharma concerning their cloud computing strategy.

Case Study

A GLOBAL OPERATING MODEL THAT EXPLOITS CLOUD COMPUTING SERVICES

by Mark Skilton

The global pharmaceutical market is a multibillion-dollar dynamic worldwide business ranging from consumer health care products to advanced medical devices and biotechnology research. Many aspects of the marketplace are interconnected by the need for constant research and rapid market trials through to dynamic scaling up and down of collaborative product manufacturing and diverse distribution supply chains to deliver to residential, wholesale, and retail marketplaces. The industry is regulated through regional and global governance standards ranging from patent laws for products and drug licensing through to compliance standards including the US Food and Drug Administration, as well as specific health data protection laws such as the US Health Insurance Portability and Accountability Act.

The Global Pharma company competes in these conditions through a wide and expansive organizational structure spanning 100,000 direct employees; 250 business units (bus) operating in the Americas, Europe, Middle East, Asia Pacific, and South American markets; and a wide partner channel ecosystem network. Its products span consumer health care, medical devices design, manufacture, distribution, and biomedical product research, and commercialization.

The following operational capabilities are essential to Global Pharma:

- The ability of front-end business operations to adapt and offer products and services quickly in response to market and consumer demands
- Creating research patents and rapidly moving research to market test trials
- The ability to build operational cost efficiencies into the infrastructure through shared services
- Rapid movement of existing and new business operations and resources to locations to enable flexible market entry and withdrawal to build and expand capacity and shrink and remove capacity as needed to pursue market opportunities

▶

▶
- Strong security and compliance partitioning and controls over business units
- Partner networks to enable effective collaboration and yet guard security compliance and corporate societal values.
- The development of brands and pricing strategies across diverse market geographies to exploit patents and market buying behaviors for long-term shareholder value in the brand and revenue share

Global Pharma's IT hardware and software assets and staff are consolidated into regional data centers connected by a corporate global network. A small central corporate IT function coordinates policy and strategy, which is largely distributed down to the business unit–based IT functions to meet local market and business service requirements. The use and development of the business applications and infrastructure are focused onshore by region. Large-scale corporate systems are developed in each data center, and some are replicated across other regional data centers. Significant investment in virtualization has addressed the operational efficiencies of the data center as the pharmaceutical market environment continues to change rapidly. At present, because of the cultural and organizational diversity, regional business units own IT strategy and delivery.

Steps toward adopting cloud computing

In 2009 the Global Pharma IT board saw that many of pharmaceutical industry characteristics aligned well with the capabilities found in cloud computing. This resulted in a cloud strategy plan and assessment of current investments in data centers and a number of strategic pilots to test public, private, and hybrid cloud solutions and to learn more about cloud technology and business models. By the middle of 2010, these investigations had focused on a complete global private cloud and recommended developing pilots to accelerate the design of the private cloud data center solution.

In terms of operating model, moving to cloud computing redefines the need for each region and business unit to develop certain types of IT service onshore. Common services hosted in a secure private cloud-based data center provide the possibility for many business units to move to an offshore shared model that Global Pharma saw as an opportunity to improve its organizational efficiency. While agility in individual markets and business units is still essential to competitiveness in Global Pharma's specific markets, Global Pharma sought to

▶

▶

support this by targeting cloud computing services for specific business activity needs.

Global Pharma developed a vision of an operating model using cloud computing:

- Flexible front-end IT services to enable the IT function to support rapid business demand in disparate dynamic markets
- Alignment of IT modernization programs of data centers, networks, and applications to become on-demand and with shared cost efficiencies
- Coordinated modular data centers and service centers for operating efficiencies from a one-to-many service for business units

Defining the right type of cloud operating model

Given the strategic decision to move to private cloud computing, Global Pharma had already invested extensively in infrastructure virtualization technology and a global data center network. Cloud computing, however, introduced the need for a modular infrastructure. The plan of work by the end 2010 was to modernize the infrastructure with modular data centers and networks, enabling a new operating model for IT resources and software applications to align with business capacity needs across the global operation and to deploy to meet specific business units.

In the distributed user groups in Global Pharma's business units, there is a range of business processes that may be supported by common administration services such as e-mail, storage, and collaboration. These are candidates for shared services. Other specific services defined for each business unit or as strategic platforms are mission critical and differentiating for the company. Hosting these business activities required cloud infrastructure services dedicated to these services and potential assembly of specific application services to meet differentiated service levels.

Thus, in parallel with the modular data center concept, the analysis of corporate and business unit enterprise software applications hosted in the modular data center identified different types of business activities that were classified into groups of cloud computing services that could be moved to a cloud computing environment. Business activities that represent commodity services across many user groups in

▶

▶

one-to-many fashion (such as e-mail and content management) and do not require much data storage and consumption of computing power were grouped into horizontal cloud services. Specific high-resource intensive business activities (with high computing power and data storage consumption) that include both one-to-many and one-to-one niche specific services for markets were grouped into vertical cloud services. Business activities that involve collaborative business transactions that are common across business units but more complex and more resource intensive than commodity services (e.g., the general functionality of customer relationship management and enterprise resource planning) were grouped together as candidates for shared service cloud-based computing environment:

- *Business activities for horizontal cloud services (one-to-many):* E-mail, market trial tests, storage, enterprise portals, content management, and human capital management
- *Business activities for vertical cloud services (one-to-one and one-to-many):* Engineering, research simulation and processing, business intelligence, niche enterprise resource planning, customer relationship management (industry specific), and supply chain management (planning and scheduling)
- *Business activities for shared cloud services (one-to-many):* Global enterprise resource planning, customer relationship management (online stores), supplier relationship management, product life cycle management, and global supply chain management

Impact of cloud services on Global Pharma

As a result of the modular approach that created data centers and services for common cross-business unit services, specific high-resource-intensive business activities and specific business capability platforms hosted in cloud were given to alternative data centers. To manage these cloud services, Global Pharma created employer competency centers for skills, training, and investment programs. Other competency groups were set up to support common shared services around specific technologies such as Microsoft, Oracle, and SAP.

Furthermore, movement to modular data centers and grouping of business activities into classes of cloud application services enabled support for business activities to be managed between onshore and

▶

▶
offshore cloud data centers where permitted. Moreover, migration of the existing applications and services to cloud-based data centers requires changes in service management practices. Existing service center operations dedicated to specific business units need to develop cross-business unit cloud services and align to specific cloud platform service support needs.

Because compliance issues related to data movements across borders prohibit the use of offshore cloud data center services, Global Pharma is facing difficulties in using public cloud.

Issues hampering forward movement for Global Pharma

Global Pharma is facing a number of issues related to cloud computing. At the strategic level, Global Pharma needs to amend its business strategy to maximize the benefits from cloud computing and incorporate cloud computing strategy into the business strategy. At the operational level, Global Pharma is struggling to decide what operations and business processes should be moved to public, private, or hybrid cloud options and how the global operating model needs to change to get the benefits of cloud computing. In addressing these issues, Global Pharma has identified specific challenges:

- *Managing multiple clouds and required capabilities:* If Global Pharma chooses a private cloud, it needs to recognize that running a cloud service as a provider is different from consuming a cloud service. The skills required for the transformation are more complex because an understanding of all of the components of cloud architecture does not typically reside in just one vendor. The business unit stakeholders also need to engage with the common services to build the one-to-many usage patterns to enable return on investment from the cloud and avoid fragmentation and multiple clouds.
- *Offshoring in the cloud:* Global Pharma is already operating in an onshore and offshore distributed model enabled through its data centers. However, the move to distributed cloud hosted business services enables one location to distribute a business activity to another region. Locations of business activities that become business services still need to be controlled for compliance and security management for the regional and business unit.

▶

▶

- *Security and operational concerns:* Specific security and compliance issues for the US Food and Drug Administration (FDA) and data controls such as Safeharbor Knowledge Solutions, which prohibits medical data movement off-premise and offshore, and Federation of Security access to supplier partner networks that need multiple identity and authentication control must be handled appropriately. Partitioning specific business activities for FDA security compliance into specific data center domains is one approach to contain a dedicated cloud resource to focus performance and security controls of critical systems. This requires specific cloud rules for control and access. Alternatively, Global Pharma may consider partitioning applications into different cloud services types – for example, an FDA application cloud, an ERP cloud, a Microsoft cloud, or an Oracle cloud to support specific vendor licensing and performance issues.
- *Outsourcing, in-house, or hybrid service delivery:* With private cloud, Global Pharma becomes a service provider delivering on-demand services to its own business units. An alternative to doing everything in-house is the use of third parties. However, it is not clear how these third parties can participate as alternative private clouds. In particular, how would third-party outsourcers with cloud data centers be certified for pharmaceutical company use? And how would external private clouds be integrated with internal company private clouds?
- *Payment structure and license reengineering:* The licensing issue is not clear. The use of pay-as-you-go consumption models of applications and infrastructure resources may not be compatible with existing licensing based on usage per user instance. If this is virtualized and not specific to a physical instance of hardware, the software license model breaks down. Alternatives may be found through reseller license models or license pooling for the corporation. How will individual vendors need to be handled on a case-by-case basis? How will umbrella contract agreements for existing vendor software licenses be affected if they are moved to a cloud-based hosted environment?
- *Stakeholder engagement:* In distributed user groups in the Global Pharma business units, a range of cloud services needs to be defined for each business unit and market-facing operation. Focusing on common services versus variations of service needs to involve different stakeholders from these groups to build the one-to-many opportunities that cloud can support.

▶

▶
The cloud service provider also needs to address some issues. This means that if Global Pharma decides to create a private cloud, the internal unit delivering the cloud services and any third parties need to clarify the following issues:

- *Alignment of modular business services with demand:* The use of modular business activity (service) hosted in specific data centers requires control and demand forecast planning of capacity availability. Demand aggregation and request management processes need to accommodate a shift to a catalog-style provisioning model. This includes a portal strategy for self-service. From Global Pharma's perspective, the cloud provider (or the internal unit providing services in the private cloud) needs to be able to forecast shifts in demand in order to meet that demand. From the cloud provider's perspective, the ability to forecast demand capacity is essential to ensure the service can meet operational demands.
- *Alignment with modular business services and supply capacity:* The standard operating environments hosted as various templates for cloud resources have to be aligned with the types of applications and usage patterns for the allocated capacity. This introduces new operating practices for traffic and load balancing.
- *Power efficiencies and facilities certification:* Efficiency of power consumption in cloud computing can be affected by a large-scale burst in demand. In certain circumstances, the power demand in the cloud data center needs to be planned to be available to prevent insufficient energy to support operations. And efficient green energy and certification of services are as essential in cloud operations as in conventionally managed hosting.

Software as a service

SaaS is a model of software deployment where an application is hosted as a service provided to customers across the Internet (i.e., a Web-based application). It is based on the principles of cloud computing but takes a commercial form. The application, or service, is deployed from a centralized data center across a network, and this center provides access and use on a recurring-fee basis. The distinction between SaaS and earlier applications delivered over the Internet (as part of the application service provision model that was popular in the late 1990s and early 2000s) is that

SaaS solutions have been developed specifically to leverage Web technologies such as the browser, thereby making them Web native (an example is Microsoft). Furthermore, SaaS is distinct from a traditional server-client approach due to its significant potential for economies of scale in its deployment, management, support, and the software development life cycle.

Many types of software are well suited to the SaaS model for customers with little interest or capability in software deployment but with substantial computing needs. The model can be applied within different segments of the market. At the higher end of the market, providers may offer applications such as ERP, CRM, and e-commerce, as well as selective industry-specific solutions. Low-end applications include solutions for small and medium enterprises that the users can easily configure.

Crowdsourcing

Crowdsourcing is the act of taking a job traditionally performed by employees and outsourcing it to an undefined, generally large group of people in the form of an "open call" (Howe, 2008). This sourcing model has been widely adopted in the open innovation movement (e.g., by InnoCentive, TekScout, IdeaConnection, and many other open innovation marketplaces and communities). A large number of new business ventures have emerged through crowdsourcing, mainly by creating an opportunity for anybody to submit an idea (examples are products such as photos to iStockphoto.com or T-shirt designs to Threadless.com) and let the community of users or potential buyers decide whether a particular creation is worth buying. The following case study describes the crowdsourcing phenomena and provides examples of crowdsourcing firms.

Case Study

CROWDSOURCING

by Onook Oh and Rajiv Kishore

The crowdsourcing phenomenon

With the development of Web 2.0 technologies, entrepreneurs are continually creating and experimenting with innovative e-business models. One of the recent e-business models that has gained popularity

▶

▶

and recognition in a short span is crowdsourcing. This business model harnesses the potential of a heterogeneous and globally dispersed online crowd to meet a variety of business needs. As with any new major business development, crowdsourcing has spawned a new and emerging vocabulary including terms such as "prosumers" (producers + consumers) or "produsage" (production + usage). A key implication of these new coinages is that consumers are no longer passive buyers who simply consume end products. Rather, they are active "prosumers" who directly or indirectly participate in cocreating the goods and services they consume. As a result, the line between producer and consumer indeed becomes blurry in the crowdsourcing phenomenon.

Crowdsourcing may be best understood as a variant of the outsourcing phenomenon in that both sourcing mechanisms use resources from outside the organizational boundaries to meet internal business needs. However, a major difference between the two sourcing mechanisms is that while traditional outsourcing relies predominantly on a handful of established professional services firms, crowdsourcing turns to a much larger heterogeneous, online crowd of individuals to meet their internal business needs. The main driver that made reaching to a multitude of potential virtual workers and crowdsourcing possible is the collection of Web 2.0 technologies that enable individuals to actively participate and engage in cocreation activities through the 24/7 interconnected virtual technological environment. Further, a crowd of individuals that is highly connected through this technological environment makes it possible for organizations to aggregate individual profiles and create a large virtual workforce of varied skill sets that they can search and match for meeting specific business needs, and then contract with specific individuals, all in real time.

Examples of crowdsourcing firms

InnoCentive: Oil Spill Recovery Institute (OSRI) was formed to find ways to remove oil from contaminated areas in response to the catastrophic 1989 Exxon Valdez oil spill in Alaska, and it continues to be engaged in cleaning up all the remaining oil from affected areas. While dozens of barges have diligently pumped oil from iceberg cracks into barge tanks, the mixture of pumped water and oil quickly freezes to a sticky state making it difficult to separate oil from water.

▶

▶

OSRI posted a challenge on the InnoCentive Web site. Within two weeks, a cement expert, John Davis, came up with a simple solution that surprised OSRI scientists. John applied tools and techniques widely used in the concrete industry. The concrete industry uses a vibration tool to keep cement from becoming solid during massive cement pours. John's solution was to attach a long pole and insert it into the oil recovery tanks, and to vibrate this pole to prevent oil and water from freezing. Using this simple vibrating tool, OSRI could remove oil from water, and the challenge solver, John, was rewarded $20,000.[1]

InnoCentive Web site is comprised of seekers, solvers, and InnoCentive open innovation marketplace. Seekers – corporations or nonprofit organizations – can post their Research and Development (R&D) challenges to InnoCentive's Open Innovation Marketplace Web site. Each challenge has solution submission deadline and is assigned a cash reward ranging from $10,000 to $100,000. Any registered InnoCentive solver can enter the online project room to gain access to the posted challenges, and work on any project that she may want to solve. The seeker reviews submitted solutions after the deadline, awards the announced cash reward to the best solver, and pays an agreed commission to InnoCentive.

Launched in 2001, InnoCentive has solved 200 challenges out of the 600 posted using the above described crowdsourcing model. In contrast to technology services firms working with a handful of highly skilled scientists and researchers, InnoCentive is working with 125,000 anonymous solvers from 175 countries. To solve problems, InnoCentive is using crowd's collective creativity and the power of scale of the knowledge community. InnoCentive counts Proctor & Gamble, Boeing, DuPont, LG, and other large and famous brand names as its seeker customers. InnoCentive has 25 employees and their revenue has increased 75 percent annually during the past 6 years.

Cambrian House: Michael Sikorsky raised $10.1 million from 2006 to 2007 for his new venture firm, Cambrian House Inc. As a Web 2.0 platform-based crowdsourcing start-up, his vision was to create "low-cost software quickly." For its first video game product, Gwabs, he believes that "from concept to finished product, it will have taken the volunteer team six months and cost $200,000. Producing it with in-house staff, says Sikorsky, would have taken 50 percent longer and cost

▶

▶

three times as much."[2] Cambrian House mixes open source software development model with a traditional company format. It outsources market research, product design, and development to its 10,000 strong member community, which is still growing. The company focuses on project management, sales, and marketing. With transparent compensation schemes and respect for its community members, Cambrian is utilizing the collective knowledge of online community members in a creative and cost-effective way.

The product development process works as follows: Any individual can submit his/her idea for a fresh, new software to CambrianHouse.com. Then Cambrian community members discuss, research, and vote on that idea. On a regular basis, Cambrian issues 100 Cambros (Cambrian's virtual money) to the individual who submits the best idea. This individual can form a project team using Cambrian community members. Cambrian on its part creates a demo Web site for the selected idea and conducts market research using Google's pay-per-click advertising. Using Google analytic tools, Cambrian analyzes market demand by gathering statistical information about "How many people are searching for your idea right now? How many visit your site? Do they ask for more info? Would they pre-order your product?"[3] If the idea shows market demand, they invest in the project themselves, otherwise cancel it.

Once the project is completed and is put into production for public use, Cambrian takes 50 percent of the revenue generated for project management, sales, and marketing. Each contributor to the project receives "royalty points" for as long as the product generates revenue. Cambrian expects modest revenue of $1 million in 2007, and $5 million in 2008 along with its community member of 100,000.

OhMyNews: For many newspaper companies, the Web is simply another channel to deliver and/or sell their news content that is created by professional journalists. Launched in February 2000, a Korean online news media company, OhMyNews, innovated the way in which news content is created and delivered to consumers. As an online newspaper, this company finds and generates news content through citizen reporters instead of professional journalists. The founder, Yeonho Oh, says that he "wanted to start a tradition free of newspaper company elitism where news are evaluated based on quality, regardless of whether it came from a major newspaper, a local reporter, an educated journalist, or a neighborhood housewife."[4]

▶

▶

In 2005, OhMyNews had more than 40,000 citizen reporters out of South Korea's total population of 46 million. Typical citizen reporters write a story or two per week. Once the story is submitted online, it remains as a "Saengnamu" article before being accepted by the OhMyNews copyeditor team. During this period, the article is subjected to intensive screening for sentence construction, factual errors, or value of news, and goes through the copyediting process by professional internal editors. When an article is approved, citizen reporters can monitor the number of readers' clicks or comments, and collect monetary rewards in virtual "tip jar."

In OhMyNews business model, readers are not passive consumers of news content. They are both active producers and consumers. This citizen reporter model turned out to be quite effective, as it can deliver the same news content much faster and with a unique perspective. However, high-quality news content does not come for nothing. To enhance their news quality, OhMyNews actively involves its citizen reporters in online conversations. For citizen reporters' news to be placed as a headline, they have to persuade OhMyNews' frontline copyeditors. Also, OhMyNews organizes regular seminars for citizen reporters to help write high-quality news and give copyright advice. OhMyNews was so successful that in 2005, nearly 70 citizen reporters were contracted to write books. In May 2006, OhMyNews was invited as a special guest to Google's Zeitgeist media forum in London along with the world-renowned media companies such as Reuters and Le Monde.[5] This model of news reporting is now being adopted by mainstream news media organizations because of its unique value proposition. CNN has developed a community of iReporters who provide first person accounts of breaking news in areas where it does not have its own professional reporters at the time.

---

[1] http://www.innocentive.com/crowd-sourcing-news/2007/11/20/innocentive-solver-develops-solution-to-help-clean-up-remaining-oil-from-the-1989-exxon-valdez-disaster/. Accessed December 15, 2010.

[2] Spence R. Cambrian House: The wisdom of crowdsourcing. *Canadian Business Online.* http://www.canadianbusiness.com/entrepreneur/managing/article.jsp?content=20070212_14 0822_6416. Accessed December 15, 2010.

[3] http://www.cambrianhouse.com/how-it-works/crowds-test-it/. Accessed December 15, 2010.

[4] Min JK. Journalism as a Conversation. *Nieman Reports* (Winter 2005) 19–21.

[5] http://www.ohmynews.com/nws_web/view/at_pg.aspx?CNTN_CD=A0000333935 (Korean version)

Microsourcing[1]

Similar to the emergence of large numbers of business-to-customer and customer-to-customer online marketplaces that bring together buyers and sellers (e.g., Amazon and eBay), online marketplaces for sourcing customized products and services have emerged. Such marketplaces allow customers to contract a vendor (an individual or a company) to develop and deliver a product or service based on the customer's specific needs. Different from online auctions such as eBay and uBid, and e-malls such as Amazon, which sell ready goods, sourcing marketplaces provide clients a suitable supplier for a product or service delivery. Marketplaces such as vWorker, Elance, and oDesk serve as intermediaries that provide legal and project management support in the form of standard contracts that include copyright protection, payment protection, and basic project management stages to facilitate interactions between client and supplier. This sourcing model is called *microsourcing* because it is suitable for only relatively small and well-defined tasks such as Web site design, software development to implement small product features, proofreading, or indexing. Client and vendor rely exclusively on online interactions and usually never meet face-to-face.

While microsourcing is characterized by small-size contracts, individuals and firms that discover microsourcing often decide to engage in several microsourcing contracts and find themselves managing multiple vendors (we discuss the multivendor trend in detail in Chapter 6).

Online microsourcing represents a somewhat unknown slice of the global sourcing landscape. *Online sourcing environments* (OSE) are online spaces where buyers and suppliers of services can meet, offer, and apply for jobs; carry out project-related tasks; and conduct financial transactions. The prominent examples of OSEs are marketplaces such as Elance, Guru, vWorker, and oDesk.

All OSEs have three main stakeholders: buyers, suppliers, and (online) platforms. Buyers are companies or individuals who come to OSEs because they are interested in outsourcing a part of their workload. Historically most OSE buyers and suppliers have been small – usually entrepreneurs and small firms with fewer than one hundred employees, mostly from the nations, and especially English-speaking countries. Suppliers are also represented primarily by small service firms and individuals, with the

---

[1] This section on microsourcing was written by Evgeny Kaganer, Erran Carmel, Rudy Hirschheim and Sandra Sieber.

latter being either moonlighters or independent professionals. They participate in OSEs to market their skills and services to potential buyers. The population of suppliers is a more geographically distributed than that of buyers – the US, however, contributes a significant portion. In addition, certain countries have become somewhat specialized in specific project types – for example, India, Romania, and Pakistan dominate the IT category. The third stakeholder is the intermediary, the marketplace itself, which we label *platforms*. These are the Web sites that provide an environment where buyers and suppliers can interact.

A new project in OSEs usually starts with the buyer formalizing its work needs and converting them into project requirements. These requirements are then communicated to suppliers typically in the form of a job, project (a request for bid), or competition announcement. The buyer selects a supplier to work on the project. This may be done on the basis of proposals (bids) submitted by suppliers or an actual project deliverable submitted as a part of a competition or contest. Once the job is awarded, the buyer oversees its completion and, when the final deliverable is deemed acceptable, pays the supplier for services rendered. The final step in the buyer work flow is to rate the supplier and, sometimes, provide additional qualitative feedback on the project.

Suppliers register with OSEs by building a personal profile. Most OSEs today allow rich supplier profiles that include personal and contact information, educational and employment history, job history on the platform, and, in many cases, skill evaluation data (tested or self-reported). Once the profile is in place, the supplier can start searching and applying for relevant job or project announcements.

The mechanics of the application process may vary from one OSM platform to another, but usually it is set up as either a reverse auction or a competition. Once selected, the supplier starts working on the project. The work is usually facilitated by the platform, which provides communication, collaboration, and project management tools. Once the job is completed, the supplier collects the payment and provides feedback on the buyer.

We distinguish three main types of OSEs: *directories,* which provide listings of projects, supplier profiles, and contact information, but deals are usually done offline; *marketplaces,* which connect buyers and suppliers and facilitate their interaction throughout the entire sourcing life cycle; and *communities,* which aim to build a network of talented and skilled individuals in a particular field, such as creative design or computer programming. Their key characteristics are summarized in Table 2.1.

Table 2.1 Characteristics of OSE directories

	Directory	Marketplace	Community
Main focus or objective	Help buyers discover suppliers by providing supplier listings with profile and contact information.	Connects buyers and suppliers of services throughout all stages of the work flow.	Help members (i.e., suppliers) develop professionally through community interaction and paid client (i.e., buyer) engagements.
Nature or structure of deals	Deals are done offline. The platform is not involved.	Deals are done online, usually through a reverse-auction type of process. The platform is involved in both legal and financial aspects of the deal.	Deals are done online and usually structured as contests or competitions. The platform is involved in both legal and financial aspects of the deal.
Platform's role in facilitating buyer–supplier interaction	No buyer–supplier interaction takes place on the platform. Buyers may have an option of posting projects online, but all the ensuing activities take place outside of the platform.	The platform facilitates buyer–supplier interaction with a focus on project completion.	The platform facilitates buyer–supplier interaction with a focus on learning and community building.
Revenue model	Advertising, sponsorship	Project commission paid by suppliers. Buyers and suppliers may sign up for premium membership	Project commission/fee paid by buyers
Platform examples	Infolancer, Chinasourcing	Elance, Guru, oDesk, vWorker	crowdSPRING, TopCoder (Direct)

Boundaries among the three OSE types often blur or change over time. For example, a platform may start out as a directory, but, over time, features are added with the objective of gradually evolving into a marketplace. Similarly, some platforms in the marketplace category are starting to adopt elements from the community category. For example, marketplace platforms Elance and oDesk have made significant efforts to engage with and foster the community of suppliers (e.g., both platforms maintain blogs and are active on Twitter).

Why do buyers come to OSEs?

OSEs afford buyers instant global reach. Neither buyers in search of talented people nor suppliers are bounded by their region or country. Buyers benefit from low costs that result from global supplier competition. The differences in bids submitted to the same project description are usually due to lower wages and costs in the supplier countries or regions. OSE programmers in India, Bangladesh, and Pakistan usually submit bids that are much lower than those by their competitors in wealthy nations.

Another advantage OSEs offer to buyers is the ability to quickly launch and scale up projects. Once a buyer posts a project, it is common to get 20 to 30 proposals from suppliers within the first two or three days. For larger projects, OSEs can help buyers mobilize the supplier community to start working in parallel on the individual tasks comprising the project. Community-type platforms like crowdSPRING and TopCoder do an especially good job at that.

Finally, buyers can take advantage of an established framework provided by OSEs for initiating and managing the sourcing projects (i.e., a comprehensive suite of online tools and services that help buyers manage all aspects of the sourcing relationship).

What challenges do OSE buyers face?

Trust is key to any successful buyer–supplier relationship, especially in OSEs that lack personal contact and face-to-face interaction, with cross-cultural and language differences creating additional obstacles to developing trust. A buyer needs to have confidence that the supplier it selects will complete the project on time and that the final deliverable will be of acceptable quality. The buyer also needs to be assured that in case problems arise effective mechanisms are available within the platform to address the issue. Thus, trust must be established at two levels: the supplier level and the platform level.

At the supplier level, the general strategy has been to make the OSEs more transparent, open up communication channels between buyer and supplier, and provide tools to monitor project progress. For example, in the early years of OSEs, suppliers had anonymous user profiles and aliases instead of real names. Over time, OSEs realized that this approach is counterproductive in terms of helping the parties build trusting relationships. Today most platforms allow suppliers to build rich profiles providing detailed personal and contact information, educational and employment history, skill evaluation scores, and often a portfolio of previous work. In addition, to make up for the lack of personal recommendations common in traditional offline environments, platforms have introduced sophisticated rating systems and feedback mechanisms. Buyers can also see a complete history of projects the supplier has worked on, along with earnings and project completion statistics.

With respect to opening up communication channels, platforms such as Elance and oDesk offer built-in online communication services, including chat, discussion forums, Web conferencing, and phone integration. These tools can be used to interview a supplier at the selection phase or facilitate collaboration between the two parties throughout the project. Similarly, many platforms now offer project management tools enabling buyers to establish milestones and link payments to milestone completion.

Fostering trust at the platform level is based on the idea that since it is virtually impossible to ensure the trustworthiness of each individual supplier in a global context, the platform itself should become the guarantor that buyers will trust. Two primary mechanisms are used to accomplish this goal. The first includes initiatives seeking to reduce the perception of risk for the buyer. Escrow accounts (the project payment is held by the platform until the work is completed and approved by the buyer), arbitration services, and mandatory intellectual property (IP) agreements for suppliers provide the most common examples.

The second mechanism focuses on grooming the supplier pool. Here, the rationale is that by weeding out poor suppliers and promoting high-quality ones, the platform will build up a trustworthy reputation for itself. For example, Elance encourages all buyers to take advantage of its project management module. Once the critical mass of projects goes through the module to create some benchmark history, a platform-wide monitoring system can be established to identify and warn suppliers who regularly underperform. Similarly, Guru's sophisticated rating system takes into account a variety of criteria, such as paying-employer acquisition rate, average earnings per employer, and employer retention rate, to identify best suppliers and help them win more projects.

Considerations for outsourcing and offshoring

An activity can be sourced as an overall set of processes or as smaller parts of it. The tasks and business processes that can be outsourced or offshored vary. In order of increasing complexity, they are:

- Low-cost simple back office functions such as infrastructure and data management
- Customer-facing services such as call centers or help desks and telemarketing
- Business functions such as human resources, finance, and accounting, and procurement

- Strategic knowledge-intensive processes, such as business intelligence, market research, and various R&D activities

Using the scope of outsourcing as a criterion (i.e., the degree to which a process is managed internally or by a third party), we distinguish three models:

- *Total outsourcing*, which refers to transferring more than 80 percent of a function's operating budget to external providers
- *Total in-house sourcing*, which refers to retaining the management and provision of more than 80 percent of the function's operating budget within the organization
- *Selective outsourcing*, which refers to sourcing selected functions to external parties while managing 20 to 80 percent of the function's operating budget internally

Along these lines, Metters (2008) has suggested that offshoring and outsourcing decisions should be seen as a spectrum rather than as distinct categories. With regard to the offshoring decision, Metters explains that initially, it may appear categorical as a process performed either in the home country or offshore. However, Metters also emphasizes degrees to the level of offshoring that are related to the amount of risk a firm undertakes. For example, we could consider a US firm that would like to lower the costs of a back office process related to keying in handwritten English text to a computer system. Modern information and communication technologies enable the performance of this process from various remote locations in a more cost-effective way. In the decision relating to where to offshore, a number of factors may play significant roles, depending on the company's business model. Metters focuses on the case of electronically transferrable services and identifies labor costs, cultural distance from data source, and quality of infrastructure as some of the most important factors to consider when making offshoring decisions.

If we take into account the labor costs of clerical workers, the most favorable cost alternative is offshoring the process of keying handwritten English text to a computer system to China. As illustrated in Figure 2.2, China is the most attractive destination for a US customer in terms of labor costs. However, non-English-speaking Chinese workers use character recognition rather than understanding English as a language. For this reason, undertaking this process would require two or even more employees to independently key characters and ensure that the process is performed correctly. Another choice might be India, where English-speaking Indians

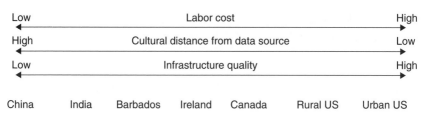

Figure 2.2 Spectrum of single-facility offshoring choices for a US customer
Source: Metters (2008)

would perform the keying. This choice would entail higher wages than in China, but only one-fifth the level of US wages. Furthermore, this choice would entail a relatively lower level of language and cultural barriers between the client and the supplier organization. An even more expensive option might be to offshore the process to Barbados, where English is the prevalent spoken language and salaries are 20 to 50 percent of the US levels. Another option might be to offshore (more precisely, to nearshore) the work to Canada, where wages are lower relative to the US yet higher than the other destinations mentioned. A further option might be using homeshoring or rural outsourcing by sending the work to lower-wage rural regions within the US. Finally, the firm can engage in offshoring to multiple destinations and perform the same process within different facilities around the world. On this basis, the cost of labor, the cultural distance, and the quality of infrastructure are the most relevant factors in the choice of an offshoring option.

In contrast to electronically transmitted services, viewing offshoring options as a spectrum is more complex if we consider nonelectronically transmitted services such as manufacturing. For such processes, factors such as tax regimes, tariffs, and government regulations make costs highly specific rather than general.

In terms of contractual agreements between client and vendor companies, most popular ones are *time-and-materials*, *fixed-price*, *fees-for-service*, and *partnership-based* contracts. These contract types support different pricing models of services delivered by the vendor, and rely on different measurement instruments to indicate whether contract conditions have been met.

Time-and-materials contracts rely on fixed hourly or daily fee and costs of the materials that the vendor needs to purchase to accomplish the work. Under this contract the supplier typically provides services that complement the customer's capabilities and service delivery is managed in-house.

This is the most common sourcing model and poses the least risk to the customer. A common example is consulting projects, such as the implementation of an ERP system.

Fixed fee is a core principle of *fixed price* contract and *fee-for-service* types of contract. The main difference between these two contract types is the volume of work for which fees are fixed.

Fixed-price contracts specify fixed fee for large work packages (e.g., fixed monthly or annual fee for maintenance of a portfolio of applications or systems) to agreed SLAs (service-level agreements), regardless of how much time the vendor will spend on this work package in a given period of time. Such contracts are also popular for one-off implementation and integration of IT projects, where clients prefer fixed fee for project completion. Such contracts often lead to win-lose situations. For example, vendor is "winning" if the amount of time the vendor eventually spends on maintenance of the client's systems is lower than the estimated workload when the fixed fee was calculated. However vendor might be "losing" if the actual amount of work in the end is higher than the estimated workload.

Fee-for-service contracts specify fixed fees for small well-defined work packages, often referred as *tickets* which rely on actual rather than estimated volumes of work. *Tickets* are associated with instances in which vendor need to provide help (i.e. resolve a problem). Per-ticket service contracts are measured by SLAs that specify time for resolving a problem. Such contracts would usually have a breakdown of fees per ticket, specifying different fixed fee per ticket for different volumes of tickets. For example, for the first 50 tickets, a client will pay $1 per ticket and if the number of tickets exceeds 50, the client will pay 80 pence per ticket. Breakdown of fees and ticket volumes captured in the contract provides vendors with incentives to invest in various improvement initiatives that may reduce ticket volumes, which may result in savings for the client and better margins for the vendor.

Joint ventures (JV) are one of the most popular partnership-based contracts. In this partnership model, the contract defines how client and vendor firms contribute resources to the new venture and states how profits will be shared. The partners define the mission and objectives for the joint venture, provide funding, initial physical assets, intellectual capital, staff members, and management capabilities. In most cases, the strategic objectives behind the formation of a joint venture include overcoming entry barriers into new markets, faster access to new markets and new technologies, economies of scale, risk sharing, and getting access to complementary assets (tangible and intangible) located outside its boundaries (Koh and

Venkatraman, 1991; Hennart, 1988), as well as pursuing an offshoring strategy at lower risks and costs associated with setting up an offshore captive center.

When client and vendor form a joint venture, they usually pursue one of the following goals:

- *New business ventures:* Aiming at developing new and innovative solutions and services for the clients' vertical markets,. such JV often take the form of an offshore development center that has similar mission as a captive offshore R&D center for the purpose of developing new products or services. Profit sharing incorporated in the contractual agreement keeps both parties engaged and motivated to maximize the profits.
- *Transformation of large-scale complex business functions and processes of the client firm:* Risk sharing helps clients to deal with uncertainty and complexity of the changes and for the vendor it provides motivation to perform well to materialize the profit-sharing option. The joint venture between Commonwealth Bank of Australia and Electronic Data Systems formed in 1997 to manage the bank's IT and processing activities is one example that illustrates such considerations (Oshri et al., 2009).

Identifying the right processes for outsourcing and offshoring

Information technology is a major subject of sourcing and has created an entire industry around it. The more a firm is operationally dependent on reliable and real-time IT functions, the more attractive outsourcing becomes as an option. However, careful analysis must be made in the selection of an appropriate and reliable vendor that will provide consistent and trustworthy service delivery. (Different types of vendors and vendor selection criteria are discussed in detail in Chapters 4 and 6, respectively).

Outsourcing constitutes a venture with fewer risks when IT-related operations include mainly maintenance work or projects that are valuable but not vitally significant to the firm. However, as new systems become increasingly important in delivering distinctive competencies to the company's business model, the outsourcing decision comes under more and more scrutiny. In such cases, the potential loss of control and flexibility can have detrimental effects and become cause for concern.

McFarlan and Nolan (1995) developed a strategic grid framework that provides major insights into firms that are considering outsourcing IT.

The framework assesses two dimensions of IT activities: current dependence on information (also referred to as the impact of IT on core operations) and importance of sustained, innovating information resource development (also referred to as the impact of IT on core strategy).

For IT services that have a high impact on operations but relatively low impact on strategy (e.g., maintenance of customer-facing applications), the outsourcing assumption is "yes" unless the company is large in scale and exceptionally well managed. Through economies of scale, vendors should provide significant cost savings to client firms if risks of operational failure are mitigated.

For IT activities that have low impact on both core operation and strategy, McFarlan and Nolan (1995) recommend outsourcing. Outsourcing of such activities poses low risk of losing control and offers significant savings, especially to large firms.

For IT activities that have low impact on core operations but are highly dependent on up-to-date and innovative IT functions, the outsourcing assumption is "no" because of risks associated with high strategic risks.

Finally, for IT activities that are of high significance for operations and are dependent on a highly innovative IT infrastructure, the outsourcing assumption is again no, because it would represent handing out processes that are key to the sustainability of competitiveness.

These suggestions by McFarlan and Nolan (1995) received some criticism from Levina (2006), who has suggested that this framework provides little guidance in the case of offshoring. For example, Levina highlighted the fact that in the offshore context, if an IT activity has a high impact on operations, then at least part of this activity has to be kept onshore (e.g., first-level support to customer-facing applications). In cases where IT has a low impact on both core operations and strategy (e.g., migration of legacy applications that are heavily linked with other applications), the decision to outsource is again problematic because some activities of this type may require deep domain knowledge that offshore providers may not possess and might be difficult to acquire. Although IT activities, such as IP and data-security-sensitive applications, should be kept in-house according to McFarlan and Nolan (because of their low impact on core operations and high impact on core strategy), Levina has suggested that such activities could be considered for outsourcing under careful management. She explains that there are large vendors in countries such as India that specialize in IP and data security systems and would have a strong motive to perform well because their reputation would be at stake. Finally, Levina suggests that a company may decide to invest in a captive unit if a particular IT capability is poorly served in the offshore market and the company has the knowledge and resources to deliver it.

Factors influencing the suitability of processes for outsourcing and offshoring

Understanding the core of each sourcing model and what it has to offer is of vital significance for engaging in effective sourcing strategies. However, in the case of outsourcing and offshoring (including offshore outsourcing and captive models), it is of equal importance to identify which processes should be transferred to another provider (domestic or offshore) or another country as part of the business of a captive center.

According to Metters (2008), firms typically consider those activities for outsourcing or offshoring that are not critical for the company's operations or holding onto its competitive advantage. The reason is that when a task is being outsourced, the institutional knowledge concerning the task is also leaving.

The scale of the process is also important in deciding if outsourcing is an appropriate solution. The costs associated with searching and selecting an appropriate vendor, establishing service-level metrics, creating and managing the contract, monitoring the ongoing outsourcing relationship, and enforcing the contract may be significant. In the case of offshoring, these costs are even more significant because of the complexity of these ventures. However, a process can also be too large for outsourcing to be effective. When a process is too large, outsourcing may represent only an additional layer of management, thus complicating operations and adding costs.

Processes influenced by rapidly changing technologies constitute good candidates for outsourcing, unless they are critical to the company's business model and operations. The reason is that small in-house units have a relatively limited capability to keep up with the rapidly changing technological environment. Firms that dedicate themselves to these activities (e.g., IBM, Accenture, Computer Sciences Corporation, Infosys, and Tata Consultancy Services) can be more innovative because they specialize in this business.

Furthermore, outsourcing (or insourcing) is appropriate for activities that have a high degree of variance – for example, they require 50 people one day and only 10 people the next day. Hiring 50 people for this activity when they are only occasionally needed constitutes a significant cost for the firm. An outsourcer can mitigate this variance by serving several countercyclical clients.

With regard to offshoring, Aron and Singh (2005) note that most companies do not make decisions systematically and rigorously enough and in fact repeatedly make at least one of three fundamental mistakes. First, although many companies spend time choosing countries, cities, and suppliers and put significant effort into negotiations, they do not spend time evaluating which processes should go offshore and which should not. It appears that most companies have difficulty in distinguishing core processes that they must control, critical processes that they must buy from expert vendors, and commodity processes that they can outsource.

Second, most organizations do not fully consider the risks associated with offshoring. Financial managers and senior executives make calculations in relation to the costs and benefits of offshoring without taking into account that, after signing the deal, the supplier might gain an upper hand. Most outsourcing customers appear to disregard any risks related to the power relationship between the two partners and make choices that eliminate the savings from outsourcing.

Third, a number of companies do not understand that outsourcing is not an all-or-nothing choice; rather, there is a range of sourcing models that they can follow.

Metters (2008) suggested that processes that require substantial levels of communication between the client and the supplier do not constitute good candidates for offshoring. Time zone differences, language, and other sorts of communications barriers can shrink the benefits of offshoring. However, Aron and Singh (2005) appear to be more concerned with how processes are ranked in terms of their value to the organization. They suggest that there must be a careful consideration between business processes that constitute good candidates for offshoring and those that do not. Processes that are important for the creation of value should not be offshored.

Along these lines, Aron and Singh (2005) suggest that executives should rank organizational processes along two dimensions: their potential for value creation and for value capture. More specifically, executives should consider how crucial a process is in the creation of customer value compared to other processes. Furthermore, they should consider the extent to which each process enables the organization to capture some of the value created for customers. For the processes that are ranked high, such as working capital management and cash-flow forecasting, offshoring is not suggested. Processes that are ranked lower (e.g., payment authorization and invoice verification) appear better candidates for offshoring.

It is important to note that one of the two dimensions can be more important for certain industries or specific companies. In this case, rankings must be calculated taking into account the relative weight of each of these dimensions. Ranking all of the company's processes creates a value hierarchy that reflects which processes should go offshore and which should not. The higher the rank of a process is, the more crucial its role is to the company's strategy, and thus the less it should be considered for offshoring or outsourcing.

Willcocks et al. (2002, 2011) suggested a similar process to evaluate which processes are good candidates for outsourcing and which are not. They suggest that business activities should be assessed in terms of their contribution to business operations (which can be compared with Aron and Singh's (2005) concept of value creation) as well as in terms of their contribution to competitive positioning (which matches the concept of value capture of Aron and Singh).

As is illustrated in Table 2.2, "order winners" are activities that contribute greatly to the company's business operations and its competitive positioning. These activities in essence constitute the basis of the firm's differentiation relative to its competitors and should be kept in-house. For example, such activities for Dell include those that maintain and enhance the speed of operations and its focus on core business. "Qualifiers" are activities that are critical for business operations yet do not contribute to the company's competitive positioning in a major way. These activities should best be sourced, which could include the involvement of a third party if it meets the right cost and quality criteria. For example, aircraft maintenance systems are a minimum requirement for airlines to compete in the industry, but they do not constitute an important differentiator between airlines. "Necessary evils" are activities that do not contribute significantly to the company's business or its competitive positioning. These activities constitute good candidates for outsourcing. For example, in the case of Dell in the early 2000s, such activities include administration, inventory, and payroll tasks. "Distractions" are failing attempts to differentiate a company from its competitors. These activities should be eliminated or migrated to

Table 2.2 Decision-making matrix on outsourcing

		"Qualifiers" (Best to Source)	"Order Winners" (In-House)
Contribution to Business Operations	Critical		
	Useful	"Necessary Evils" (Outsource)	"Distractions" (Migrate or Eliminate)
		Commodity	Differentiator
		Contribution to Competitive Positioning	

Source: Willcocks, Petherbridge, and Olson (2002)

another quadrant. For example, Dell in 1989 opened retail outlets, but soon it discovered that its major distinctive competence was the direct model of selling.

Having identified activities that are outsourcing candidates, Willcocks et al. (2002) suggest another matrix to evaluate whether the market can service the requirement. If the market is not cheap, capable, or mature enough, then the organization will need to seek a largely in-house solution. Table 2.3 captures the major elements for consideration and plots the cost efficiencies and capabilities the market can offer against carrying out the activity internally.

Where the market can carry out a task cheaper and better, then outsourcing is the obvious decision, but only for "qualifiers" and "necessary evils." As an example, Federal Express provides customer delivery for Dell. Where the market offers an inferior cost and capability, then in-house sourcing will be the best alternative (assuming that "distractions" are best not sourced at all). Where the market offers a better cost deal, then this should be taken, but only for nonkey activities ("necessary evils"). Where the market offers superior capability but at a premium price above what the in-house cost might be, there may still be good reasons for buying in

Table 2.3 Strategic sourcing by market comparison

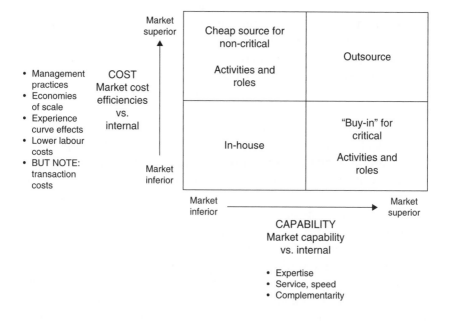

or close partnering with the third party, not least to leverage and learn from their expertise, and apply it to "qualifying" and "order-winning" tasks.

Impact of operational and structural risks on outsourcing and offshoring decisions

Another aspect to consider while deciding which processes can be off-shored or outsourced is related to two major types of risk that companies face: *operational risk,* which refers to the danger that processes will not function properly and operate smoothly after offshoring, and *structural risk,* which refers to the danger that the relationship between clients and suppliers may not work as expected. With regard to operational risk, it is of great significance to evaluate the extent to which processes can be codified and measured. Aron and Singh (2005) distinguish transparent, codifiable, opaque, and noncodifiable processes.

Transparent processes (e.g., transaction processing, telecollection, and technical support) can be clearly measured in terms of quality and are the tasks that can be fully codified. Consequently, the operational risk of off-shoring and outsourcing in this case is very low.

Codifiable processes can be measured to some extent in terms of the quality of their execution, and most of the work can be codified. If firms can measure the quality of the final outcome to a satisfactory extent (e.g., for processes such as customer service and account management), then the operational risk of offshoring and outsourcing becomes more manageable. However, if measuring the final outcome is not possible (e.g., for processes such as equity research, yield analysis, and litigation support), then the operational risk becomes very high.

Opaque processes can be codified in terms of the work being done, but the quality of the process outputs is difficult to measure (e.g., for processes such as insurance underwriting, invoice management, and cash-flow fore-casting). Although the risks of offshoring these processes are moderate, companies can monitor the work being done and inspect samples to ensure that the outcome meets their expectations. This, however, could be rather troublesome and expensive. If a company can specify how the supplier should do the work, it can lower the risk of offshoring by establishing a performance-based reward system and penalties.

Noncodifiable processes, as the term implies, cannot be codified; examples are supply chain coordination and customer data analysis. In addition, often they cannot be measured in terms of the quality being achieved (such as pricing and working capital management). For this reason, such processes usually carry a high amount of operational risk. If an organization chooses to outsource such processes, it should closely supervise the vendor's work.

The ability to monitor work and the precision of metrics used to measure process quality define the degree of structural risk that outsourcing presents to a client firm (Aron and Singh, 2005). For example, transaction processing and insurance claims processing are typically easy to monitor, with precise metrics to measure their quality. Therefore, these activities present low structural risk. Activities like product design and research and development are high risk because it is difficult to monitor outcomes and challenging to define a precise quality metric.

While engaging in an outsourcing relationship, most companies assume that their supplier will behave in a collaborative way. This is not necessarily true, however, even in the case of companies that are buying services from captive centers that they own. For example, structural risk may arise because a vendor does not update the processes of performing certain tasks, does not invest in employee training, and does not hire the most qualified people. Another problem is that service providers often exert much less effort in getting the work done than they originally agreed to. Structural risk also arises when contractual terms are altered after clients have handed over processes to providers. Once a company has handed a set of processes to a supplier, it is not easy to take it back in-house at short notice. Providers are aware of this and thus may use their power position to demand higher prices.

It is also important to consider that when firms source processes that require the transfer of a large amount of knowledge, they have to invest time and effort to pass this knowledge on to the supplier's employees. Furthermore, some processes take a long time to stabilize when they are offshored. In both cases, the cost of switching providers is very high.

Nonetheless, structural risk can be mitigated in a number of ways. First, firms must establish contractual clauses that will impose on the provider the obligation to continue to deliver the service at a certain price after the contract's expiration date. Usually this period is 150 percent of the time that it would take for the provider to deliver output that matches the organization's requirements and quality standards. Furthermore, companies should try to split their business between two or more providers. Working with multiple suppliers provides a strong element of power for a company for at least two reasons. First, if a supplier underperforms, it becomes easier to transfer the work to a supplier that is already executing the same processes. Second, working with multiple providers will generate a competitive climate among them that, if managed carefully, can become very beneficial for the customer in terms of price and the quality of service delivered.

Aron and Singh (2005) suggest that firms should base their outsourcing and offshoring decisions on the assessment of operational and structural risks. For activities that present high operational and structural risks such as corporate planning, they recommend executing in-house and onshore. For activities that present moderate operational and structural risks such as supply chain coordination, they suggest outsourcing carefully, using extended organization offshore, and monitoring closely in real time. (*Extended organization* is a hybrid organizational form where the client company specifies the quality of services it wants and works closely alongside providers to get that quality by managing the providers carefully and monitoring the agents' work to ensure that things are done properly.) Activities with low operational and structural risks such as transaction processing are suitable for outsourcing to offshore service providers. Table 2.4 provides the full spectrum of organizational forms and locations and several example of activities suitable for each combination of operational and structural risks (each being low, moderate, and high).

Table 2.4 Choosing location and organizational form

Operational risk		Structural risk	
HIGH	Outsource to service provider located nearby (nearshore) *Litigation support*	Set up captive center nearby or onshore *R&D, design*	Execute process in house and onshore *Pricing, corporate planning*
MODERATE	Outsource to offshore service provider over time *Insurance claims processing, customer support*	Outsource carefully, using "extended organization" offshore, and monitor closely in real time *Supply chain coordination*	Set up captive center offshore *Equity research*
LOW	Outsource to offshore service provider *Data entry, Transaction processing*	Outsource carefully, using "extended organization" offshore *Telecollection, technical support*	Outsource carefully, using "extended organization" offshore, and conduct frequent process audits *Customer data analysis, market research analysis*
	LOW	MODERATE	HIGH

Structural risk

Source: Aron and Singh (2005)

Complex and problematic business processes

In addition to the value-creation and value-capture criteria that certain processes present, as well as the relative operational and structural risks in outsourcing, Aron and Clemons (2004) suggest that the complexity of processes plays a significant role in offshoring decisions. They provide a useful set of criteria for evaluating process complexity that can help executives make appropriate sourcing decisions:

1. The codifiability of the data that must be transferred so that the process can be performed by the external party in a reliable way and with adherence to the required quality standards
2. The amount of training that must be provided to the employees of the supplier so that they become competent in performing the work
3. The cost of monitoring performance levels
4. The difficulty in assessing managers' level of confidence that their quality assessments will be accurate and reliable
5. The desired educational level for the employees of the supplier
6. Revenue per vendor working on the assigned task
7. Number of subtasks associated with the task
8. A single overall measure of task complexity used to assess the accuracy of ratings and the weight associated with different factors

Taking a different perspective, Puryear and Detrick (2006) suggest that the main problem with offshoring is that many managers regard it as a panacea for operational processes. Instead of diagnosing and correcting deficiencies, many managers seek to move the problems somewhere else. In most cases, however, this tactic is counterproductive. For this reason, the authors suggest that before considering offshoring, firms should determine the factors that inhibit performance. On this basis, they suggest three steps:

1. *Revamp business processes:* Increased complexity is a fundamental factor causing organizational deficiencies and poor performance. Offshoring is not always an answer to the problem. Managing complexity and eliminating unnecessary complications can bring significant cost reductions, without engaging in the risks of offshoring. This is what Brother International Corporation did when dealing with its problematic frontline call center operations. The company received approximately 1.8 million calls on an annual basis, which took too long to process. To make matters worse, customer profiles were lost in online databases, and representatives were able to resolve fewer than half of the queries from new customers. However,

instead of misdiagnosing the problem as a simple customer service problem that could be solved by offshoring it to an external cost-efficient party, executives tried to dig deeper. They discovered that solving the issue of managing customer complaints could actually benefit the organization if the insights gained with regard to their customers' profiles and tastes could be shared and used to improve marketing and product design. For this reason, they did not consider offshoring call center operations, but instead decided to improve them. The division consolidated paper manuals into an online directory and integrated its records into a CRM database. Within a year, product returns had dropped by one-third and the time needed to resolve customer problems dropped by 43 seconds on average. The new CRM enabled the company to capture insights with regard to its customers that it used in the development of its new products and marketing strategies.

2. *Reinforce credibility and trust:* Sourcing strategies often mask dysfunctional relationships between departments and business units. For this reason, it is important to make sure that different divisions and units within an organization are collaborating effectively and that their goals are aligned. For example, at the brokerage firm Charles Schwab, IT had long been viewed as a source of competitive advantage. But while the IT budget remained strong, pressure to deliver new applications meant less spending to update infrastructure and reduce complexity. Over time, the firm's IT efforts drifted. When a major two-year initiative to develop a new portfolio management system failed, trust in IT plummeted. In response, the company launched a business-led IT project in 2004 geared to restructuring the IT infrastructure. The alliance and collaboration between the business and the IT department was fundamental for the effective execution of the project.

3. *Find the scale-economy sweet spot:* Contemporary organizations can benefit significantly from the consolidation of activities to the regional or global level. For example, one global financial services company reduced its cost structure significantly by consolidating its scattered customer service centers. The company had to deal with a host of inconsistent procedures across its centers. However, the standardization of the technology and the connection between the locations by a routing software boosted both efficiency and customer satisfaction. The overall savings of the company reached $200 million.

Summary

This chapter reviewed key models for making decisions regarding outsourcing and offshoring. Although many dimensions must be considered, firms mainly concern with the following questions: which parts of the business to outsource and to what locations. This chapter brings together the considerations regarding these two aspects to offer a comprehensive analysis of the options available for firms.

Relevant teaching cases

Applegate, L. M. (2002). "Xerox: Outsourcing Global Information Technology Resources." *Harvard Business Online*, no. 9-195-158.

CHAPTER 3

Country attractiveness for sourcing

This chapter discusses the maturity of various geographical locations worldwide and the factors that clients and suppliers take into account when deciding on their offshoring and offshore outsourcing strategies. We focus on the following aspects:

- An overview of sourcing destinations
- Criteria for selecting locations
- The advantages of nearshoring as a sourcing option

An overview of sourcing destinations

Both clients and vendors consider sourcing destinations, but with different goals in mind. Vendors are interested in locations where they can set up global delivery centers. Client companies are interested in outsourcing or in setting up captive facilities abroad for R&D or customer support to service their own organization or their customers.

Together with India, which in 2008 attracted some 65 percent of ITO and 43 percent of the BPO market (Willcocks and Lacity, 2009), Brazil, Russia, and China (BRIC) are considered the most attractive (tier 1) sourcing destinations for ITO and BPO. This is mainly because of the scale of services, available skills, and the maturity achieved with regard to sourcing activities. Vendors as well as captive centers based in these countries, in particular in India, tend to move up the value chain, departing from specific and repetitive tasks that are usually captured by new entrants – the so-called tier 2 and tier 3 countries. By 2011, over 125 offshore locations were providing ITO and BPO services.

The relative attractiveness of BRIC and non-BRIC countries as sourcing destinations is dynamic. Their attractiveness needs to be understood in the context of long-term global sourcing trends and the current global economic climate. In this regard, spending will continue to rise in all global sourcing markets through recessionary as well as growth periods, but spending on BPO will overtake spending on ITO within the next five years. BPO expenditures will be in areas such as the human resource function; procurement; back office administration; call centers; legal, finance, and accounting; customer-facing operations; and asset management. In line with this trend, a highly competitive global services market presents opportunities for countries that can offer the right mix of costs, skills, and reliable service (see the trends in Chapter 1).

Emerging sourcing destinations are trying to differentiate their offerings from BRIC countries and from tier 2 and tier 3 rivals when competing for a contract. For example, Egypt is promoting itself as a low-cost destination for call centers that specialize in European languages. Dubai and Singapore present their IT security systems and legal systems as an advantage, particularly with regard to the outsourcing of high-security and business-continuity services. The Philippines, a former US colony, stresses its long cultural ties with the US and the excellent English skills of its population to attract English-speaking call centers. Morocco is trying to attract French-speaking European clients to set up call centers, while Central and South American Spanish-speaking countries are hoping to establish call centers that can provide services to the Hispanic market in the US (Reinhardt et al., 2006). In fact, recent studies have shown that some non-BRIC destinations have been successful in competing with BRIC by positioning their specialized skill sets in particular areas and often by offering lower costs than other potential destinations (Kotlarsky and Oshri, 2008).

While tier 2 and tier 3 outsourcing destinations are improving their position, India has gained in the area of ITO and BPO services recently. Many global clients (large multinational corporations) view India as a center of excellence for ITO and BPO, and not merely as a low-cost destination. Many US and European clients initially engaged Indian suppliers to provide technical services such as programming and platform upgrades (e.g., to help with compliance at the turn of the century). However as these relationships matured, Western clients assigned more challenging work to Indian suppliers, such as development and support tasks for critical business applications. From our research, we learned that Indian suppliers now wish to assume higher-value activities, including R&D and KPO.

However, India and, to a lesser extent, China, Brazil, and Russia, are already experiencing upward pressure on wages, combined with rising, and sometimes high, attrition. There is in fact a war for talent within each of the BRIC countries, which suppresses the key factors that made these countries attractive destinations for outsourcing in the first place. For example, many firms from India and China have relocated offshore activities from these countries to more attractive locations. And major Indian suppliers such as TCS are setting up global delivery centers in China mainly because the supply of engineering skills and the proficiency in English has significantly improved in recent years in China.

To put these views into context, China's $142.3 billion investment in ICT in 2006 aimed at improving its competitive position in the offshoring service market. Willcocks and Lacity (2009) predict that China's ITO and BPO service capabilities will be strong. However, the main ITO and BPO suppliers in China are either large US-based suppliers such as Accenture, Capgemini, Dell, HP, and IBM, or large India-based suppliers such as Genpact, Infosys, and TCS. Still, similar to the development of the Indian services supply base, many Chinese suppliers do not want to compete solely in terms of low-level technical skills. Now they are trying to address the full range of the service value chain.

Nevertheless, many client organizations are cautious of China's ITO and BPO services because of language and cultural barriers and fears over losing intellectual property. The Chinese government and business sectors are well aware of these barriers and are seeking ways to address them. An investment of $5 billion in language skills by the Chinese government is one example of the attempts to overcome such barriers. In 2009, the Chinese government redressed the lack of attention to the services outsourcing industry by establishing 20 service outsourcing base cities (Lacity, Willcocks, and Zheng, 2010).

Developing countries other than India and China are becoming players in the IT services market. Many US clients already use Central American suppliers for Spanish-speaking business processes such as help desks, patient scheduling, and data entry. Synchronous time zones are one of the drivers for US firms that outsource work to Central or South America. Furthermore, access to skills and scale are two factors that clients consider in their assessment of attractive locations. In this regard, Brazil has the advantage of a large population, the innovative creativity of its engineers, and government programs supporting the outsourcing industry, while Chile and Uruguay have exploited their time zone advantages, back office proficiencies, and government incentives to attract outsourcing work.

While South America is emerging as an attractive destination for offshoring and offshore outsourcing, today organizations from Western Europe are increasingly sourcing IT and businesses services to providers located in Central Eastern Europe (CEE). Among the key drivers of such a trend are the closer proximity to the supplier, limited time zone differences, and lower transaction costs than those incurred through using Asian alternatives. Furthermore, latest research on captives by Oshri (2011) shows that the CEE region is becoming a popular nearshore captive destination for

Western European clients. In particular, Bulgaria, Czech Republic, and Hungary have attracted large numbers of R&D centers, making them a hub for business innovation and high-value knowledge-intensive professional services.

In sub-Saharan Africa, several countries are actively seeking to become players in the global ITO and BPO markets. For example, countries such as Botswana and Kenya have quickly established their economies partly on the competitiveness of IT and IT services. Another example is South Africa, which is exporting IT and business services primarily to UK-based clients, because of similar time zones, cultural similarities, English-speaking capabilities, and a good infrastructure. Mediterranean North Africa already exports IT services to Europe. For example, Moroccan IT suppliers are favored by clients in France because of the common language, similar time zone, and cultural capability.

Criteria for selecting locations

Selecting a location is one of the major challenges when making offshoring and outsourcing decisions. A decision to relocate a business function or set up a new captive facility (for clients) or delivery center (for suppliers) abroad is based to a large extent on the attractiveness of the sourcing locations. However, in some outsourcing decisions, it is no less important to consider the attractiveness of the suppliers. This is mainly because some suppliers, though they are associated with a particular location, have a global presence, which can be a factor that a client would appreciate far more than the home-base advantages of the supplier. (We discuss supplier evaluation and selection criteria in detail in Chapter 6.)

Several frameworks for selecting offshoring and offshore outsourcing destinations are set out in the academic and professional literature to help managers assess the attractiveness of countries and regions. All of these frameworks consider costs, business environment, availability of labor resources, and specific skills. Some frameworks (e.g., Carmel, 2003; Farrell, 2006) are more detailed than others (e.g., A. T. Kearney Global's three factors) in terms of the factors they consider when comparing potential sourcing locations.

In our view, the most effective frameworks are the six factors that Farrell (2006) identified: costs, skills, business and living environment, quality of infrastructure, risk profile, and market potential. We describe these factors in Table 3.1 and discuss them in detail below, providing an example of how each of these factors can be used to compare the attractiveness of

Table 3.1 Factors for assessing country attractiveness for outsourcing and offshoring

Cost	Labour costs (average wages for skilled workers and managers)
	Infrastructure costs (unit costs for telecom networks, Internet access and power, and office rent)
	Corporate taxes (tax breaks and regulations and other incentives for local investment)
Skills	Skill pool (the size of the labor pool with required skills). Required skills may include technical and business knowledge, management skills, languages, and the ability to learn new concepts and innovate. The scalability of labor resources in the long term (i.e., the ability to supply sufficient labor resources to meet growing demand) is a major issue to consider when choosing a sourcing destination. An indication of the scalability of labor resources in a country is the annual growth in the number of graduates with desired skills. Countries that offer scalability of labor resources are also more likely to keep wages relatively low due to the constant supply of new graduates
	Vendor landscape (the size of the local sector providing IT services and other business functions). For clients looking to outsource IT or business processes, it is imperative to evaluate the vendor's landscape in terms of the general skills set (or capabilities) and competencies of vendors
Business and living environment	Governance support (policy on foreign investment, labor laws, bureaucratic and regulatory burden, level of corruption)
	Business environment (compatibility with prevailing business culture and ethics)
	Living environment (overall quality of life, prevalence of HIV infection, serious crime per capita)
	Accessibility (travel time, flight frequency, and time difference)
Quality of infrastructure	Telecommunication and IT (network downtime, speed of service restoration, and connectivity)
	Real estate (both the availability and quality)
	Transportation (scale and quality of road and rail networks)
	Power (reliability of power supply)
Risk profile	Security issues (risks to personal security and property-related issues such as fraud, crime, and terrorism)
	Disruptive events (including the risk of a labor uprising, political unrest, and natural disasters)
	Regulatory risks (the stability, fairness, and efficiency of the legal framework)
	Macroeconomic risks (such as cost inflation, currency fluctuation, and capital freedom)
	Intellectual property risk (strength of the data and protection regime)
Market potential	Attractiveness of the local market (the current gross domestic product and its growth rate)
	Access to nearby markets (in both the host country and adjacent region)

Source: Based on Farrell (2006)

several non-BRIC tier 2 countries for the sourcing of IT services and BPO. The countries we compare are CEE countries such as Romania, Bulgaria, Poland, Slovakia, Czech Republic, and Belarus; Egypt, Morocco, and Tunisia in Africa; Costa Rica and Venezuela in the Americas; and several Asian countries, such as Vietnam, the Philippines, and Thailand (see the detailed country comparison in Willcocks et al., 2009).

Factor 1: Costs

Companies considering outsourcing IT or business processes typically compare a range of costs, including labor costs (average wages for skilled workers and managers), infrastructure costs (unit costs for telecom networks, Internet access and power, office rent), and corporate taxes (tax breaks and regulations and other incentives for local investment) across potential outsourcing locations. In addition, they are now also looking at value-added dimensions for how they might benefit over time.

Example: Comparing costs

Among the 14 countries compared, the highest salaries are in CEE. Within CEE, salaries in Bulgaria are the lowest (46 euros per week) compared to Czech Republic (205 euros), Hungary (114 euros), Poland (144 euros), and Slovakia (232 euros). These are the median gross private sector wages for early 2010. This situation is beginning to change, however, as markets change and the skills base develops further within particular economies. As a result, costs within these countries are increasing more rapidly than in Asia. A contributing factor is that the property prices in CEE vary significantly. In some places, such as Prague, monthly rent is on par with any other Western city. Typically the rent of commercial space in high-tech business parks located near a capital or other major city is significantly higher than in the more remote business parks, and prime locations within major cities are more expensive than on the outskirts. As a result, secondary locations are emerging in CEE countries (e.g., Katowice, Poznan, Wroclaw) that are close to major universities to ensure a supply of skilled graduates and yet benefit from the relatively lower property prices.

Labor costs in Asia are lower than in all the other countries we have compared, with Vietnam being the cheapest (among the countries compared, Indonesia has lowest salaries in Asia).

The costs of the telecommunications infrastructure and Internet are relatively low in all the countries compared.

Although all CEE countries are offering preferential tax policies and support for investment, the governments of countries in the Middle East and Africa, Asia, and the Americas offer even higher incentives than CEE countries do. Some provide complete tax exemption. For example, Morocco promotes its so-called Morocco value proposal, which offers a set of unique incentives, including tax credits, value-added tax exemptions for exports, and subsidies for training purposes. Beyond financial incentives, the Philippines government recently liberalized visa requirements for certain categories of investors and IT professionals, making it easy for expatriate employees to be based in the Philippines.

Factor 2: Skills

This factor encompasses the skill pool (the size of labor pool with required skills) and the vendor landscape (the size of the local sector providing IT services and other business functions). Required skills may include technical and business knowledge, management skills, languages, and the ability to learn new concepts and to innovate.

Labor resources

The scalability of labor resources in the long term (i.e., the ability to supply sufficient labor resources to handle growing demand) is a major issue to consider while deciding on a sourcing destination. An indication of the scalability of labor resources is the growth in the number of graduates with desired skills that the country is able to produce each year – for example, technical and business knowledge, management skills, languages, and the ability to learn new concepts and innovate. Countries that offer scalability of labor resources are also more likely to keep wages relatively low owing to a constant supply of graduates.

For companies considering expansion to offshore or nearshore locations, it is important to evaluate the gap between desired and available skills. Furthermore, these companies should assess the efforts by various stakeholders to bridge such skill gaps, for example, through various specialized in-house training programs.

Vendor landscape

Clients looking to outsource IT or business processes must evaluate the vendor landscape in terms of the skill set (or capabilities) and competencies of vendors. In this regard, clients should assess each vendor's ability to respond to the customer's ongoing needs (a delivery competency), radically improve service in terms of quality and cost (a transformation competency), and be willing and able to align its business model to the values, goals, and needs of the customer (a relational competency). Countries that have suppliers able to demonstrate such competencies to clients are in a better position to attract clients looking to outsource high-value complex, knowledge-intensive, and strategic activities. The vendor landscape combines both local vendors and international suppliers that have a presence in the country (e.g., have set up a delivery center). The maturity of vendors in a country can be assessed based on 12 capabilities that are grouped into three key areas of competencies: relationship, transformation and delivery (these are discussed in detail in Chapter 4).

Example: Comparing availability of skills

The education systems in CEE countries have become strong in the sciences, technology, and engineering and accessible to the vast majority of the population. During communist rule, secondary education was made compulsory for the entire population of these countries. In contrast, in countries in the Middle East, Africa, Asia, and the Americas that we have examined, a large part of the population still lives in rural areas and is not well educated. The level of literacy in these countries is significantly lower than in CEE countries. Therefore, while CEE countries are on average much smaller in population than Egypt, the Philippines, Venezuela, Thailand, Vietnam, and Morocco, the percentage of their population that is being educated and is becoming a highly skilled workforce is much higher. However, in numbers, this higher percentage of educated population still is lower than the number of graduates in large countries such as Egypt and Philippines.

In particular, CEE countries have a highly skilled workforce with technical skills and training in research and the applied sciences;

however, the labor pool of these countries is limited. For example, in 2010, Bulgaria, which has a higher percentage of university graduates than any other CEE country, had about 39,000 students enrolled in a technical program, with nearly 5,800 graduates that year. Egypt, in contrast, has 330,000 new graduates, from all disciplines, every year, with 31,000 of them receiving technology, science, and engineering degrees. The Philippines has 380,000 new graduates each year, but only 15,000 are focused on technology studies. The main difference in the skills base that Egypt and the Philippines are offering is in the variety of languages (English being the main language offered by the Philippines, and a variety of European languages offered by Egypt). The impact of this continuous stream of well-educated graduates is that it ensures stability in labor costs and a choice of skills and languages for local and international labor markets.

Although some countries have developed specific language skills (Morocco) or technology-related knowledge (Vietnam), one key challenge that all 14 countries examined face is the lack of management skills – in particular, project management. Vendors from these countries tend to solve this problem by retaining management roles with the Western client or partner.

To examine this topic more thoroughly, we look at a case study from Costa Rica.

Case Study

PANGENESIS: A CREATIVE COSTA RICAN APPROACH TO THE PERSISTENT IT LABOR CRUNCH

by Erran Carmel

"We have an innovative workforce solution for offshore outsourcing," asserted Carlos Apéstegui, head of PanGenesis's Costa Rican operations. "We have a unique apprentice program to tap young Costa Rican students and a special approach to importing highly qualified labor into Costa Rica. We have created a formula that allows us to lower charge rates, perform faster development – and all this in this attractive small nation." He finished his sentence by waving at the

▶

▶
many tropical plants around him in the garden of the hotel hosting a large technology conference.

His guest was Paul Matzurski, a deputy CIO at a large American corporation who was visiting Costa Rica for the first time in search of new destinations for offshore outsourcing. Matzurski sipped his drink and said, "I didn't know the extent of the tight labor market here and even the rest of Latin America." He continued: "You know, labor scarcity, the search for talent, and a tight labor market are all issues we deal with a lot in the USA. We hear about the tight labor markets in India and elsewhere. I was surprised to learn this is the case here in Costa Rica. Even [Costa Rican] President Arias spoke of spending more on education during his keynote address to this conference yesterday."

PanGenesis's CEO, Richard W. Knudson, spoke up: "Let me tell you the details of PanGenesis's workforce and pricing plans," he said to Matzurski. "Do you have a sheet of paper? I will explain." Fifteen minutes later, Matzurski had a much clearer appreciation of PanGenesis's ambitious plans.

Matzurski leaned back and pondered the PanGenesis value proposition for offshore outsourcing. *This is certainly creative, intriguing, and ambitious,* he thought, *but will it work? Will the program provide the apparent substantial improvement in productivity and quality at a lower cost with quicker delivery? Will the plan generate enough skilled employees? How many more years will it take to get the kinks out of this new workforce method?*

In 1997, Costa Rica's president, José María Figueres, flew to California to visit Intel's headquarters in Santa Clara, California. This was an unusual visit: the president of a tiny Central American country was coming to press his case that Intel, one of the world's most important tech companies, would choose Costa Rica as the next location of its semiconductor plant.

The Intel gamble clearly paid off. Costa Rica is now a high-tech star. Intel alone employs 5,500 people in country. The other major multinational corporation player in the country is HP, which employs a similar number. Dozens of other foreign tech companies, including those in the life sciences, have set up operations in Costa Rica, and hundreds of indigenous Costa Rican firms have sprouted up selling their products and services to clients in the region, as well as to North America and to Europe.

Until its rise as a tech center, Costa Rica was best known for its coffee, bananas, rain forest, and, most interesting, abolishing its standing army in 1948.

▶

▶

Costa Rica has only 4 million people and so the boom in high tech has led to an unusual high-tech labor crunch with escalating salaries. Of the labor force, there are about 7,500 software professionals (or as many as 25,000 if broader assumptions are used) and another 20,000 employees in a related boom sector: call centers.

Costa Rica has nurtured good schools and universities, both public and private, resulting in being a country with one of the highest literacy rates in the world. In addition to the major public universities, one of its leading private universities, Universidad Latina, has established a number of computer-related programs that help train software professionals.

And its timing has been right. By 2007 the global tech boom was in its second decade, with an accelerating global demand for software professionals in both wealthy and emerging nations and an ensuing labor crunch and a related problem of turnover as people jumped from job to job in the hot market seeking higher salaries. At the same time, baby boomers in Europe and the United States were racing toward retirement, with US Labor Department estimates that by 2020, there will be a shortage of 28 million people in the labor force. And so, after looking at the overheated markets in India and China, and the upcoming crunch in the US, many have turned to labor markets in Latin America to fill the void. PanGenesis is one of the companies that was in the right place.

PanGenesis is an IT services firm targeting and servicing multinational clients. Thus, its foreign clients outsource IT support offshore (nearshore) to PanGenesis. PanGenesis was founded in 2002 and is headed by three experienced leaders. American CEO and founder Richard W. Knudson is an old hand in offshoring, having lived in India for seven years consulting to the Indian IT industry. Among his many accomplishments, Knudson was involved in early capability maturity model (CMM) evaluations in India and China. The firm's president is Jim Kamenelis, the former CIO of Xerox Palo Alto Research Center, one of the most venerated R&D centers in modern US history. Carlos Apéstegui heads operations in Costa Rica. He is a native of Costa Rica and has 20 years of successful IT business operations in Costa Rica.

PanGenesis is building several programs for tapping inexpensive but well-trained IT labor.

▶

► **Apprentice program**

CEO Knudson and President Kamenelis began working with the newly elected Able Pacheco government in 2002 to create apprentice programs. Working with influential people in Costa Rica and making his case directly to the president and the science and technology minister, Mr. Pardo-Evens, many of the elements of the program were in place in 2007.

At its core, the program targets young, poor students out of high school. There are many excellent students who are not funneled through career tracks for various reasons. Typically they are busy working to contribute to the family income. Only about 20 percent of 2,500 applicants who apply at the state-funded public university computer science (CS) program are accepted, with the remaining 80 percent ripe for an apprentice program. Of those who are accepted into the CS programs, 60 percent are unable to finish. A related source of apprentices are the 450 students who finish the strong high school IT track of 2,500 hours. In spite of their computer prowess, many seek structure in their computer career plans.

All of these students can be turned into productive software engineering professionals through the apprentice program. The students undergo a rigorous six-month training program that includes English immersion; intensive programming concepts; configuration management using well-known software; quality assurance audits; nightly code reviews; training in documentation; and teamwork, scheduling, and statistical analysis. Once the training is successfully completed, the graduates become engineering apprentices and are assigned to support a seasoned software engineer four hours a day. This pair acts as a development team. The qualification for an apprentice is modeled in the following diagram.

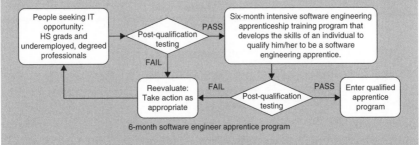

6-month software engineer apprentice program

▶

The apprentice relieves the software engineer from having to perform important but nonengineering housekeeping tasks that take up a substantial amount of time. This frees the engineer to focus on high-impact software engineering tasks.

While fully educated and experienced software engineers are "charged out" at up to $30 an hour, an apprentice is charged to the client at a much lower rate. PanGenesis's income for the apprentice is used to fund the apprentice's living expenses, pay the university for the apprentice's four-year university education to receive a software engineering degree, and sponsor grants for underprivileged students and support university classrooms and labs.

To remain an apprentice the student must pursue a university degree as a software engineer, maintain a high grade point average, properly and diligently perform his or her apprenticeship assignments, and commit to work for PanGenesis after graduating from the university. The apprentice works four hours each day and attends the university the remainder of the time. This program is modeled in the following diagram.

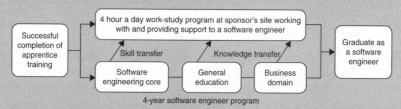

As shown in the table that follows, the apprentice model allows PanGenesis to significantly underbid competitors while substantially reducing project and development costs and delivery times. In addition to schedule and cost benefits, the services and products receive a substantial improvement in quality due to 100 percent code reviews and frequent quality audits conducted by the well-trained apprentices. This value added to quality and project cost is not factored into the savings already achieved by the apprenticeship model.

Costs and charges for apprentice-supported teams

Software engineer productivity: The workday breakdown

Typical Engineering Tasks	Hours
Core engineering work	4.0
Productive housekeeping tasks: configuration management, code review, quality audits, scheduling, statistical analysis, etc.	2.5
Social time: Phone calls, long lunch, breaks, nonbusiness conversation	1.5

▶

▶

In the traditional model, assume a typical project with the following parameters:

Traditional model	Metrics
Total project hours	10,000
Rate charged in offshore outsourcing	$30 per hour
Skills needed: Engineers experienced in J2EE, Web applications	5 or more years experience
Number of engineers assigned	5
Effort per week	200 hours per week
Duration	**50 weeks**
Total charge to customer	**$300,000**

In the PanGenesis apprentice model, the apprentice takes over some of the software engineer's productive housekeeping tasks:

	Metrics
Number of total productive hours (1,000 hours added for apprentice management)	11,000
Apprentice daily work hours	4
Engineering rate	$30 per hour
Apprentice rate	$9
Total weekly charge to customer of a team of engineers and apprentices	$1,380
Charge rate by PanGenesis (engineers with five or more years of experience)	$23 per hour
Effort per week (engineers and apprentices)	300 hours
Duration (total hours/weekly burn rate)	**37 weeks**
Total cost to PanGenesis of team of engineer and apprentice (hours × average rate)	**$253,000**

Underemployed university graduates

According to the government's estimate, Costa Rica has 47,000 underemployed or unemployed university graduates. The Arias government's minister of science and technology, E. Flores, would like to retrain them for IT. Therefore, PanGenesis has included a fast-track program for these professionals using the apprenticeship program model. These professionals have experience in business that would add value to their role as a software engineer.

▶

▶

The PanGenesis program is an accelerated two-year program: working while attending the core software engineering courses to qualify for a degree in software engineering. The accelerated pace is based on having met prior university general education and elective requirements from the employee's previous degree. Income from the client for the degreed professional/apprentice is used in the same way as the income from high school graduates who cannot afford the university.

Labor importation

The last element of the PanGenesis model is to build a large, scalable, highly qualified engineering workforce. To accomplish this, it is augmenting Costa Rican labor with guest workers from other nations. PanGenesis has established an international IT sourcing capability, hiring skilled software engineers from Eastern Europe, the Philippines, and Latin America. This initial workforce will serve clients and will be the first mentors to the apprenticeship workforce being developed.

Of particular interest to the firm is the Philippines, which has a relatively large and mobile IT professional labor pool. Its engineers are well trained and speak excellent English and are also familiar with Spanish.

Filipino employees will enjoy income tax exemption because they are working outside the Philippines. They will be working for an affiliate company of PanGenesis. PanGenesis pays their social security tax due on salary received in Costa Rica, and provides them with room and board expenses.

Factor 3: Business and living environment

This factor considers governance support (policy on foreign investment, labor laws, bureaucratic and regulatory burden, level of corruption), the business environment (compatibility with prevailing business culture and ethics), the living environment (overall quality of life, prevalence of HIV infection, serious crime per capita), and accessibility (travel time, flight frequency, time difference).

Example: Comparing business and living environment

Governments try to attract foreign investment, and therefore some offer special development zones such as the free trade zone in Egypt, the offshore programming zone in Belarus, and the nearshore center in Morocco. These free trade zones offer tax breaks, simplified administrative procedures, and, in some cases, more flexible labor rules. However, although such an investment incentive might be appealing to Western firms, corruption remains a problem in many of the tier 2 and tier 3 countries. The European Union, for example, has been monitoring corruption in its member states to ensure that local governments also fight this phenomenon.

In terms of business environment, CEE countries are the most attractive destinations for European companies looking to outsource or nearshore business processes or services. Culturally these countries provide a good fit with Western cultures, the time zone difference is limited, and most destinations are easily accessible by air or ground transportation.

Countries in Asia and the Americas require longer commutes and offer wider time zone differences for clients based in Europe. For call centers that operate 24 hours every day, time zone differences do not necessarily create major challenges. However, for offshore outsourcing projects that involve software development and the collaboration of globally distributed teams, time zone differences may result in coordination challenges.

For North American clients, CEE countries provide a reasonable cultural fit; however, in terms of travel time and time zone differences, these countries are too remote; alternative destinations such as Central America or the Caribbean countries are more attractive.

In terms of the living environment, this factor mainly affects the attractiveness of the outsourcing destination for expatriates. This is particularly common where the client establishes a presence in the destination country in the form of a captive center or as a support provided to the vendor's service team. In this regard, CEE countries, where the standard of living is relatively high and the cultural fit with Western countries is reasonable, are most attractive for expatriates. Vendors from countries that are less attractive to expatriates have been attempting to expand their presence in Western countries. For example, there is a large Vietnamese expatriate community living and working in developed IT markets worldwide, providing a connection between Western customers and Vietnamese developers and helping to reduce cultural and language barriers.

Factor 4: Quality of infrastructure

Quality of infrastructure includes telecommunication and IT (network downtime, speed of service restoration, connectivity), real estate (availability and quality), transportation (scale and quality of road and rail network), and power (reliability of power supply).

Example: Comparing quality of infrastructure

CEE countries are rapidly catching up to Western European countries in terms of the quality of telecommunications and IT infrastructure. Bulgaria, Czech Republic, and Slovakia, for example, have excellent telecommunication infrastructures. Romania's domestic telecom infrastructure is still poor but improving. The Romanian government aims to transform Romania to become the Internet hub of the Black Sea region. In the past few years, the country has had one of the largest growths in mobile communications in Europe.

In contrast to CEE, where the quality of telecommunications and IT infrastructure is comparable across the countries, the availability and quality of telecommunications and IT infrastructure in non-CEE countries vary significantly. It is common to find an advanced IT infrastructure in business parks and large cities, but a limited IT infrastructure in rural areas – or none at all. For example, Tunisia has a large number of high-tech parks (called technopoles) with state-of-the-art IT infrastructure and telecom facilities, while Morocco has a better telecom infrastructure than Tunisia has but only in special development zones. The Philippines stands out as having a particularly good telecom infrastructure with a reliable domestic and inter-island service because of the US military bases there. In Vietnam, where telecommunications and power need improvement, infrastructure is the major barrier to the growth of IT.

Transportation systems in CEE are considered to be advanced, as compared with other regions. Roads in CEE are in fairly good condition, and most public transport systems consist of rail, metro, and buses. Countries in Asia, the Middle East, Africa, and the Americas have developed transportation infrastructures around areas where a workforce with the required skills is available, and often only near international airports and major cities. Such high-tech islands, often surrounded by slums or a desert, provide a high-quality IT infrastructure, have better roads, and offer high-quality office space and other facilities such as cafeterias and fitness centers. However, the workforce in these countries mainly relies on private transportation, typically company buses that collect staff in the morning and take them back at the end of the workday. Western visitors typically need a car and a driver to get around. This situation, which seems rather negative compared to CEE, is not different from India in any respect and does not prevent Western counterparts from visiting local facilities. Hotels and company-owned houses offer high-quality living standards for visitors from the West. Companies own cars and employ drivers (and interpreters if needed) to ensure that the transportation and communication needs of foreign clients or staff are satisfied. Such arrangements for living and working compensate for the poor transportation system and infrastructure in the rest of the country.

Factor 5: Risk profile

This factor assesses security issues (risks to personal security and property-related issues such as fraud, crime, and terrorism), disruptive events (risk of labor uprising, political unrest, natural disasters), regulatory risks (stability, fairness, efficiency of legal framework), macroeconomic risks (cost inflation, currency fluctuation, and capital freedom), and intellectual property (IP) risk (strength of data and IP protection regime).

Example: Comparing risk profile

CEE countries, in particular those that have recently joined the European Union, have been considered by Western partners as safer to live in and visit than countries in the Middle East, Africa, and some countries in Asia and the Americas. The Czech Republic, for example, is considered one of the most stable post-communist countries. Furthermore, CEE countries have suffered less from natural disasters than countries in Asia and the Americas. For example, the flooding in Prague in 2002 caused minor damage compared to the damage caused to Thailand and its population following the 2004 earthquake in the Indian Ocean that hit the country through a series of devastating tsunamis.

Terrorist attacks also affect the attractiveness of a country for trade to the business community. For example, Egypt's image was damaged as a result of the terrorist attacks on resorts of Dahab in April 2006 and Sharm el-Sheikh in July 2005. There is a perception in some quarters, notably the US, that Egypt is unsafe, which affects its choice of business destination. The Egyptian government is trying to reverse this perception by enforcing security measures, with cars and packages being thoroughly checked and people being searched for weapons or explosives on entry to office buildings and hotels. In fact, the 2008 survey by Black Book Research rated Cairo as the world's tenth safest outsourcing city in 2008. In the 2010 survey, however, Egypt does not appear in the 25 safest cities list. In 2010, the safest cities were in Czech Republic and Poland (see Table 3.2).

There are risk issues as well concerning piracy, IP rights protection, and copyright laws that affect a country's attractiveness for trade and outsourcing. In Venezuela, for example, the software piracy rate in 2010 was reported at 87 percent. Vietnam, which has a stable and secure environment, is known for its extensive illegal copying of software and a culture of software piracy (85 percent software piracy rate). Among CEE countries in 2010, Bulgaria and Romania scored highest (68 percent) in software piracy rate.[1] Governments in many countries, including Romania, Costa Rica, and the Philippines, are taking steps to strengthen and enforce IP rights protection and copyright laws.

Table 3.2 Top ten safest and riskiest cities for offshore outsourcing, 2010

	Top ten safest cities for offshore outsourcing, 2010	Top ten riskiest cities for offshore outsourcing, 2010
1	Prague, Czech Republic	Karachi, Pakistan
2	Warsaw, Poland	Medellín, Colombia
3	Brno, Czech Republic	Juarez, Mexico
4	Kraków, Poland	Cali, Columbia
5	Toronto, Canada	Tijuana, Mexico
6	Halifax, Canada	Lahore, Pakistan
7	Singapore, Singapore	Jakarta, Indonesia
8	Dublin, Ireland	Lagos, Nigeria
9	Kiev, Ukraine	Dhaka, Bangladesh
10	Chennai, India	Chittagong, Bangladesh

Source: Black Book research (2010)

---

1 Software piracy rate figures are based on http://www.nationmaster.com/graph/cri_sof_pir_rat-crime-software-piracy-rate.

However political risk has a significant impact on country's attractiveness. Political unrest and government change in Egypt in early 2011 is an example of how the image of Egypt as an attractive offshoring destination (which in 2009 for the first time have been included in the Gartner's top 30 countries for offshore services list) has changed momentarily as Western companies based in Egypt started pulling out work following the unfolding crisis and Egypt's Internet and mobile network shutdown on January 28, 2011. It is doubtful that Egypt will be able to quickly recover from the tarnished reputation as an attractive offshoring destination following these events.

Factor 6: Market potential

Market potential can be assessed based on the attractiveness of the local market (current gross domestic product and gross domestic product growth rate) and access to nearby markets (in the host country and adjacent regions). This may take one or more forms:

- Whether the local market is attractive for setting up a captive operation (client consideration) or delivery center (vendor consideration) that would use local labor, infrastructure, and resources
- Whether the local market is populated with sophisticated local service suppliers (client and vendor consideration)
- Whether local or nearby market have demand for outsourcing services (vendor consideration for setting up a service center)

Example: Comparing market potential

In CEE, the Czech Republic and Poland stand out as countries with notable market potential. Each already has $500 million a year in revenues from ITO and BPO service exports. They are attractive as both captive and outsourcing locations. Although the Czech Republic has language and cultural compatibility with Western European companies as well as good infrastructure, its low wages are rising, as are property costs, and it has a low level of service maturity. Its main threats are other CEE countries that will seek to penetrate further into the adjacent Western European market. Poland is also a strong nearshore destination for Western European companies and is strong in R&D

and infrastructure, with a well-educated if small-sized IT workforce. It faces similar threats and opportunities as the Czech Republic. Romania has a smaller market potential and starts at a lower base – some $100 million from ITO/BPO exports in 2008. It has attractive cost competitiveness and strong software development capability, but a small labor pool that needs more investment in IT skills and education.

In terms of ITO/BPO services, the market is growing as CEE countries become more Westernized, and the quality of life in these countries moves toward those of Western European countries. Local CEE demand for software and IT-related products and services is expected to continue growing, which means that Western European companies already present in CEE are able to take advantage of their good access to such markets.

The Middle East and Africa are less attractive than CEE for Western European companies, partly because of a lack of knowledge and partly because of perceived language and cultural differences. However, this is changing as Morocco and Tunisia focus on French- and Spanish-speaking countries to attract potential clients and Egypt targets Western European and US clients through its multilingual workforce.

In the Asian countries, in particular Vietnam and the Philippines, demand for software and IT-related products and services from the local market is growing, but much more slowly than in CEE. This demand mainly comes from the major cities.

Case Study

THE GIANT AWAKENS: SHEEN SOFTWARE SYSTEMS CONSIDERS CHINA FOR OFFSHORE IT OUTSOURCING

by Erran Carmel

Frank Xin and Zhang Chang were ordering dinner at M on the Bund, the stylish eatery overlooking the dazzling Shanghai riverfront. "I'm bullish on China and particularly on Shanghai," said Xin. His friend, Chang, vice president (Information Systems) at a major Shanghai bank, was more careful. "Look, Xin, as a friend, I think you're taking some major risks in setting up shop across the ocean. And this stuff about lightweight methodologies seems lightweight to me."

▶

▶
Frank Xin goes to China

Xin had made up his mind that China was where his offshore outsourcing unit would be located. He had monitored the recent emergence of the offshore outsourcing industry in China. His deliberation was only on where and what form his Chinese operations would take. He considered Shanghai because of the buzz and because of some family ties in the city. Shanghai is a good strategic point to grow, he thought. And in answer to his own hesitations, he continued: "If Shanghai itself continues to get expensive, I can move to one of the nearby cities with tech parks such as Suzhou or Hangzhou [each is 12 hours by train from Shanghai]."

Operations

Xin wasn't sure how to set up China operations. He saw two options: setting up his own captive office that would be a subsidiary of Sheen-USA or partnering with an existing firm. In that arrangement, he would sign an agreement with a Shanghai firm whereby the Shanghai firm would allocate some of its staff to Sheen. Xin saw advantages to each. If he decided to lease an office, he had a number of choices. His first interest was in the software park in Pudang, a newly built area in eastern Shanghai. But the facility was already full. Pudang costs are very low for Shanghai, at 55 cents per square meter versus about 70 to 80 cents in the rest of the city. Being a member of the software park, even if he did not reside there, would give Sheen other financial benefits: a tax holiday for the first three years (on profits) and a 50 percent reduction on taxes in the subsequent five years. Xin was not sure what profits would be allocated to his Shanghai office, though.

Xin began planning his offshore strategy by attending the 2003 Global IT outsourcing summit[1] in downtown Shanghai, a few minutes walk from the Bund. The two-day conference was one of the first in China that focused on offshore outsourcing. It was organized by the Shanghai Municipal Foreign Economic Relations and Trade Commission, the Shanghai Municipal and Formalization Commission, the Shanghai Software Industry Association, and several other organizations.

At the conference, the vice mayor of Shanghai welcomed the attendees. About 200 people attended the conference, most of them from

---

1 Link to conference site: http://www.cnoutsourcing.com/English/index.asp.

▶

▶

Chinese software companies. Several foreign firms had sent their representatives, including ADP-Asia and Siemens. Conference speeches included those by the heads of Microsoft China and Shanda (a leading computer game maker based in Shanghai) and the CTO of WebEx, an American firm with R&D in Shanghai. The summit was covered on the next day's English-language *Shanghai Daily* with the headline, "China's software outsourcing industry is expected to shorten its gap with India in about 3 years."

By 2003, the Chinese software market had been growing at a fast pace for several years. Unlike the Indian industry, which most see as its main competitor, China's industry enjoyed a strong demand domestically from an economy that had been growing over the past decade at double-digit compound annual growth rate. Beginning roughly in 2000, Chinese firms had begun to set their sights on augmenting the domestic demand with foreign markets. In 2003, China was expected to export roughly $1 billion in software and software services. The Shanghai metropolitan area accounted for roughly 12 percent of the total software exports. Shanghai was also home to software R&D centers for HP and Ericsson as well as support centers and localization centers for Microsoft and other multinationals.

Xin and Sheen

Frank Xin is reflective of many global software entrepreneurs: as an "overseas Chinese," he is able to bridge East and West. His home has been in Los Angeles for 15 years. Having grown up in Taiwan, Xin speaks Mandarin and can be understood in Shanghai; however, he is still trying to master the local Chinese dialect, he says. Prior to founding Sheen, he was at PeopleSoft.

Xin founded Sheen in 2000 to provide customized solutions for the business and entertainment industries. His large clients include Disney and 20th Century Fox, but most of his clients are small and medium-sized enterprises. In all cases, the development teams assigned to projects are small and nimble – usually three to six technical staff. Most of his clients are local, but some have been based elsewhere in California and the United States.

Sheen has four permanent employees and a dozen regular consultants and contractors brought in when needed. He runs a small, lean shop that relies on the combined technical abilities and sales abilities

▶

►

of the principals. "My strategy is to grow," said Xin, "to capitalize on our strengths and the strengths of the Chinese."

In Sheen's client engagements, the firm uses its own adaptation of agile methodologies, also known as "lightweight methodologies," the most famous of which is Extreme Programming (XP). The "agile movement" is a reaction to the "heavy" methodologies exemplified by the Software Engineering Institute's CMM, which emphasizes controls and documentation, both of which are anathema to independent-minded programmers.

Xin said, "We've found that most clients don't have the bandwidth to do full-blown systems analysis and design, so agile methodologies are better suited. Agile approaches are much better suited to more and better communication between client and developers with lots of end user participation and small, nimble teams of developers. By working closer with the developer, the client gets over the xenophobia of working with the foreigner, the unknown."

The other part of Xin's strategy is to use the strength of the Chinese. While the Indian outsourcing industry has mastered the factory approach of software production, the Chinese software industry is only slowly, and perhaps reluctantly, following that lead. About 20 Indian firms have attained the highest process standards of software development: CMM level 5. India's success is all the more noteworthy because its firms represent roughly 50 percent of all global firms that have attained this standard. "When we bid against CMM level 5 Indian firms, how do we beat them? We have to offer something different," reflected Xin.

Chinese programmers are educated in computer science programs with a tradition of theory and algorithm development. Students coming out of this educational system are not interested in working in factory environments in which they are handed specifications. They want to work with the customer to solve problems. "Agile programming is a much better fit to Chinese work culture than the stifling procedures embedded in the CMM," said Xin.

One of the cornerstones of agile methodologies is tight teamwork and close interactions between client and developer. Sheen's approach to teamwork is to place people at the client site as much as possible. Sometimes this can be for as much as half of the project duration. When the client wants the team at its site for longer periods of time, this adds to the project cost, and Sheen passes the cost to the client. "In China, everyone wants to be their own boss, people are less conformative, so when you use agile methods, you allow everyone on the team to give feedback."

The A. T. Kearney Global Services Locations Index (2011), shown in Table 3.3, illustrates a different approach to assessing the attractiveness of a location for outsourcing and offshoring. Its approach provides a score for each factor (financial attractiveness, people skills and availability, and business environment), which are summed to create a final score. We believe that a qualitative assessment should be combined with a quantified approach to decide on the attractiveness of a location for outsourcing.

Finally, those who are comparing potential sourcing destinations must consider the influence of certain cities on such a decision. The rationale for this is that costs, availability of skills, and infrastructure may vary significantly across cities within the same country. Even factors such as the environment, risk profile, and market potential can present varying results when examined in each city of the same country. The Global Services Tholons Report (Vashistha and Khan, 2008) argues that comparing countries is superficial because "no two cities of a country would be at the same level of skills maturity or offer the same cost advantage." For example, some cities graduate more engineers, others more accountants. Therefore, sourcing decisions can be more accurate if these assess the attractiveness of potential locations such as cities rather than countries.

One approach to assessing the attractiveness of cities for outsourcing is that proposed by Farrell (2006), in which the scale and quality of workforce, business catalyst, cost, infrastructure, risk profile, and quality of life are among the more critical factors. Vashistha and Ravago (2010) have compared a large number of cities and have come up with a list of the top ten global outsourcing cities: six are in India, and the others are Manila and Cebu City in the Philippines, Dublin in Ireland, and Shanghai in China. They also found that among emerging global outsourcing destinations, Kraków in Poland, Beijing in China, Buenos Aires in Argentina, Cairo in Egypt and São Paolo in Brazil are the top five on this list.

Nearshoring and beyond

Nearshoring is an activity in which a client outsources work to a supplier located in a foreign low-wage country and yet the vendor is close in distance and in terms of time zone differences. Compared to offshore outsourcing, the benefits of nearshoring include lower travel costs, fewer time zone differences, and closer cultural compatibility. Canada, for example, is a significant nearshore destination for US clients. Indeed, some analysts argue that US clients can have lower costs when nearshoring work to Canada as compared with the strategy to offshore-outsource to India.

Table 3.3 A. T. Kearney global services location index, 2011

Rank	Country	Financial attractiveness	People skills and availability	Business environment	Total score
1	India	3.11	2.76	1.14	7.01
2	China	2.62	2.55	1.31	6.49
3	Malaysia	2.78	1.38	1.83	5.99
4	Egypt	3.10	1.36	1.35	5.81
5	Indonesia	3.24	1.53	1.01	5.78
6	Mexico	2.68	1.60	1.44	5.72
7	Thailand	3.05	1.38	1.29	5.72
8	Vietnam	3.27	1.19	1.24	5.69
9	Philippines	3.18	1.31	1.16	5.65
10	Chile	2.44	1.27	1.82	5.52
11	Estonia	2.31	0.95	2.24	5.51
12	Brazil	2.02	2.07	1.38	5.48
13	Latvia	2.56	0.93	1.96	5.46
14	Lithuania	2.48	0.93	2.02	5.43
15	United Arab Emirates	2.41	0.94	2.05	5.41
16	United Kingdom	0.91	2.26	2.23	5.41
17	Bulgaria	2.82	0.88	1.67	5.37
18	United States	0.45	2.88	2.01	5.35
19	Costa Rica	2.84	0.94	1.56	5.34
20	Russia	2.48	1.79	1.07	5.34
21	Sri Lanka	3.20	0.95	1.11	5.26
22	Jordan	2.97	0.77	1.49	5.23
23	Tunisia	3.05	0.81	1.37	5.23
24	Poland	2.14	1.27	1.81	5.23
25	Romania	2.54	1.03	1.65	5.21
26	Germany	0.76	2.17	2.27	5.20
27	Ghana	3.21	0.69	1.28	5.18
28	Pakistan	3.23	1.16	0.76	5.15
29	Senegal	3.23	0.78	1.11	5.12
30	Argentina	2.45	1.58	1.09	5.12
31	Hungary	2.05	1.24	1.82	5.11
32	Singapore	1.00	1.66	2.40	5.06
33	Jamaica	2.81	0.86	1.34	5.01
34	Panama	2.77	0.72	1.49	4.98
35	Czech Republic	1.81	1.14	2.03	4.98
36	Mauritius	2.41	0.87	1.70	4.98
37	Morocco	2.83	0.87	1.26	4.96
38	Ukraine	2.86	1.07	1.02	4.95
39	Canada	0.56	2.14	2.25	4.95
40	Slovakia	2.33	0.93	1.65	4.91
41	Uruguay	2.42	0.91	1.42	4.75
42	Spain	0.81	2.06	1.88	4.75
43	Colombia	2.34	1.20	1.18	4.72
44	France	0.38	2.12	2.11	4.61
45	South Africa	2.27	0.93	1.37	4.57
46	Australia	0.51	1.80	2.13	4.44
47	Israel	1.45	1.35	1.64	4.44
48	Turkey	1.87	1.29	1.17	4.33
49	Ireland	0.42	1.74	2.08	4.24
50	Portugal	1.21	1.09	1.85	4.15

Note: The weight distribution for the three categories is 40:30:30. Financial attractiveness is rated on a scale of 0 to 4, and the categories for people skills and availability, and business environment are on a scale of 0 to 3.

Source: A. T. Kearney Global Services Location Index™, 2011

In their study of nearshoring, Carmel and Abbott (2007) argue that distance still matters and point to customers choosing the nearshore option to gain benefit from one or more of the following constructs of proximity: geographical, temporal, cultural, linguistic, economic, political, and historical linkages. Their study identifies three major global nearshore clusters based around clients in North America, Western Europe, and a smaller cluster in East Asia (see Table 3.4).

Nearshoring represents a major way in which non-BRIC countries can compete with India for market share. The top Indian firms now offer a variety of location choices to their clients, which mitigates some of the currency costs incurred in uncertain markets. For example, India-based TCS can offer its British clients services that are "farshore" (India), nearshore (Budapest, Hungary), and onshore from their offices in London,

Table 3.4 Global distribution of nearshore destinations

	Client cluster in North America	Client cluster in Western Europe	Client cluster in East Asia
Client location only	US	EU13 Norway Switzerland	Japan Singapore
Both client and offshore or nearshore location	Canada	Ireland Spain Israel Russia	Korea
Nearshore only	Mexico Guatemala El Salvador Nicaragua Costa Rica Panama Honduras Colombia Guyana Venezuela Peru Brazil Chile Uruguay Argentina Bahamas Jamaica Dominican Republic Puerto Rico Barbados	Poland Hungary Czech Republic Slovakia Croatia Serbia Slovenia Bulgaria Romania Armenia Ukraine Belarus Morocco Algeria Tunisia Egypt South Africa Turkey Malta Cyprus	China Malaysia

Source: Based on Carmel and Abbot (2007)

Nottingham, or elsewhere. Another Indian firm, Infosys, has "proximity development centers" and like other Indian firms has also refined its internal processes in mitigating time zone difficulties (Carmel and Abbott, 2007).

Willcocks and Lacity (2009) argue that, in addition to the continuing nearshoring trend, there is what can be called a "bestshoring" trend. The concept of bestshoring can be explained through the example of the outsourcing contract between TCS and ABN AMRO (Oshri et al., 2007a, b). In this contract, TCS provides IT services to the bank from offshore locations (Mumbai and São Paulo), from nearshore locations (Budapest and Luxembourg), and from an onshore location (Amsterdam). The client and the vendor assess the most appropriate location to provide services based on some of the criteria outlined above (e.g., availability of skills, language, cost). Our research suggests that clients and suppliers are increasingly moving to such an arrangement for either insourced or outsourced IT and business services (Oshri et al., 2007).

We believe that nearshoring is less likely to dominate the offshoring strategy in the coming years. In our opinion, nearshoring will be only one component within the bestshoring strategy. According to Willcocks and Lacity (2009), locations in CEE and Mediterranean Africa will be attractive to clients in Western Europe and Gulf States; in Asia Pacific to China, India, and Japan; those in Central and South America to North America. Shared language, culture, or history will continue to influence purchasing decisions. Clearly the BRIC countries themselves are increasingly interested in non-BRIC services and locations.

Summary

This chapter has provided an extensive review of the factors that affect country attractiveness for outsourcing and offshoring. Through examples, the chapter has illustrated the comparative advantage of certain locations within the context of the nature of the function outsourced. As such contexts change, the attractiveness of a location may change as well.

Relevant teaching case

Vietor, R. H. K., Rivkin, J. W., and Seminerio, J. (2008). "The Offshoring of America," *Harvard Business Online*, no. 9–708-030.

Building Sourcing Competencies

CHAPTER 4

Supplier core capabilities and strategies for sustainability and growth

As we have illustrated, the global sourcing market is large, and the services it offers range from relatively simple processes or call centers to the radical transformation of entire back office functions. The supplier base is equally diverse, ranging from locally based firms that specialize in particular services or industries to offshore or global providers that promise to offer a high quality of service at a low cost. Tables 4.1 to 4.3 identify the dominant players in the sourcing market: the top ten outsourcing companies (Table 4.1), the top ten outsourcing advisors (Table 4.2), and the top ten BPO companies in India (Table 4.3). These rankings can provide important information regarding the expertise of a number of vendors and thus help clients identify potential partners. Of course, these rankings are quite dynamic as existing, developing, and new players compete increasingly across global geographies.

This chapter provides an overview of suppliers and intermediaries. Vendor landscape will therefore be discussed in terms of firm size, areas of

Table 4.1 Top ten outsourcing companies, 2010

Rank	Company	Key strength
1	Accenture	Customer references
2	Infosys Technologies	Demonstrated competencies
3	Sodexo	Balanced performance
4	Wipro Technologies	Management capabilities
5	IBM	Management capabilities
6	ISS	Demonstrated competencies
7	TCS	Management capabilities
8	Aramark	Balanced performance
9	CSC	Demonstrated competencies
10	Convergys	Customer reference

Source: International Association of Outsourcing Professionals

Table 4.2 Top ten outsourcing advisors, 2010

Rank	Company
1	TPI
2	EquaTerra
3	Alsbridge
4	KPMG
5	Kirkland & Ellis
6	Quint Wellington Redwood
7	Morrison Foerster
8	Baker & McKenzie
9	Gartner
10	Booz & Company

Source: International Association of Outsourcing Professionals

Table 4.3 Top ten BPO companies in India, 2010

Rank	Company
1	Genpact BPO
2	WNS Global
3	TCS
4	IBM–Daksh
5	Wipro Infotech
6	Firstsource Solutions Ltd.
7	Aditya Birla Minacs Worldwide
8	Aegis Ltd.
9	Infosys Technologies Ltd.
10	HCL BPO

Source: NASSCOM

specialization, and location. The chapter focuses on a supplier's core capabilities and discusses suppliers' strategies for sustainability and growth.

In this chapter, we focus on:

- The role of suppliers and intermediaries in sourcing arrangements
- A supplier's core capabilities for sustainability and growth

Overview of vendors and intermediaries

In addition to choosing a supplier that specializes in a particular line of services, it is of vital importance to choose the right configuration for the outsourcing arrangement. The different configuration options for the client are the sole-supplier model, the best-of-breed model, the panel model, and the prime contractor model.

Sole supplier: In this model, a single supplier provides the entire service. The main benefit of this model is the sole accountability of the supplier, which makes the governance of the venture easier relative to other configuration models. Its main risk is associated with the high danger of compromising service quality because no supplier is outstanding in all areas. However, over the past five years, the practice of bundled services outsourcing has grown, stimulated by better-integrated supplier capability and client moves to rationalize and reduce their multiple-supplier bases. Willcocks, Oshri, and Hindle (2009: 1) define *bundled services* as "a mix of business process and/or information technology services purchased separately or at the same time from the same supplier where synergies and efficiencies are sought in end-to-end processing, governance, relationship management, cost and performance." They analyzed 865 bundled outsourcing contracts signed between 2003 and 2009. The value of bundled outsourcing contracts signed in 2003 was $38 billion. This rose to a peak of $95 billion in 2006 when 204 such contracts were signed. In 2007, 200 contracts were signed at a value of $46 billion. Willcocks et al. found that 75 percent of the deals were for bundled services across two or more IT towers, with the rest either IT and BPO combined or mixed BPO contracts.

Best-of-breed: In this model, the organization has a number of suppliers and plays the role of the head contractor. Willcocks, Lacity, and Cullen (2006) have emphasized that this type of configuration constitutes a low-risk outsourcing option and has become a prevalent outsourcing model. According to their research findings, in 2006, 75 percent of UK and 82 percent of US organizations used the best-of-breed of model as an approach to mitigate outsourcing risks. Willcocks et al. (2009) pointed out the trade-offs on operational and management costs, supplier capabilities, risks, and control when comparing best-of-breed versus bundling outsourcing models.

Panel: In this arrangement, a company compiles a list of preferred suppliers that work in continuous competition. Every supplier constantly competes for a project or a contract. This approach is very common in applications development, hardware purchasing, and consulting, as the requirements differ from one initiative to another, and thus it makes more sense for client firms to have a list of preferred suppliers and call them for the work they are best at.

Prime contractor: This model consists of a network with several suppliers that operate under the control of the head contractor. The head contractor is accountable for the delivery of the service and liable for this under the terms of the contract. The subcontractors are firms with expertise in a specific area relative to the head contractor that operate in regions in which the head contractor does not or that offer a combination of both of these factors (superior expertise and geographical coverage).

In every outsourcing venture, there are service-level arrangements (SLAs) that specify the level and quality of service that the supplier is contractually obliged to deliver. If the supplier does not deliver, the risk is high that it will have to suffer the imposition of service credits. In the case of multiple-supplier settings, operational-level agreements are in place to ensure that each supplier is aware of the commitments of other suppliers. (These issues are further discussed in Chapter 8.)

While competition for cost arbitrage in the global sourcing market is growing, offshore intermediation is gaining momentum as a tactic for managing the complexity of offshoring ventures. Mahnke, Wareham, and Bjorn-Andersen (2008) explain the value of intermediation in outsourcing and offshoring and provide an overview of services that intermediaries offer to clients and vendors:

1. *Mitigation of cultural disparities*: Cross-cultural tensions such as differences in language and organizational practices can cause turbulence in offshoring ventures. If an outsourcing firm does not understand and manage these differences and the tensions that arise because of them, substantial conflicts are likely to emerge that can reduce the benefits of the venture. Along these lines, an intermediary with experienced staff and managers who are aware of the cultural specifics of both regions can more easily foresee and manage the tensions that arise as a result of different communication styles.
2. *The mitigation of cognitive distance:* Cognitive distance can result from different mind-sets and different ways of thinking, processing information, and communicating. More often in the offshoring context, cognitive distance arises when relatively less-skilled clients attempt to exploit the high technological expertise of an offshore vendor at a relatively low cost. This is a major area where an offshore intermediary can add value. In particular, the offshore intermediary may offer services such as specialized translations between perceived client needs and vendor requirements and codified interfaces so that systems can be connected and contracts can be designed and managed. Furthermore, intermediaries can contribute to the creation of sufficient common ground to facilitate mutual understanding and avoid conflict.
3. *Comprehensive preparation of the client for an offshoring venture*: A number of offshoring ventures have led to disastrous results because the

client lacked knowledge, experience, and maturity in offshore vendor selection and negotiations. An offshore intermediary can help an organization be prepared for offshoring ventures in a number of ways, including creating awareness of objectives, establishing common expectations with the vendor, and contributing to contract formulation and negotiation.

4. *Facilitating and managing the ongoing relationship between the client and the offshore vendor*: Offshore relationships are not static, and relative to domestic ventures, they are more prone to unforeseen situations and contingencies. Especially in offshoring ventures in which project outcomes are hard to identify (and thus the performance of the vendor is more difficult to measure), the role of offshore intermediaries is key. More specifically, the offshore intermediary can contribute significantly to the detection of misunderstandings and the resolution of conflicts. Furthermore, it can create relational awareness by generating mutual understanding, clarifying implicit assumptions, and defining a common vocabulary from which joint future action can proceed. Finally, the intermediary may, if necessary, work with the client to make sure that appropriate communication structures are in place so that the interfirm governance mechanism can be tailored to relational requirements.

A number of consultancies (e.g., Deloitte, TPI, KPMG) and law firms (e.g., DLA Piper, Berwin Leighton Paisner) play the role of an intermediary in outsourcing ventures and provide services in domestic and offshore operations. Their services range from strategy consulting, program management, and change management to contract design, contract management, and dispute resolution.

Core capabilities of suppliers

While supplier configuration is highly significant for the outcome of the venture and firms must analyze extensively which model best fits their purposes, another critical area for consideration is the actual capabilities and competencies that selected suppliers can demonstrate.

Levina and Ross (2003) have provided a useful categorization of supplier capabilities:

1. *Client-specific capabilities:* These are related to the routines and resources that align the vendor's practices and processes to the client's goals. More specifically, these capabilities are associated with the knowledge that a vendor must have of the client's business model and industry, as well as of the specifics of the client's operations.

2. *Process capabilities:* These are concerned with task delivery routines and resources that accomplish software design, development, and execution. Six Sigma and the capability maturity model (CMM) are some of the better-known methodologies that aim to improve software development processes.
3. *Human resource capabilities:* These are related to recruitment, training, and mentoring practices; designing jobs that will expose individuals to a variety of tasks and thus enable them to broaden their skills; and developing performance appraisal and compensation systems.

Feeny, Lacity, and Willcocks (2005) have identified 12 key supplier capabilities (see Figure 4.1) that clients should take into account when looking for a vendor:

1. *Leadership:* Leadership refers to the capability of delivering the desired result throughout the lifetime of the deal. Feeny et al. found that individuals who occupied supplier leadership roles had a considerable impact on the success of an outsourcing venture. More specifically, they found that although individual supplier firms were consistent in the way they contracted and governed, 76 percent of the deals under study were identified

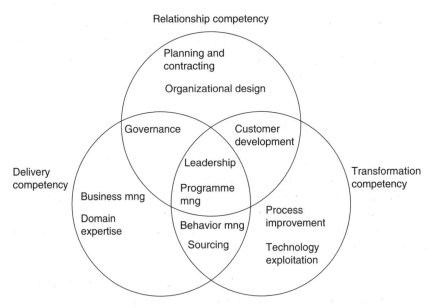

Figure 4.1 Twelve supplier capabilities

Source: Willcocks et al. (2006)

by the interviewees as successful and 24 percent were seen as unsuccessful. The main differentiating factor between success and failure was the individual who was leading the supplier account teams. Feeny et al. found three patterns that emerged when they examined how these leaders could make a difference to the outsourcing result. First, in unsuccessful cases, the leader of the supplier team was often too focused on business management issues such as delivery and meeting SLAs while delivering the required profit margin to the vendor. These issues are important, but they are distinct from leadership. Second, the quality of the relationship between the leaders of the supplier's and the client's teams has an impact on the wider client–supplier relationship. Third, the relationship between the leader of the supplier's team and the top management of the supplier's organization can be a critical success factor. Because most suppliers tend to create more of a front-end team rather than a full-function business unit when serving a client, the local team is extremely dependent on its leader's relationship with headquarters to gain access to key resources and approval for client-aligned business policies.

2. *Business management:* This is the capability of delivering products and services according to the agreement and the business plans of both parties. If either of the two parties is dissatisfied with the sourcing arrangement, the venture will fail. Often clients try to fully exploit their power position at the expense of the vendor, but this tactic erodes the relationship and undermines the sourcing result. As the contract manager of an Australian public sector agency noted, "Suppliers have to make a reasonable margin to stay in business. You don't want them to lose money because the worse their business gets, the worse your business gets" (Feeny, Lacity and Willcocks, 2005, p. 44)

3. *Domain expertise:* This is the capability to retain and apply professional knowledge. The key issue is not only the supplier's technical expertise or know-how, but also the ability to understand and manage the customer's business needs. A number of suppliers acquire domain expertise by transferring employees to the client's site. For example, Deutsche Bank moved its procurement people to Accenture, and Barclays transferred check processing staff to Unisys. Such arrangements have two advantages for customers. First, it becomes the supplier's responsibility to adjust capacity and use the best people. Second, both parties are reassured that the operating staff not only have the required expertise but also understand the specifics and particularities of the client's service.

4. *Behavior management:* Behavior management refers to the ability to motivate and inspire people to deliver services of high value. It is highly significant for customers to evaluate the extent to which a supplier has

acquired this capability – in other words, how competent the supplier is in motivating and managing people to deliver service with a front office culture. Different suppliers use different methods to acquire this capability. For example, CGI Group of Montreal puts employees who will be transferred to client's sites through a process that it calls "harmonization." A CGI partner explained that this process is much more than an orientation to the client. The goal is "to show every employee – not just a subset – this is what we do, how we do it, the timing. We want to set the stage for good behavior management beforehand, not react to bad behavior afterwards."

5. *Sourcing:* This is the ability to access the necessary resources. This ability may take the form of generating economies of scale, using a superior infrastructure, or turning to of efficient procurement practices. For example, the procurement services deal between BAE Systems, a British defense, security, and aerospace company, and Xchanging, a business processing company, was based on two key areas: the superior ability of Xchanging to attract high-level professional skills for certain procurement categories (such as office suppliers, health plans, and training) and its ability to generate economies of scale by aggregating BAE's part-time needs with those of other clients.

6. *Process improvement:* This is the capability to change processes in a way that generates a dramatic improvement. Supplier track records can be useful resources in the evaluation of their capabilities for improvement. Most clients are familiar with Six Sigma methodologies or alternatives such as CMM and are looking for these. However, it is important to look beyond such tools to consider the people and behavioral aspects. Key areas for consideration include who has the critical skills, who owns the change process, who defines what an "improvement" is, and who benefits. It is important to note that, often, improvements appear on the surface to be targeted to the needs of the customer, but in fact are intended for the convenience of the supplier.

7. *Technology exploitation:* This refers to the capability of rapidly deploying new technology, one of the key capabilities to be considered for BPO (Lacity and Willcocks, 2009). This capability requires careful evaluation from the customer's perspective and should go beyond the supplier's pure technical skills. Significant areas for consideration include the values and behaviors the supplier brings to using technology, the processes that are followed, and the infrastructure.

8. *Program management:* Program management refers not only to project-level capabilities but also to the capability of delivering a set of interrelated projects. More specifically, it involves prioritizing, coordinating,

mobilizing the organization, and promoting a series of tasks that aim toward change and improvement. Feeny et al. (2005) highlighted the fact that this capability has played a major role in clients' decision to expand the use of a particular supplier for more projects.

9. *Customer development:* This is the capability to enable clients to become customers who can make informed choices about their business needs, service levels, and costs. Feeny et al. (2005) suggested three steps that suppliers should take to achieve the reorientation from user to customer: (1) establish personal contact with a number of end users to understand what sort of service they want to use and how (this will also lead to trust development); (2) cooperate with client managers to arrive at an agreement on the provisions of the service; and (3) work toward relationship development by which the end user becomes a customer who feels fully informed of service functionalities, options, potential enhancements, and associated costs.

10. *Planning and contracting:* This is the capability to plan resources and deliver "win-win" results for both the supplier and the customer. The planning component involves envisaging potential rewards for both vendor and client and figuring out way to achieve these rewards. For example, in the outsourcing arrangement between Deutsche Bank and Accenture, Accenture committed to fund and create a new platform for procurement, with 200 people assigned to its development. It expects to gain good revenue from Deutsche Bank, as well as the opportunity to attract other clients to the service. Deutsche Bank estimates that the plan will deliver 15 to 20 percent savings through the consolidation, standardization, and restructuring of its 14 procurement units. The contracting component defines how rewards will be shared during the execution and delivery of the plan. Many possibilities exist. For example, the Bank of America and Xchanging structure their major deals as profit-sharing arrangements, while the Bank of America chose to take an equity stake in Exult during its HR outsourcing arrangement.

11. *Organizational design:* This is the capability required to design and implement successful organizational arrangements. Feeny et al. (2005) found that a number of major deals took approximately two years to reach an organizational fit between a client and a supplier. Often in these deals, clients were experimenting with various organizational arrangements without fully understanding the supplier's design strategy. In this regard, suppliers greatly vary in terms of their organizational approach, the choices they make, and their levels of flexibility. For example, some emphasize a thin front-end client team, interfacing with consolidated service units

(silos) that have ownership and the responsibility for profit and ownership of most of the resources. Though such arrangements may lead to the generation of significant economies of scale, they can also limit a supplier's ability to deliver the business plan for a specific client. By contrast, other suppliers allocate most of their resources to enterprise partnership units created for each major deal. These units are responsible and accountable for the delivery of the business plan and have their own chief executives, senior executive teams, dedicated staff, and resources. Clearly the supplier's organizational design and its fitness with the client's operational mode will affect the success of the outsourcing project (Lacity and Willcocks, 2009).

12. *Governance:* This refers to the governing processes and structures that facilitate the alignment of the client's objectives and strategies with the vendor's delivery system. Key areas for consideration are that the structures will be in place to ensure that the supplier is delivering according to the contract and that decision making is visible and accountable, that procedures are set out for dealing with problems, and that the governance structure addresses powers and authorities.

These 12 core capabilities of the supplier can be leveraged into three key competences (Feeny et al., 2005; Lacity and Willcocks, 2009; see Figure 4.1):

1. *Delivery competency:* This is based on the supplier's ability to respond to the customer's ongoing needs. This competency primarily involves the supplier's leadership, business management, domain expertise, behavior management, sourcing, program management, and governance capabilities.
2. *Transformation competency:* This is based on the supplier's ability to deliver radically improved service in terms of quality and cost. It primarily involves the supplier's leadership, behavior management, sourcing, process improvement, technology exploitation, program management, and customer development capabilities.
3. *Relationship competency:* This is based on the supplier's willingness and ability to align its business model to the values, goals, and needs of the customer. The key capabilities are leadership, customer development, planning and contracting, organizational design, governance, and program management. Among these, the planning and contracting capability present the major challenge, because it is not easy to align the goals and incentives of the two sides.

With regard to the management of suppliers' capabilities and competencies, Willcocks, Cullen, and Craig (2011) have identified eight key lessons that reflect on suppliers' capabilities that have emerged from their 15-year research into more than 1,200 organizations. These lessons can affect suppliers' ability to win outsourcing contracts:

1. During the phase of supplier selection and negotiation, the bargaining power is in the hands of the client. If the client does not use this power wisely, the risk that problems will occur subsequently is high. For example, clients who accept the vendor's suggestion that some SLAs in the contract can be defined in a later stage and after the contract has been signed may suffer from supplier's opportunism resulting in a dispute.
2. Customers need to focus on the supplier's competencies and capabilities rather than on the extent of its resources.
3. Choosing the right supplier configuration is critical to the outcome of the venture.
4. Clients should examine a supplier's capabilities and competencies in relation to the business context. Not every business context requires the suppliers to rank high in all 12 capabilities and three competencies. In the evaluation of the suppliers, there are three sets of criteria: mandatory, qualitative, and price.
5. CEOs must understand that deals that excessively favor the client are not viable in the long run. The deals with the best outcomes are those in which the client is getting the best value for a fair price.
6. Tendering is the most common and effective strategy in choosing suppliers. Joint decisions among the CEO, business executives, and IT managers are also the most effective. Going straight into negotiations without tendering or competition among the suppliers might be appropriate only for very experienced clients.
7. Effective and ongoing communication and transparency between the client and the potential supplier during the negotiation phase set the stage for a good relationship.
8. The client CEO has two fundamental roles to play: (1) selecting the right supplier for the right price and contributing to the development of a relationship and (2) ensuring that the organization selected is properly staffed so that the supplier can perform to the best of its capabilities.

The following case illustrates the evolutionary path that Tata Consultancy Services have followed developing capabilities imperative to successfully compete in the IT outsourcing industry.

Case Study

TATA CONSULTANCY SERVICES: BUILDING CAPABILITIES

Credibility: 1970s–1990s

In 1968, Tata Sons in India established Tata Consultancy Services (TCS) as a division to service its electronic data processing (EDP) requirements and provide management consulting services. Over the next few years, a few young engineers at TCS realized that they were staring at a potential new business opportunity and started offering data processing services to clients outside the group.

India's first-generation computer experts felt handicapped by an outmoded computing environment in the country. When TCS started, there were only 17 computers in the entire country. The first breakthrough in India came in 1969 when TCS won a contract from Central Bank of India to automate branch reconciliation processes. But progress was slow because India's foreign exchange laws made it difficult to import hardware.

As a result, TCS became the exclusive distributor for the mainframe computer maker Burroughs and simultaneously started doing programming for the hardware maker's customers in the US. Using its export revenues, TCS was able to bring in new computers, enabling the fledgling company to keep pace with the evolving needs of its growing client roster in the US.

The defining moment for the Indian software industry came in 1974 when TCS won a large export project for the Detroit Police Department. This was followed by other projects in the US and UK, and thus the notion of offshore services, or the ability to provide services from remote locations, was born. Without an adequate telecommunication infrastructure, programmed tapes were sent on weekly flights to the US, while software requirements came through the postal services.

In 1977, the Indian government enacted a legislation forbidding foreign firms from operating fully owned subsidiaries in India. As a result, IBM chose to leave India, a decision that opened up a new window of opportunity in India: as its core competency, TCS

▶

▶ installed hardware and systems software and created and ran data centers.

From the 1980s, TCS expanded aggressively. The average size of its deals grew beyond 25 person-years to over 100 person-years. In 1988, with improvements in telecommunications, TCS began to drive the offshore business by installing a water-cooled IBM 3090 mainframe, an aggressive move for a company that decided to invest heavily in a single machine with substantial export guarantees to the government. The gamble paid off and eventually led to a complete redefinition of the business model that in turn sparked the creation of today's $60 billion Indian IT industry.

With its business growing steadily in the 1980s, TCS became the hub for new technology knowledge in India. It started creating opportunities for Indian IT professionals with focused academic–industry partnerships beginning with IIT Bombay and IIT Kanpur, followed by new engineering colleges with course design and faculty developmental programs. By the end of the 1980s, a robust system was in place for the education and research needs of the country's IT professionals.

In 1981, TCS established India's first IT R&D division, the Tata Research Design and Development Centre, at Pune. Simultaneously TCS worked closely with the Indian government on regulatory issues.

Because computers were still scarce, the improvement of processes to increase productivity became a focus for TCS. Quality became a cornerstone for TCS first and subsequently for the entire IT industry in India. The relentless pursuit of excellent quality began to draw the attention of customers and competitors alike.

Scale: 1990s–2004

With the end of the century approaching and the impending Y2K problem looming ahead, TCS was becoming known for its software factory, a development that helped it leapfrog into the global environment. TCS spread its footprint worldwide by setting up global development and nearshore delivery centers in Hungary, China, Uruguay, Brazil, Japan, the US, and Canada. By the 1990s, the dot-com boom had the IT industry on steroids making it a highly lucrative sector.

By the 1990s, the dot-com boom was firmly entrenched, and it became a period of exponential growth for TCS, which saw its first change of the guard. The visionary Massachusetts Institute of

▶

▶

Technology (MIT)-trained electrical engineer who had started TCS, F. C. Kohli, stepped down as he passed the leadership to Subramaniam Ramadorai who had the drive, rigor, and passion to lead TCS through its next phase of growth. Taking over as CEO in 1996, Ramadorai made organizational changes beginning with a more empowered management style. Having grown from the ranks and served TCS in different departments, his understanding of the organization was deep, and his vision was to take TCS into the global top ten league of IT services companies.

Under his leadership, TCS was restructured into a domain-led organization, capabilities evolved to deliver end-to-end solutions, and uniform organization-wide quality processes were introduced and reinforced.

TCS became the world's first organization to achieve an integrated enterprise-wide maturity level 5 on both the capability maturity model and people capability maturity model (frameworks conceptualized by the Software Engineering Institute at Carnegie Mellon University to benchmark and appraise the software process and people management process of an organization).

As the offshore model of software development gained currency among global corporations, Ramadorai played an active role in establishing offshore development centers in India to provide high-end quality solutions to major corporations such as HP and GE. Under his leadership, technology excellence centers were set up in India with a vision of remaining abreast with changing technologies at all times.

TCS's internal operational efficiency was given a boost by an enterprise-wide digitization initiative. A turning point in 1989 was SEGA, a project that involved designing, building, and implementing on a turnkey basis a new system for the Swiss Corporation for Securities, Clearing and Settlement. The 350-person-year project went live on schedule and established TCS as a global technology partner with unmatched credentials for delivery excellence. This provided a platform for TCS to build India's financial and capital market infrastructure, including the state-of-the-art National Stock Exchange, among the biggest exchanges in the world in terms of volume, as well as a national securities depository that made the Indian stock markets paperless.

New horizons emerged for the business, including addressing the Y2K problem before the end of the millennium, and developing e-business, BPO, and engineering services. TCS's global growth saw

▶

▶

an expansion in its customer list, its global network and presence, and increased interaction with professional groups, and it earned a greater presence in the Indian government on policy matters.

In 2003, TCS became India's first billion-dollar IT services company. The following year, it went public through an initial public offering that at that time was the largest ever such offering.

Leadership: 2004–2011

As the Indian economy continued to grow, the need for technology to drive growth became part of the national agenda. TCS, which had been investing in the domestic IT market since its inception, was well positioned to help the government at the central and state levels in its new initiatives. India's largest IT company was firmly in the spotlight, not only as the jewel in the Tata Group's crown but also because of its growing global presence.

Strategic acquisitions were also playing a role to position TCS for future growth. TCS had acquired CMC in 2001, prior to the IPO, to expand its presence in the domestic market and joint ventures in the BPO space. In 2005 and 2006, it acquired FNS, an Australian software products firm, and Comicrom, a BPO company in Chile.

Together with other growth initiatives, including expansion into Brazil, Mexico, China, and Hungary, and setting up strategic units to pursue new opportunities in the financial services products space or new services such as remote infrastructure management and platform-based BPO, TCS set the stage for positioning its brand and its offerings to global customers.

Concurrently, a strong talent localization initiative was being undertaken: the number of non-Indian employees rapidly increased to over 10,000 at the end of 2008–2009, including 1,200 in China and over 6,000 in Latin America, creating a multinational, multicultural global organization. The company's greatest asset is its young workforce, whose synergy and vitality extend beyond TCS and into the community. Employee engagement channels like Maitree, for example, offer employees the opportunity to contribute to their communities in a number of ways – education, health care, and conservation, among other areas.

Despite its size, TCS has stayed true to its roots of building collaborative models of development, reaching out to work with partners, venture capitalists, academia, and government in order to innovate.

▶

▶

These reflect the new models of innovation where global teams work virtually to create and build new solutions and ideas. Being at the hub of this system, TCS has been able to leverage its relationships to build a network of innovation labs and create new solutions to address customer challenges.

In 2009 a new leader emerged: N. Chandrasekaran, popularly known as Chandra, assumed charge as the CEO and MD. He had been at the helm of several key strategic transitions at TCS since 2002 when he took over the role as head of global sales. As the chief operating officer, he had been the architect of the new organizational structure unveiled in 2008, which created multiple agile business units focusing on domains and markets, as well as built strategic business units in order to pursue new initiatives.

Chandra personifies TCS's commitment to customer satisfaction and high-quality deliverables. Through his experience in a variety of operating roles across TCS, he has built a reputation in the IT services industry for his exceptional ability to build and develop new businesses and nurture long-term relationships. He has also been a champion of software and business quality for the industry.

Under his leadership, TCS pioneered the creation of its unique Global Network Delivery Model across five continents and ventured into new markets, including Europe, China, and Latin America, and it added new business lines. At the end of 2009–2010, over 25 percent of TCS revenues came from new services like BPO, infrastructure, assurance, and asset-leveraged solutions, reflecting the effectiveness of this strategy.

Chandra has also driven domain diversification as TCS has entered new areas like media and information services, as well as high technology. All of these have matured into sizable businesses under his guidance. In 2008, the company went through an internal restructuring exercise designed to bring agility to the organization. All of these have matured into sizable businesses under Chandra's mentorship and guidance. The philosophies of leadership and delivery excellence and the promise of "experience certainty" are pillars on which the success of TCS is cemented.

Four decades ago, when TCS began to promote the concept of global sourcing in IT and application services, it was a market-defining model. Today it is the mainstream model for the global IT industry. TCS has the same opportunity to create new business models for the future.

Summary

This chapter explored the role of the vendor and intermediaries in sourcing arrangements. Particular attention was given to the core capabilities vendors should develop to maintain their competitive position and to ensure their ability to provide quality services to their clients.

Relevant teaching case

Burgelman R. A., and Aneesha, C. (2006). "Infosys Consulting in 2006." *Harvard Business Online*, no. 9-SM1-51.

CHAPTER 5

Leveraging knowledge and expertise

What happens to knowledge when an organization outsources? Despite the rapid growth of ITO and BPO, there is still a considerable time lapse on grasping the implications for knowledge and expertise management in these processes. Organizations often have limited understanding of how new knowledge can be created and exploited, especially when outsourced activities are considered noncore services. As Willcocks et al. (2004) point out, in an increasingly commoditized outsourcing market, with ever-more-demanding client companies, competing on leveraging knowledge-related value may well become the new game in town.

In this chapter, we discuss what happens to knowledge and expertise in outsourcing arrangements and how to realize benefits of knowledge creation and exploitation to achieve better performance and innovation. We focus mainly on the following topics:

- How organizations leverage knowledge in outsourcing relationships
- How vendor firms integrate diverse domains of expertise to facilitate knowledge transfer between on-site and offshore teams and across projects
- How to manage expertise within and between projects

Integrating knowledge and outsourcing strategy

Researchers find that do-it-yourself sourcing or using management consultancy are both limited in terms of leveraging knowledge assimilation and creation. Similarly, in ITO, client organizations often make inadequate investments in retaining core knowledge capabilities, which sometimes lead them to lose control over the destiny of their IT function and can result in belated re-insourcing of these capabilities. In BPO, which is often conducted on a fee-for-service basis, knowledge implications are just as often neglected, although they may well be disguised by improvements in real cost and service (Willcocks et al., 2004; Willcocks, Oshri, and Hindle, 2009).

Quinn (1999) advises companies to develop an integrated knowledge and outsourcing strategy to mitigate these risks. The key is to identify and build up selected areas of a company's competitive strength to a best-in-world level. The most effective core competency strategies focus on a few cross-functional, intellectually based service activities, or knowledge and skill sets critical to customers. Such strategies allow the company to build selective specialized capabilities and provide a flexible platform for future innovations. Quinn points out that at least one of these competencies should be related to the notion of customer and market knowledge. On such a basis, integrating knowledge and outsourcing strategy into organizational core competency strategies will enable companies to:

- Focus and flatten their organizations by concentrating their limited resources on a relatively few knowledge-based core competencies through which they can develop best-in-world capabilities
- Leverage their internal innovation capabilities through effective personal, IT, and motivational links to outside knowledge sources
- Eliminate the inflexibilities of fixed overheads, bureaucracy, and physical plant by conscientiously tapping the more nimble resources of both their customer chain downstream and their technology and supply chain upstream
- Expand their own knowledge and physical investment capabilities by several orders of magnitude through exploiting the facilities and program investments of outside sources

Intellectual capital and social capital

How do companies effectively tap into knowledge sources from outsourcing vendors? Willcocks et al. (2004, 2009) argue that outsourcers should have knowledge management strategies that enable the creation and exploitation of intellectual capital. Creating intellectual capital is more than simply hiring bright people or buying knowledge management software. Stewart (2001) suggests three essential elements or assets that contribute to the development of intellectual capital:

- Structural capital, which refers to the codified bodies of semipermanent knowledge that can be transferred and the tools that augment the body of knowledge by bringing relevant data or expertise to people
- Human capital, which represents the capabilities of individuals to provide solutions to customers.

- Customer capital, which is linked to shared knowledge, or the value of an organization's relationships with the people with whom it does business

The mere possession of these assets is not enough. Intellectual capital can be generated only through the interplay between these essential elements. Therefore, as Willcocks et al. (2009) suggested, there should be a fourth kind of capital, *social capital,* which helps bring these elements together and encourages interplay among them. Examples of social capital are trust, loyalty, and reciprocity within a community, that is, the values created from social networks. There is a reciprocal relationship between social capital and intellectual capital: the former facilitates the development of the latter, which in turn strengthens social capital.

Social capital has three dimensions: structural, cognitive, and relational. Since social capital to a great extent involves social connections, mutual respect, shared identity and culture, trust, and common motivation, organizations are in a better position to generate these qualities than markets are. However, outsourcing often disrupts and reduces social capital by disembedding people, systems, and institutional knowledge from the client organization. Therefore, attention should be paid to cultivating social capital.

Rottman (2008) conducted a case study with a US manufacturer and its offshore outsourcing partner in India. Using the three dimensions of social capital, he derived eight practices from the case study that facilitate effective knowledge transfer:

Structural (network ties and configuration)
1. Use multiple suppliers to strengthen network ties and increase social networks.
2. Increase network use and frequency, and maintain multiple connections by breaking projects into small segments.
3. Ensure knowledge retention and transfer by requiring suppliers to have shadows for key supplier roles.

Cognitive (shared goals and culture)
4. Strengthen cultural understanding by visiting the offshore supplier and project teams.
5. Clarify goals by communicating the offshore strategy to all parties.
6. Integrate the supplier's employees into the development team.
7. Cotrain internal employees and supplier employees to communicate goals and increase cultural awareness.

Relational (trust)
8. Increase internal trust by understanding and managing the talent pipeline.

Rottman shows in the case study that managing the structural, cognitive, and relational dimensions of the relationship allowed the partners in the strategy alliance to increase network stability, reduce cultural barriers, share and understand common goals, and strengthen network ties.

Management control to capture intellectual capital

To leverage benefits from knowledge and expertise, Quinn (1999) suggests that companies should carefully set up management controls to:

- Ensure goal and value congruence
- Build a professional and highly trained procurement and contract management group
- Develop a strong strategic and operations information system at the strategic and operations levels
- Include all insourcing transaction costs and measure the benefits intended from the outsourcing relationship
- Develop feedback systems to leverage and share knowledge and innovation in both directions
- Create a mutual three-level contact system for top managers, middle-level managers, and operating-level personnel. Such a contact system allows personal relationships and knowledge exchanges to take place and helps to stave off problems

Willcocks et al. (2009) suggest that enterprise partnership, which often involves risk-and-reward and joint ownership arrangements, is a promising way to leverage cost and quality gains as well as knowledge creation and exploitation. They present the example of Lloyds of London, which outsourced its back office policy and claims settlement systems to the supplier Xchanging. This example illustrates how intellectual capital is generated and retained through the formation and continuous maintenance of the partnership. Willcocks et al. introduced three key innovations:

1. *An enterprise partnership business model*: This entails setting up multiple joint governance bodies that engage both the client and the vendor in a continuous process of planning and decision making, thereby establishing trust and mutual obligation and reinforcing the institutional relationship. Relating this model to the notion of intellectual capital, we can see elements of customer capital and the structural dimension of social capital being leveraged.

2. *An Xcellence competency model*: The Xcellence model helps in building up a community of practice to facilitate the sharing of tacit knowledge and its

conversion to explicit knowledge in the form of detailed competency manuals. The model exemplifies the involvement of human capital and structural capital and helps to establish the cognitive dimension of social capital.

3. *A four-phase implementation model*: The phases of preparation, realignment, streamlining, and continuous improvement not only help employees make the transition from client to vendor organization but also create a new culture of a dynamic, profitable business. Group identity and trust are built in this process, as well as a sense of mutual obligation. This model represents the relational dimension of social capital.

Knowledge transfer between on-site and offshore teams

To leverage the value of knowledge and expertise of both sides in an offshore partnership, a crucial element is to ensure effective knowledge transfer between on-site and offshore teams. Knowledge that is not transferred gets lost. Despite advances in information and communication technologies, breakdowns in the transfer of knowledge across distributed sites still constitute a major challenge. Oshri and associates identified the following factors that contribute to the difficulty of transferring knowledge between remote sites, especially across national boundaries:

- The diversity of local contexts, which exacerbates the stickiness of information, a notion developed by von Hippel (1994), which refers to tacit knowledge rooted in action, commitment, and involvement in a specific context
- Different local routines for working, training, and learning that obstruct the development of shared understanding of practices and knowledge
- Differences in skills, expertise, technical infrastructure, development tools, and methodologies
- Changes in membership
- The lack of prior experience of working together between the distributed teams

Organizational learning processes in offshore sourcing

One way to achieve successful knowledge transfer from the onshore to the offshore organization is through effective organizational learning processes. Huber (1991) suggests four key constructs and processes in organizational learning: knowledge acquisition, information distribution, information interpretation, and organizational memory. Knowledge acquisition refers to the process by which knowledge is obtained, and it can be broken down into the following subprocesses:

- Congenial learning – getting the organization's inherited knowledge from its creators
- Experiential learning – acquiring knowledge through direct experience
- Vicarious learning – observing and copying successful routines from other organizations
- Grafting – hiring new members with new knowledge from other organizations
- Searching and noticing – acquiring information through scanning, focused search, performance monitoring, awareness of the external environment, and internal conditions of performance

Chua and Pan (2008) conducted a case study of a global information systems department in a multinational bank that was transferring its business application support and development experience to an offshore location. They examined how different types of knowledge were transferred and identified the following types of knowledge (Iivari, Hirschheim, and Klein, 2004): technical knowledge, application domain knowledge, information system (IS) application knowledge, organizational knowledge, and IS development process knowledge. They showed in their case study that depending on the type of knowledge required, different learning subprocesses are needed (see Table 5.1). While some areas of the IS knowledge

Table 5.1 Organizational learning sub-processes in different IS knowledge areas

IS knowledge areas	Learning sub-processes
Technical knowledge Application domain knowledge	Grafting of staff with as much of these two knowledge areas as possible will form the basis to which new knowledge will be added
Organizational knowledge	Experiential learning and vicarious learning were carried out through presentations, support simulations, on-the-job training, and playback. Self-appraisal techniques such as quizzes and individual and team appraisals were used to check whether learning was effective.
IS development process knowledge	A separate training programme for analysis design, using the same knowledge transfer mechanisms as above, was created for the more experienced members of the offshore team. Offshore staff have to be retained to enable continued offshore learning.

Source: Based on Chua and Pan (2008)

can be easily grafted, some require intense, vicarious, and experiential learning using rich data. Certain types of knowledge, which are "sticky" and difficult to codify, are also difficult to transfer.

A Transactive Memory System between on-site and offshore teams

So what can we do about sticky knowledge that is embodied in experts in the area of knowledge and is thus difficult to transfer between distributed teams? While colocated teams may develop various memory systems that support knowledge transfer, globally distributed teams face various barriers in developing such systems that may facilitate the transfer of contextual and embedded knowledge. A Transactive Memory System (TMS) is the combination of individual memory systems and communications (also referred to as "transactions") between individuals that enable the shared division of cognitive labor used to encode, store, and retrieve knowledge from different but complementary domains of expertise while being engaged in collective tasks (Wegner, 1986). A group-level TMS consists of individuals using each other as a memory source.

Individuals encode information for storing and retrieving in a similar way that a librarian enters details of a new book in a particular library system before putting it on the shelf. Three core TMS processes – directory updating, information allocation, and retrieval coordination – enable the formation and further operation of a TMS. *Directory updating* is associated with learning about areas of expertise of team members and creating awareness about "who knows what" in the team or organization. Through this process, knowledge is categorized (i.e., assigned labels that reflect the subjects of the knowledge) for systematically storing the location of the knowledge, but not the knowledge itself. *Information allocation* is about communicating information to the relevant experts for processing and storage. Individuals store this information internally (building their own memory), or externally (storing it in artifacts or indirectly in other people's memories). *Retrieval coordination* implies knowing whom to contact for which information and in what sequence so that the retrieval process is effective and efficient (Wegner, 1995). Through this process, information about the location of the knowledge or expertise is retrieved when someone else asks for it. Retrieval thus consists of two interconnected subprocesses: person A communicates the need for information with person B; person B retrieves the information (Oshri, van Fenema, and Kotlarsky, 2008).

In practice, the development and activation of the core TMS processes is supported by knowledge directories that point to where knowledge and expertise reside. Oshri, van Fenema, and Kotlarsky (2008) differentiate two types of directories: *codified* (e.g., information systems and technologies) and *personalized* (e.g., personal memory or other people's memories). Table 5.2 details how codified and personalized knowledge directories support TMS processes in globally distributed teams.

Oshri, van Fenema, and Kotlarsky (2008) suggest that in order to overcome differences derived from the local contexts of the on-site and offshore teams (e.g., different work routines, methodologies, and skills), organizations should invest in developing a TMS. In particular, they recommend specific mechanisms supporting the development of codified and personalized TMS directories to help develop a TMS between on-site and

Table 5.2 Transactive memory system processes and codified and personalized directories in globally distributed teams

TMS processes	How knowledge directories support TMS processes	
	Codified directories	Personalized directories
Directory updating Having a shared "cataloging" system.	Creating a shared system to categorize information. Developing a set of rules of how to label the subject and location of the expertise.	Creating a shared understanding of context and work-related processes, terminology and language.
Information allocation The way in which the information is organized in physical locations and in the memories of dispersed team members.	Storing information about the subject and location of the knowledge. This can be achieved by creating pointers to the location of knowledge in an expertise directory. Storing up-to-date records of available documents and expertise.	Storing information about "who knows what" and "who is doing what" in individuals' memories.
Retrieval coordination Knowing where and in what form information is stored in the dispersed team. Being able to find required information through determining the location of information, and, sometimes, the combination or interplay of items coming from multiple locations.	Developing search capabilities (e.g., keyword-based) for effective and efficient search and retrieval processes.	Developing interpersonal channels through which individuals can search for information about who has expertise and in which areas, and where this expertise resides.

offshore teams and keep it updated. These include the standardization of templates and methodologies across remote sites as well as frequent tele-conferencing sessions and occasional short visits (see Table 5.3). These mechanisms contributed to the development of the notion of "who knows what" across on-site and offshore teams despite the challenges associated with globally distributed teams, and supported the transfer of knowledge between on-site and offshore teams.

In order to enable the transfer of knowledge between remote sites, organizations should consider the mechanisms we have noted that support the development, management, and coordination of collective expertise and enable the transfer of knowledge between on-site and offshore teams. In doing so, they should consider two key aspects with respect to work division. First, they should attempt to select project members based on their shared histories of collaboration in their respective area of expertise. In this way, remote counterparts who already know each other have developed a meta-knowledge relating to their counterparts and have established procedures for working together. Such a staffing approach is likely to speed the development of the TMS because procedures, codified routines, and social ties have already been established. Second, an expertise-based division of

Table 5.3 Organizational mechanisms and processes supporting the development of a TMS in globally distributed teams

TMS processes	Codified directories	Personalized directories
Directory updating	Standard document templates (for product deliverables and process phases)	Rotation of on-site and offshore team members
	Glossary of terms to include unique (e.g., product-specific) terminology	Joint training programs
		Team-building exercises
		Social activities
Information allocation	Central project repository	Expertise-based division of work
	Standardization of tools and methods across locations	Creating complementary documentation for software components (includes the name of the developer)
	Centralization of tools on the central server; Web access	
Retrieval coordination	Standard processes and procedures (that include pointers to the location of information)	Systematic and frequent communication using email and tele- and videoconferencing
	Keywords-based search capabilities	Technologies that enable reachability when on the move and out of working hours (e.g., mobile phones, pagers, PDAs)
	Tools that enable automated notification of changes and requests (e.g., software configuration management and change management tools)	

work should be considered when members of the team have worked with each other previously and have developed shared histories. Teams that do not have shared histories, however, may benefit from a division of work that is based on geographical location for a period of time, which enables them to establish procedures, standards, and templates from the development of codified directories before changing to an expertise-based division of work approach.

The case study that follows illustrates how one IT vendor, Tata Consultancy Services, dealt with challenges faced during transition in an offshore outsourcing project.

Case Study

THE KEY KNOWLEDGE MANAGEMENT CHALLENGES IN THE OUTSOURCING PROJECT BETWEEN ABN AMRO AND TCS

When the IT industry started, it was more like a cottage industry, very much people dependent. It is now changing from being people dependent to process dependent. When this happens, knowledge management becomes part of the process itself.

Tata Consultancy Services (TCS), part of the Tata Group, was founded in 1968 as a consulting service firm for the emerging IT industry. Since then, it has expanded to become a global player with revenues of over $6.3 billion in 2010. With over 174,000 associates and 50 service delivery centers, TCS has established a presence in 34 countries. It provides various services, including BPO and IT maintenance and development, to clients around the globe.

TCS has developed a global delivery model (GDM) in which projects are handled mainly by teams located remotely from clients but often with a small team at the client site. Generally TCS's on-site and offshore teams transfer work packages back and forth to each other until the task is completed. TCS's project teams, which are based on-site, onshore, and nearshore, depend on the expertise and knowledge that reside within TCS at various locations. Thus, TCS has developed knowledge management practices to acquire and retain knowledge globally, regardless of the physical location of the expert or the knowledge seeker.

▶

▶

In late 2005, Netherlands-based ABN AMRO Bank announced a $1.2 billion outsourcing contract with five providers, including TCS, to provide support and application enhancement services. The outsourcing project organization of ABN AMRO's contract with TCS consists of three arrangements across three continents. Each arrangement type has an on-site component at the client site and a remote component elsewhere:

1. In the Netherlands, on-site TCS teams at ABN AMRO's Amsterdam locations work with corresponding offshore TCS teams in Mumbai, India.
2. In Brazil, on-site TCS teams at ABN AMRO's São Paulo locations work with corresponding onshore teams at TCS's delivery center in Campinas, 100 kilometers away.
3. In several countries (e.g., Switzerland, Germany, Monaco), on-site TCS teams communicate with an onshore TCS delivery center in Luxembourg and a nearshore TCS delivery center in Hungary.

Typically TCS team members reside in one location throughout a project – either on-site, onshore, nearshore, or offshore. Only a small number of TCS staff travel between locations for short visits. An on-site TCS team includes project members, project leaders, portfolio managers, program managers, a transition head, a relationship manager, and other functions – mainly quality assurance, human resource, and organization development personnel.

The ABN AMRO–TCS offshore outsourcing project was divided into two phases: transition and steady state. In the transition phase, the on-site TCS team learned about ABN AMRO's systems and transferred this knowledge to its corresponding offshore TCS team. In the steady-state phase, the offshore TCS teams provided the main support for the bank's systems and services and also developed applications. This multisite mode of working required the on-site, onshore, nearshore, and offshore teams to overcome two expertise management challenges: the relationship and organizational challenges.

The relationship challenge deals with the client–provider relationship. With respect to managing knowledge, the provider needs to answer the question: How can a client's knowledge be captured and retained at both on-site and remote locations to ensure uninterrupted service to the client and to develop further services for the client? This

▶

▶

challenge requires the provider to quickly and effectively assimilate the client's knowledge. TCS views success in meeting this challenge as having no knowledge gaps between its corresponding teams, that is, the pairs of on-site/onshore, on-site/nearshore, and on-site/offshore teams. TCS addresses this challenge by requiring the remote TCS team to develop the same level of knowledge as its corresponding on-site TCS team.

Eliminating knowledge gaps between on-site and remote teams is particularly important for offshore service companies such as TCS because they need to demonstrate to clients that offshoring application maintenance and development will not reduce service or application quality. As one TCS delivery manager on the offshore team in Mumbai notes: "When I had my initial discussion with the bank's portfolio managers, they asked, 'How are you going to take care of the knowledge base? We have ten, fifteen, thirty years of experience at the bank, yet you are going to join afresh. You are just going to have a knowledge transfer for a short time'. They asked, 'So how do you ensure that you have this knowledge with you? And how are you going to retain this knowledge?'"

The organizational challenge concerns the provider's mechanisms for managing knowledge within its own organization. It answers the question: How do we turn local learning and knowledge into global assets? The challenge is to capture knowledge from an on-site TCS team and then refine and reuse it globally on other teams that may need it. TCS addresses this challenge by developing knowledge-co-ordination competencies to ensure that knowledge is reapplied across the company.

TCS and other outsourcing providers are exposed to vast amounts of knowledge through their numerous outsourcing relationships. However, this knowledge often becomes the asset of just a single project. It is rarely shared with other projects that will likely confront similar challenges. The head of the learning and development department at TCS explains this challenge by saying: "How do we create a kind of customer-focused experience? How do we share this knowledge? How can we enhance our learning about banking and insurance so that we can say that we know technology and we also know about the banking industry? Basically, I need to develop specific domain knowledge and link it to other value activities, share it with the entire workforce so our employees can talk to the customer in their own language and in

▶

▶
their own domain of expertise as an expert. That is a challenge for me to create this kind of expertise."

Kamal Joshi, the TCS transition head in Amsterdam who was responsible for ensuring that the client's knowledge possessed by ABN AMRO experts will be transferred to TCS offshore teams in Mumbai, was confident that TCS would meet the client's expectations; however, he was also wondering, *Have I considered all risks involved in my knowledge management strategy? What can go wrong?*

Managing expertise within and between projects

While knowledge transfer is an important step in offshore outsourcing, the question remaining for the client's executives is where they should draw the line on outsourcing their knowledge and expertise. How can the selected provider develop the knowledge and expertise of their domain, systems, and practices to maintain continuity of service and achieve the sought-for innovation and transformation? IT outsourcing provider executives also have to ask themselves how they can quickly develop expertise in new areas, particularly where their teams are remote and dispersed, and how they can retain knowledge when people equipped with key knowledge and expertise move on.

Coordination mechanisms to facilitate knowledge processes in global teams

In offshore outsourcing, some providers adopt a multisite mode of work, often referred to as a GDM, which consists of various types of arrangements that involve an on-site component at the client site and one or several remote components somewhere else, typically in the provider home country or other locations (offshore, nearshore, or onshore) where the provider has development or customer support facilities. The idea behind the GDM is to complete the work where it can be done best, makes the most economic sense, with the least amount of acceptable risk. Large suppliers such as IBM, Accenture, TCS, and Infosys set up global delivery centers in locations where they have cost, flexibility, and time-to-market advantages and access to large pools of talent and specialized expertise. For the same

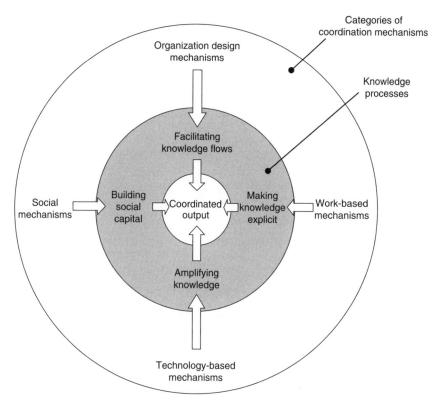

Figure 5.1 How coordination mechanisms facilitate knowledge processes to achieve coordination

reasons, many client companies, in particular large multinationals, set up captive facilities around the world.

The multisite or the GDM of work requires significant coordination. Otherwise organizational performance may encounter problems like asymmetries, knowledge that is "stuck" at a particular site, and lost opportunities in knowledge creation. Coordination mechanisms become knowledge management instruments and contribute to the coherence of knowledge processes (Kotlarsky, van Fenema, and Willcocks, 2008). Kotlarsky and associates (2008) developed a model of how each category of coordination mechanism has an impact on knowledge processes and thus ultimately on coordinated outcomes as shown in Figure 5.1. There are four types of coordination mechanisms:

- *Organization design mechanisms,* which encompass formal structures such as hierarchies, linking pins, teams, and direct contacts. They facilitate knowledge flows by providing a structure through which knowledge workers can channel their expertise. Organization design clarifies who is supposed to know what and who is supposed to communicate with whom. It therefore simplifies knowledge flows.

- *Work-based mechanisms,* which involve the specific structuring of tasks to be accomplished. They include plans, specifications, standards, categorization systems, and representations of work in progress such as prototypes and design documents. Work-based mechanisms that capture knowledge are important for making knowledge explicit, as they enable activity replication and commonality. The use of such mechanisms implies that knowledge and expectations are made explicit and thus are known and useful to other people working at different sites or times. In such dispersed organizations, knowledge must be rapidly disseminated by means of technology.

- *Technology-based mechanisms,* which amplify knowledge management processes by enabling information capturing, processing, storage, and exchange (e.g., electronic calendaring and scheduling, groupware, shared databases). These technologies not only process data and information, but also trigger new ideas and enable coordinated actions.

- *Social (interpersonal) mechanisms,* which involve communication activities, working relationships, and social cognition. They help establish social capital and facilitate the development of a TMS (knowledge about who knows and does what). Individuals are thus knowledge workers who negotiate points of view and transform their understanding to generate innovative outputs; they have relational needs that are relevant for coordinating their work.

Practices for managing dispersed expertise

Oshri, Kotlarsky, and Willcocks (2007a) point out that firms engaged in offshore outsourcing face a relationship challenge and an organizational challenge. The former refers to the client–provider relationship: how a client's knowledge can be captured and retained at both on-site and remote locations to ensure uninterrupted service to the client and to further develop services for the client. This is the knowledge transfer challenge we discussed above. The organizational challenge concerns the provider's ability to manage expertise within its own organization. In other words, the challenge is to capture expertise from an on-site team and refine and reuse it within other distributed teams. Based on their case study at TCS and its globally distributed service delivery centers, Oshri, Kotlarsky, and

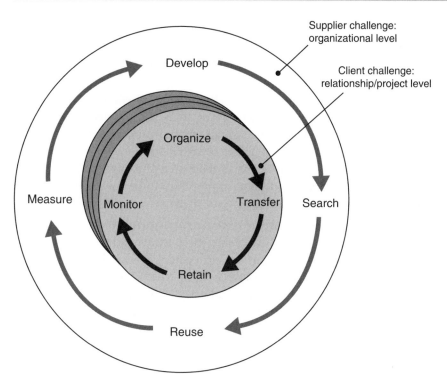

Figure 5.2 Expertise management processes at the relationship and organizational levels

Willcocks (2007a) observed that TCS employs the following practices to address these challenges (shown in Figure 5.2).

1. *Implement an organizational structure that is a mirror image of the client's structure ('organize')*: TCS uses an organizational structure that ensures that client personnel and offshore TCS personnel can easily identify their counterpart. Oshri and associates identify three types of organizational structures found in offshore outsourcing arrangements: the funnel (a single point of contact and control between client and provider), the network (multiple points of contacts and control), and the mirror. They identify the mirror as the most effective of the three in terms of organizing knowledge assimilation and transfer.

2. *Implement a knowledge transfer methodology ('transfer')*: Codifying knowledge is the key practice here. TCS's on-site team provides documentation based on standard templates and passes these templates to the offshore team. But this is only the first step. The offshore team then has

to "play back" what they learned from the documentation by giving presentations to the on-site team. Again, while codified knowledge is useful, transferring tacit knowledge, which can be obtained only through learning by doing, is more difficult.

3. *Implement a knowledge retention methodology ('retain')*: To avoid loss of knowledge due to personnel turnover, TCS has adopted a succession plan. TCS managers identify individuals who can replace them in case they leave the project or company. These potential successors are trained and back up the manager's knowledge in their area of expertise. This greatly reduces the disruption and delay resulting from turnover of key players in outsourcing projects.

4. *Monitor expertise development and retention at project and organizational levels ('monitor'):* To enable local teams to take advantage of centralized resources, TCS has set up centers of excellence (CoEs) to link project and organizational levels of expertise monitoring. The CoEs are networks of experts who have advanced know-how and experience in a particular market or technological domain. They are responsible for acquiring know-how from internal and external sources and then sharing that with project teams. CoEs serve as repositories of knowledge as well as directories that point to an expert's location.

5. *Make expertise development a key organizational value ('develop')*: In TCS, every project is supported by the CoEs – quality assurance, digitization, and codification groups. These groups provide support for the continuous development of know-how and skills. Moreover, employees receive various types of training during different phases of their career, especially in terms of where to access knowledge and expertise across team boundaries.

6. *Provide mechanisms to search for expertise at project and organizational levels ('search'):* At the project level, the on-site and remote teams keep a regularly updated expertise directory that identifies who knows what and who does what. A project portal (or knowledge base) has also been built that includes information about experts in the project, system, and project documents. Using TCS's knowledge transfer and knowledge retention methodologies, the pointers are created and constantly updated during the transition and steady-state phases of each outsourcing project, as on-site and remote counterparts interact with each other to transfer knowledge and develop their expertise. (This is an example of the development and update of a TMS system discussed earlier in this chapter.) At the company level, a broad memory system brings external expertise into a project in a timely manner. Members of CoEs in a project also serve as connection points with experts in other projects or CoEs. Finally, TCS also

organizes knowledge exchange events and seminars at different locations to facilitate communication and learning between remote counterparts.

7. *Implement a reuse methodology at the global level ('reuse'):* TCS adopts a component-based methodology of developing software components and building software systems by integrating components. Components are supposed to be self-contained and can be removed or replaced without affecting other parts of the system. They can therefore also be modified and reused. TCS makes its reusable components available on its intranet. Also made available with the components is expertise in that particular technology. It should be noted that fundamental to a reuse methodology is systematic and accurate collection of components from projects. Such practices should be cultivated and routinized so that they become part of the organizational culture.

8. *Continually measure the contribution of reusable assets ('measure'):* To reap the benefit of reusable components, firms also have to reach a certain maturity level in terms of systems development standards – for example, in design, testing, and documentation. On top of this, TCS's quality assurance group also regularly tracks how often and how well components are reused. They also optimize the process of reusing components by centralizing the process and by carefully managing the pool of reusable solutions.

Summary

This chapter reviewed the challenges that both vendors and clients face in terms of managing knowledge and expertise. We opened this chapter with a simple question: What happens to knowledge when you outsource? We illustrated how knowledge can be effectively used by both vendors and clients and how the management of knowledge and expertise can be perceived as a value-adding activity that can benefit vendors and clients alike. However, most clients have not fully captured the potential of advancing learning from such opportunities and in most cases have trusted the management of knowledge and expertise to their vendor.

Relevant teaching cases

Oshri, I., Kotlarsky, J., and Willcocks, L. (2007). "Managing Dispersed Expertise in IT Offshore Outsourcing: Lessons from Tata Consultancy Services." *MIS Quarterly Executive,* 6(2), 53–65. This is not a classic teaching case; however, it describes in detail aspects relating to knowledge and expertise in an offshore outsourcing setting

The client perspective: vendor selection strategy, retained management capabilities, and legal issues

One key factor in achieving success in global sourcing arrangements is the quality of the client–supplier relationship. Selecting the right vendor is critical to maximizing the benefits and minimizing the risks associated with the venture. In this chapter, we review the major considerations during the vendor selection process:

- The key criteria for evaluating vendors
- Which capabilities need to be developed and retained
- The critical legal issues in outsourcing and offshoring
- The role of the contract in managing risk

Vendor selection: key aspects and considerations

There are two key aspects in a client's decision to outsource: the configuration of the deal and the market in which the client would like to operate. With regard to the configuration, a client should consider the configuration that will best facilitate the objectives of the firm in this particular sourcing arrangement. Different configuration options (discussed in Chapter 4) are the sole supplier (a single supplier providing the entire service), best-of-breed (the client organization plays the role of the head contractor to manage a supplier network), panel (a list of preferred suppliers that work in competition), and the prime contractor model (a supplier network that operates under the control of the head contractor). A firm should examine thoroughly its business needs in comparison to the benefits and risks associated with each configuration model. These are summarized in Table 6.1 (Willcocks et al., 2011).

Table 6.1 Supplier configuration options and associated benefits and risks

Option	Benefits	Risks	Management issues
Sole supplier	Sole accountability Potential for the supplier to create economies of scale, the benefits of which may be passed on to the customer Streamlined contracting costs and processes End-to-end key performance metrics	Monopolistic supplier behaviors Compromise quality where the supplier is not best of breed in services, industries, or geographical locations	Extensive contract flexibility rights due to dependence on the supplier Independent expertise to avoid solution channeling and ensure value for money
Prime contractor	Single point of accountability Allows best-of-breed subcontracting Streamlined, but a bit more complex, contracting costs and processes End-to-end key performance indicators	Prime contractor should be expert at subcontracting (selection, management, disengagement) Client may desire different subcontractors Client is often required to resolve issues between the prime and subcontractors Primes and subcontractors often encroach on each other's "territories"	Contract ensuring various rights over the subcontracting (access, selection, veto) Compliance auditing ensuring the prime contractor passes obligations to the subcontractors Oversight ensuring all parties are operating as an efficient and unified front
Best of breed	Greater control Flexibility to change vendors Promotes competition and prevents complacency	Attracting the market for small slices of work Keeping suppliers interested, giving management focus, and allocating staff Interdependent services and contracts Integration complexity Tracing accountability	Designing interdependent contracts between independent suppliers Multiparty interface and handover management End-to-end process management is more difficult Multiple life cycle management
Panel	Buy services and assets when required Promotes ongoing competition Prevents complacency	Attracting the market when panel is a prequalification and does not guarantee work Adding new panel members or wanting to use suppliers not on the panel	Panel bidding process for work Ongoing ranking of panel members based on performance Managing and evaluating the total program

Source: Willcocks et al. (2006)

Multisourcing (or multivendor sourcing), which implies combining inter-dependent IT and business services from a set of internal and external providers to achieve optimal outcome, appears to be the long-term dominant trend in global sourcing. The best-of-breed and panel approaches are examples of multisourcing. Levina and Su (2008) outlined the benefits and risks associated with the multisourcing strategy. Benefits of multisourcing include increased competition among suppliers in terms of price, quality, and degree of innovation; lower operational risks and dependency (each supplier becomes less critical); and lower strategic risk (sensitive information is split amongst different suppliers; see Levina and Su, 2008). Among the risks of multisourcing are reduced incentives to make customer-specific or supplier-specific investments. Along these lines, the two parties are less willing to make investments in relationship building, technology, dedicated staff, or physical assets as the basis for enhancing their collaboration (see also Chapter 4). Furthermore, multisourcing arrangements increase management overhead as client firms incur costs associated with contracting, developing relationships with suppliers, and coordinating work.

Multisourcing arrangements can be characterized by different breadth and depth of supply relationships that constitute a supply base of a client firm. Su and Levina (in press) define *supply base* as a set of contractual supplier relationships that are directly managed by the sourcing firm for a given business function at a given time. The breadth of the supply base reflects the number of suppliers the focal firm uses for a given business function, and the depth of a supply relationship is characterized by the client's level of investment in a particular supply relationship for a given function. Figure 6.1 describes different combinations of breadth and depth of supply relationships, breadth and depth of the supply base also have a number of implications on the outcome of outsourcing arrangements (see Table 6.2).

With regard to the markets in which the client may wish to operate, the client has three main choices to consider suppliers operating in various settings:

Domestic versus offshore: When going offshore, most firms tend to use a best-of-breed approach. However, some organizations choose to establish a prime contractor to manage the offshore vendors. Typical services for which the offshore market has been shown to generate increased cost savings include applications coding, call center operations, data entry, and transaction processing. Consequently, the offshore market has tended to be rather niche oriented. However, as the larger offshoring suppliers are expanding the scope of their services as well as the geographical areas they cover, this trend

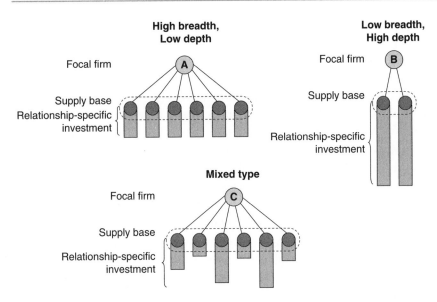

Figure 6.1 Supply base types

Source: Su and Levina (in press)

Table 6.2 Benefits and risks of supply base characteristics on outsourcing arrangement outcomes

	Advantages	Disadvantages
Increased breadth of supply base	Reduced dependency on individual vendors and therefore relatively low switching costs	Limited economies of scale and therefore higher production costs
	Access to best-of-breed vendors reduces operational risk and is likely to yield intangible benefits such as flexibility and innovation	Increased vendor management costs because more vendors need to be managed
Increased depth of supply base	Vendor is likely to invest in developing client-specific capabilities such as deeper understanding of the client's unique business practices, routines, and culture (aiming at long-term benefits from the relationship)	Higher switching costs because the vendor has deeper knowledge about the client and customized solution and cannot be easily replaced
	Reduced vendor management costs due to better communication and collaboration between the parties Deeper relationship may create opportunities for innovation and other synergies	

Source: Based on Su and Levina (2011)

appears to be changing. In doing so, they compete against existing global suppliers. On this issue, in fact, Indian service providers such as Infosys, Wipro, and TCS are gaining ground against established global suppliers such as IBM, Accenture, and HP. An interesting trend that appears to be emerging in this context is bestshoring – mixing offshore, nearshore, and onshore in the same deal. In this way, the supplier locates its resources where they are best deployed according to the notion of fair quality for a fair price.

Local versus global: In a majority of the cases where an organization follows the sole-supplier configuration, global providers are used because of their worldwide reach and the broad scope of services they offer. Such large suppliers have access to more resources and economies of scale and can deal with fluctuations in the demand for services.

Niche versus broad: Because niche suppliers offer a limited range of services, they are usually deployed in a best-of-breed configuration and are contracted either directly with the customer or indirectly through the prime contractor. The respective advantages of these two types of suppliers are illustrated in Table 6.3 (Willcocks et al., 2011).

Table 6.3 Niche versus broad suppliers

Supplier Capability	Niche Supplier	Broad Supplier
Leadership	Supplier leaders will be well known, and there will be easy access to the CEO and straightforward deployment of resources.	Harder to contact top management.
Planning and contracting	Suppliers have more vested interest in the relationship because they cannot absorb or afford failures.	The client should push hard for creative contracts, as suppliers have a greater ability to absorb risk than niche players do.
Organizational design	Less formal design is required, and the deal is based more on personal relationships.	Formal organizational design is more important.
Process improvement	Niche suppliers may rely less on processes (like Six Sigma, CMM), but make up for this with domain expertise.	Broad suppliers may rigidly use CMM.
Domain expertise	There will be better domain knowledge because of specialization, but specific elements of business knowledge will still need to be transferred to the supplier.	Clients need to pay special attention to knowledge transfer. Large suppliers can gain domain knowledge through the transfer of relevant employees.

Source: Willcocks et al. (2006)

Some client firms struggle with the supplier selection process. In particular, client firms seek a framework to guide them in making this decision. The Willcocks et al. (2006) supplier key capabilities model can help client firms to make informed decisions with regard to the selection of a global or a local supplier. As an example, in one study by Willcocks et al. (2011), the customer, a large US retailer, had an eight-year outsourcing relationship with a domestic vendor. The issue was whether to award a large project to the existing domestic supplier or to a supplier in India. The supplier in India had a major cost advantage in comparison to the domestic supplier and had performed well in some pilot projects. However, the customer underestimated the amount of effort needed to manage remote teams and the volume of rework needed because the Indian supplier did not understand the company's business. These problems eroded much of the cost savings.

As is illustrated in Table 6.4, the domestic supplier had superior capabilities to deliver the project compared to the offshore supplier. But the Indian supplier had cost advantages. The retailer decided to use the offshore supplier bid to pressure the domestic supplier to reduce its price by 10 to 50 percent. However, by forcing the domestic supplier to reduce costs the retailer weakened the business management capability of the domestic supplier – in other words, its ability to earn a profit while delivering the service. On this issue, Willcocks et al. (2006) emphasize that a number of domestic suppliers are increasingly creating offshore captive centers to compete with Indian suppliers on costs, while leveraging their domestic presence to keep customer service levels high.

It is important to stress that suppliers do not need to demonstrate high levels of performance in all 12 capabilities and all three competencies. For example, not every supplier will need to form a close partnership with a client. For this reason, the client should not be particularly concerned with the relationship competency of the supplier. But the client should pay careful attention to the levels of relationship competency demonstrated by suppliers with whom it wishes to maintain a close long-term partnership – for example, when it needs the supplier's ability to support future changes in the client's business direction or needs innovation from the supplier. A contrasting example is where a client contracts with a supplier only to maintain legacy systems. In this case, the client is likely to focus on the capabilities related to delivery competency (domain expertise, business management, behavior management, sourcing, program management, leadership, and governance capabilities) and less on other capabilities.

Clearly not every client needs a supplier to help transform its business processes and technology. However, if the objective of outsourcing is transformation, then the supplier will need requisite capabilities, including

Table 6.4 The relative capabilities of two suppliers

Supplier capability	Domestic supplier	Offshore supplier
Leadership	*Strong*	*Good*
	The supplier had named a well-respected manager with a good support team.	The supplier had named a well-respected manager but was less clear on who would serve on the supporting team.
Business management	*Strong*	*Strong*
	Given the high-cost bid, the supplier should have been able to deliver the project and still earn a profit.	Although the bid was low, the supplier cost base was low and should have been able to deliver and still earn a profit.
Domain expertise	N/A	N/A
Behavior management	*Strong*	*Weak*
	Supplier employees would ask the customer if they needed clarification. Many of the supplier staff had worked with the client before.	Supplier employees were eager to please but did not share bad news promptly. The supplier staff were mostly new to the client.
Sourcing	*Weak*	*Weak*
	It was likely that the supplier would assign low-level programmers.	It was likely that the supplier would primarily use recent graduates of Indian universities.
Process improvement	N/A	N/A
Technology exploitation	*Strong*	*Strong*
	The supplier had performed this work in the past and had automated tools.	The supplier had performed this work in the past and had automated tools.
Programme management	*Strong*	*Weak*
	The supplier had demonstrated this capability in the past	The supplier relied heavily on an on-site engagement manager who was expected to fulfill too many roles.
Customer development	N/A	N/A
Planning and contracting	*Weak*	*Strong*
	The supplier was very expensive.	The supplier's bid was 60 percent lower than the domestic supplier's.
Organizational design	*Strong*	*Weak*
	Supplier staff were primarily on-site.	The supplier staff would be offshore, with an on-site engagement manager as the contract.
Governance	*Strong*	*Weak*
	The supplier already had reporting processes in place and reported twice a week.	Although the supplier was CMM Level 5, internal supplier reports were not shared, and in the past the client had had to request daily reporting.

Source: Willcocks et al. (2006)

in reengineering and technology exploitation. Along these lines, a firm should identify and focus on the capabilities and competencies that are more relevant to its business when selecting a vendor.

In addition to the supplier's capabilities and competencies, a client should consider the extent to which the supplier would be willing to exert extra effort for its success. In other words, the willingness of suppliers to deliver capabilities and competencies depends also on their desirability to work with a particular customer.

With regard to the criteria affecting supplier selection, according to the results of a 2010 survey of the Outsourcing Institute, commitment to quality, price, and references or reputation are the top three criteria. Other factors that influence supplier selection are flexible contract terms, additional value-added capability, cultural match, existing relationship, and location of the supplier.

However, the matter at hand is not only about a client who is choosing a supplier. Suppliers also assess the attractiveness of potential clients before deciding whether to engage in an outsourcing relationship. Several factors can make a client more attractive than others for a supplier: the prestige of the customer, the degree to which the client CEO is involved in the venture, the size of the project, the potential for additional supplier revenues, the opportunity to enter new markets or business, or the opportunity to acquire new knowledge. Furthermore, the supplier's desire to obtain business from a particular customer may depend on the sales targets of the supplier's headquarters. By this, we mean that a supplier may take business from a client even when the terms and conditions of this contract are not in the supplier's favor, but are mainly to meet its sales figures. In the case where the vendor is satisfied with its current revenue stream, it is likely that the supplier will be cautious in attracting business when the terms of the contract are not in its favor. The following case illustrates the importance of long-term decision making in outsourcing and the consequences for the parties when circumstances change.

Case Study

JPMorgan Chase: to outsource or not outsource?

In 2002, JPMorgan Chase (JPMorgan) and IBM Global Services (IBM) signed a contract. The deal, to extend over seven years, was worth $5 billion, which made it the largest outsourcing contract at the

▶

time. In August 2004, one month after JPMorgan merged with Bank One, JPMorgan cancelled the contract with IBM. Austin A. Adams, chief information officer for JPMorgan, said, "After a rigorous review, the merged firm concluded it has significant scale, enhanced capabilities, tools and processes to build its own global infrastructure and services organisation."

JPMorgan was not new to outsourcing. The bank had previously contracted with IBM in 1995, and in 1996 it contracted with a group of vendors including Computer Sciences Operations (CSC), Anderson Consulting, AT&T Solutions, and Bell Atlantic to manage its data centers, desktops, networks, and some corporate applications in the United States and Europe. Clearly JPMorgan had developed strong client capabilities that allowed it to manage its vendors as well as ensure that vendors delivered value in line with the bank's business strategic road map.

Two years after the start of the contract, JPMorgan had merged with Bank One, the largest player in the consumer banking business, in order to reduce its dependence on investment banking. Bank One, however, had a history of contract termination with IT vendors. Indeed, in 2001, it had terminated a service contract with IBM and AT&T and following this successfully centralized its IT systems. Clearly, Bank One's management believed that the bank needed to keep its IT capability in-house. Outsourcing IT was not part of its sourcing philosophy.

While Bank One was restructuring its IT function in-house, JPMorgan decided to outsource its IT infrastructure to IBM with the aim of cutting costs and centralizing the IT function. JPMorgan short-listed three vendors in the search for an IT services provider – IBM, EDS, and CSC – and finally chose IBM as a sole supplier. On December 30, 2002, JPMorgan and IBM signed the outsourcing contract that would extend over seven years and was worth $5 billion. The contract specified that a large part of JPMorgan's IT services infrastructure, which included data centers, help desks, and data and voice networks, would be transferred to IBM. JPMorgan would retain application delivery and development, desktop support, and other functions in-house. It was also expected that IBM would help and host mission-critical functions such as trading applications for the securities side of the banking giant's operations. Under the contract, IBM would deliver a somewhat new service, on-demand computing services. This meant

▶

▶
that clients could buy and pay only for the IT services they used instead of buying fixed IT services and paying fixed prices. The contract also included the transfer of approximately 4,000 IT employees to IBM. This transfer of employees was planned to take place during the first half of 2003. Indeed, the transfer of employees and IT assets began in April 2003 and was completed by January 2004. By then, work had begun on consolidating data centers, upgrading hardware, and setting up a common networking infrastructure. This was scheduled to take two years to complete.

A year after the 4,000 IT staff had been transferred to IBM and two years into the contract, JPMorgan decided to backsource the IT functions that it had outsourced and bring the entire IT staff back home.

In retrospect, should JPMorgan have outsourced its IT infrastructure at all?

As we see multisourcing gaining popularity with some clients, we also see an increase in bundling services in order to reduce the number of suppliers. *Bundled services* refers to a mix of business processes or IT services purchased separately or at the same time from the same supplier from which synergies and efficiencies are sought in end-to-end processing, governance, relationship management, cost, and performance. Bundled services can help clients reduce transaction costs in a number of ways. They typically include:

- Risk reduction
- Lower levels of governance
- Simpler contracting
- Ability to move to standardized practices
- Synergies across services and processes
- Less management time getting to contract
- Lower relationship management costs

There are two types of bundled services: price bundling and product bundling (Harris and Blair, 2006). Price bundling refers to offering a discount in the sale of two or more products that are not integrated in a package. Product bundling is the integration and sale of products at any price. Studies have shown that the propensity and capability of organizations to buy and manage bundled IT services is much higher than in the case of business process outsourcing and offshoring of IT services (Willcocks and Lacity, 2006).

Three dimensions are reported to affect the customer's propensity to bundle services (Agarwal et al., 2000):

Bundle dimension: This encompasses the bundle choice, that is, the newly formed combinations of products, and the bundle size, or the number of products per bundle.

The client dimension: The following factors affect a client's propensity to buy bundled products: the tendency for single sourcing, the extent of the use, the number of products currently used, and certain client-specific characteristics.

The supplier dimension: The key factors are the perceived quality of the service and the lock-in position of the supplier (Willcocks, Oshri, and Hindle, 2009).

Table 6.5 explains these dimensions as situated in the outsourcing context.

One critical element in achieving successful bundled services is to demonstrate that the client benefits from the synergies among the various services provided by the vendor. Our research shows that most clients have not developed capabilities to evaluate their vendors of bundled services based on the synergies achieved.

Client sourcing capabilities: the retained organization

In Chapter 4, we examined the supplier capabilities that client firms should assess carefully when deciding on their sourcing strategy. In this section, we focus on the capabilities that a client firm should retain to ensure that it can exploit the business advantages of IT over time. Willcocks and Craig (2008), in revisiting research by Willcocks and Feeny (1998), have identified nine such capabilities:

1. *IT leadership:* This capability is related to the challenge of integrating IT efforts with business goals and practices. A major activity for leadership is to devise organizational arrangements in terms of governance, structures, processes, and staffing, with the aim of managing their interdependencies in a way that does not constrain or inhibit the value delivered by the IT function. Leaders can also influence perceptions with regard to the role of IT and its contribution to organizational processes and practices.

Table 6.5 Factors affecting firms' propensity to buy bundled services

	Factors affecting propensity to bundle services	Dimensions	Relevance for the outsourcing context
Bundle	Bundle choice	New or perceived new services	Clients might be more inclined to consider bundled services if they are perceived as new services (higher-value proposition). Needs to be considered from early adopter's viewpoint. Who are the early adopters in this industry?
	Joint functional compatibility	Risk associated with the performance of bundled services	Buyers might tend to add services to the package if they think the bundling will not harm additional services but will present cost advantages that nonbundled services offer.
	Bundle size	Number of products per bundle	Flexibility in bundle size may increase propensity of small firms but might have a negative effect on the supplier's cost structure.
Client	Single-sourcing tendency	Tendency to purchase from single supplier	Clients with limited resources or weak learning capabilities will tend to contract with a single source.
	Extent of use	Heavy consumers of outsourcing versus light consumers of outsourcing.	Clients for whom a large portion of their expenditure is on outsourcing will be more inclined to buy bundled services (sensitivity to discount on high value activity).
	Number of products currently used	High number of services in use	The more the client is familiar with the product, the more likely it is that the client will buy the bundled service.
	Firm characteristics	Size, performance	Large, well-performing firms will tend to buy bundled services. High spenders on IT services will tend to consider bundled services.
Supplier	Perceived supplier quality	Perceived quality across the various services bundled	Propensity to buy experienced services if quality is high or services with quality perceived as high.
	Lock-in position	The dependency between the various services	Propensity to buy or renew bundled services will increase when the dependency between the services is high (regardless of whether performance is enhanced by buying bundled services).

Source: Willcocks, Oshri, and Hindle (2009)

Furthermore, they can establish strong business and IT relationships at the executive level and exploit them for the creation of a shared IT vision.

2. *Business systems thinking:* This capability is related to the challenge of envisioning the business process in terms of its functions, efficacy, and utility as a result of technology. A business systems thinker is capable of building and communicating holistic views of current organizational activities as a basis to identify new patterns that will generate the optimal integration of strategy, process, technology, systems, and people.

3. *Relationship building:* This capability is related to the challenge of getting the business engaged in IT issues in a constructive way. It is important to note that while the business systems thinker is concerned with the integrated business or IT thinking, relationship building is concerned with the wider communication between business and IT communities. More specifically, relationship building involves helping users understand the potential of IT for the creation of value, helping users and IT experts collaborate, and ensuring users' ownership and satisfaction. For most organizations, this is a major challenge resulting from the difference in culture between "techies" and "users." Role holders with this capability have to facilitate a shared purpose and constructive communication among people engaged in business and IT functions.

4. *Architectural planning and design:* This capability is related to the challenge of creating a coherent design of a technical platform that will be able to support current and future business needs. People holding this role are involved in shaping the IT architecture and infrastructure by envisioning the type of technical platform that will best serve the firm's business and by formulating policies and processes that will ensure integration, flexibility, and efficiency in IT services. The principal challenge for the architect planner is to ensure that the organization is up-to-date with technology trends and is consistently able to operate from an efficient IT platform.

5. *Making technology work:* This capability is associated with the challenge of achieving rapid technical progress. The capability of making technology work lies in the overlap between the challenges of IT architecture design and the delivery of IT services. The role of technology "fixers" is to manage problems associated with IT and figure out how to address business needs that cannot be sufficiently facilitated by standard technical approaches. Even organizations that are engaged in total outsourcing acknowledge the need to retain this sort of capability.

6. *Informed buying:* This capability is related to the challenge of managing the IT outsourcing strategy in a way that meets the interests, priorities, and goals of the business. People involved in this role are concerned with

different tasks, including analysis and benchmarking of the external market for IT providers; the design of a five- to ten-year sourcing strategy; and tender leadership, contracting, and management processes of the sourcing venture.

7. *Contract facilitation:* This capability is associated with the need to manage and govern the relationship between suppliers and business users. Along these lines, the contract facilitator aims to ensure the success of existing contracts for IT services and provide a major point of reference through which problems and conflicts are resolved promptly and efficiently. From our experience, the need for this role is rarely identified at the beginning of the outsourcing relationship. It tends to emerge as a response to ongoing issues such as users' requesting more services or changes, the need to coordinate multiple suppliers, or the need to monitor service delivery.

8. *Contract monitoring:* This capability concerns the protection of the current and future contractual position of the firm. It involves the development and maintenance of a robust contract as a fundamental element in the governance of the outsourcing relationship. It is important to note that while the contract facilitator is mainly involved in the day-to-day operations, the contract monitor ensures that the business position is contractually protected at all times. The supplier is assessed against both the standards in the contract and external benchmarks.

9. *Vendor development:* This capability is about ensuring value-adding activities within the outsourcing relationship. The person concerned with the growth of this capability seeks to cultivate and enhance the long-term potential of suppliers to add value to the firm's operations. One major goal in vendor development is to create a win-win situation where the client receives increased value-adding services and the supplier generates better revenues and learning opportunities. One of the hidden risks of outsourcing is the costs incurred in changing suppliers. When taking into account such a risk, it would be in the client's interest to maximize the value-adding activities from its suppliers while guarding against "midcontract sag," where the supplier meets the delivery criteria of the contract but only to the minimum required.

Figure 6.2 illustrates these nine capabilities, as well as the way in which their combination contributes to the delivery of the four fundamental tasks of the IT function:

Governance: This task refers to the dynamic alignment of the activities of the IT function with those of the overall organization.

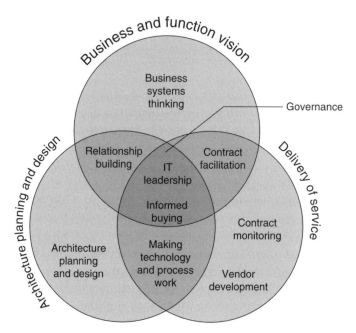

Figure 6.2 Nine core capabilities for high performing IT and back-office functions

Source: Willcocks and Craig (2008)

Business and function vision: This is a demand-driven task associated with defining the systems, information, and processes needed. This task is also geared toward exploiting such business components to improve business efficiency.

Architecture planning and design: This task is supply driven and associated with defining the architecture of the evolving technical platform and dealing with the risks related to nonroutine technical issues.

Delivery of service: This task is concerned with managing the sourcing strategy. It seeks to investigate and understand the external market and involves the ability to select, engage, and manage third-party IT resources and service delivery.

Client organizations use primarily three mechanisms to identify and develop capabilities: certain organizational processes, the firm's culture, and the firm's structure. Table 6.6 illustrates how capabilities emerge as a result of an organization's processes, culture, and structure and presents some examples.

Table 6.6 Organizational mechanisms for building capabilities

Mechanism	Definition	Examples
Processes	Capabilities emerge from problem-defining and problem-solving routines interwoven with individual skills. At a higher level, these are formally combined into organizational processes.	IT governance Strategic IT planning Contract reviews and market testing IT investment reviews Process models (e.g., ITIL) Compliance
Culture	Capabilities emerge from links across a mosaic of organizational elements, such as incentive plans, operating systems, corporate culture, or behavior-shaping practices.	Career models Reward and recognition Job families Competencies Service orientation
Structure	Capabilities emerge as a key product of the organization as an entire system. In other words, capabilities are embedded in organizational processes and are bounded by the structure of the organization.	IT organizational model Group CIO reporting line Business-unit IS function reporting lines Roles and responsibilities

Source: Willcocks et al. (2007)

Retaining the management of these capabilities is critical for the client because these capabilities offer more control over the firm's IT operations. However, developing a high-performing retained organization is not free of challenges. The following five major challenges should be thoroughly considered in this regard:

1. *Human resource challenge:* The nine roles that have already been illustrated and associated with each of the nine retained management capabilities demand high performers. Each role requires a mix of business, technical, and interpersonal skills (these are summarized in Table 6.7). However, there appears to be much greater emphasis on business skills and business orientation in nearly all roles (excluding those of technical fixers and to some extent technical architects). Furthermore, there appears to be an increased need for interpersonal skills in all roles, except in that of contract monitor.

2. *The supplier challenge*: In specific projects and services, suppliers need complementary rather than competing or duplicating skills. Furthermore, it is important to create a climate of cooperation between the in-house management team and the supplier groups. Taking into account the

Table 6.7 Skills, time horizons ,and orientations of retained capabilities

Core IT capability	Business skills	Technical skills	Interpersonal skills	Time horizons	Motivating values
IT leadership	High	Medium	High	Future and Present	Strategy Structure Individuals
Business systems thinking	High	Medium	Medium	Future	Strategy
Relationship building	Medium	High	High	Present	Structure Individuals
Architecture planning and design	Low to medium	High	Medium	Future	Technology
Making technology and processes work	Low	High	Low to medium	Present	Technology
Informed buying	High	Medium	High	Future and Present	Strategy Structure
Contract facilitation	Medium	Medium	High	Present	Structure Individuals
Contract monitoring	Medium	Medium	Low to medium	Future	Structure
Vendor development	High	Medium	Medium to high	Future	Strategy Individuals

Source: Willcocks and Craig (2008)

multisourcing trend, a supplier's ability to cooperate with other vendors is of great significance for the performance of the venture.

3. *The perennial challenge: Relationships*: The way the relationship between the supplier and the vendor evolves is a critical element that can affect the success of the project. For example, one element that affects the way the relationship evolves is the power balance between the two partners. Maintaining good relationships throughout the outsourcing project is extremely challenging because power is likely to shift from the client to the supplier over time. While it is expected that both clients and suppliers will exploit this power position, there should be a tipping point in which the goodwill and future development of the relationship is not diminished. Evidence by Willcocks and Craig (2008) shows that relationship management can create a 20 to 40 percent difference in performance.

4. *The project management challenge*: In dynamic business environments, there is an increased need for appropriate project management skills. Project management must be an organizational core capability and not an asset of a particular division or department. In the retained management capabilities framework (see Figure 6.2), candidates for the role of the project manager are most likely to be found in the relationship builder and technical fixer roles.

5. *Rising challenges:* IT security has moved up the organizational agenda not only because of the increased security risks arising from increased offshoring but also because of the growing concern of hacking and potential terrorism. Along these lines, there is a need to retain internal capability around security. On this issue, a senior IT executive of a multinational company suggested, "Clearly we don't want to do security administration. Happy for that to be outsourced. But all the monitoring and compliance, all that sort of thing, we believe we need to keep a pretty tight control over."

Legal issues

The legal issues that arise in sourcing arrangements are numerous. Some of the most common ones are related to confidentiality, security, intellectual property, and compliance.

Confidentiality

Both the customer and the vendor will want to protect their confidential information during their sourcing partnership. For this reason, each party should examine what information it regards as confidential and what safeguards it should implement. These issues should be carefully considered by both parties and resolved before the agreement is signed. In practice, both clients and suppliers appear to underestimate these issues and can run into serious problems.

It is important to note that issues with regard to the confidentiality of data are more likely to arise on termination. Often in such situations, the client will attempt to ensure access to information required for continuation of uninterrupted service by either the retained organization or a subsequent supplier. Similarly, the supplier will attempt to protect its proprietary procedures and information, which can be seen as distinctive competences critical for its competitive position.

Security

The security requirements of the sourcing partners will vary significantly from one arrangement to another depending on the nature of the customer's business, the personal data being processed, and the services being sourced. For example, it may be compulsory to include a commitment to comply with specific security standards.

The following lists present examples of common security issues (based on Lewis, 2006):

Data security
- Securing access to data to validated and authorized employees
- Taking all reasonable steps to ensure that outsourcing employees cannot and do not copy data
- Ensuring appropriate levels of authorized access with audit trails of all access being provided
- Providing access rights standards
- Holding data in a manner compliant with all legislation and best practice guidance
- Having detailed written procedures for data handling
- Keeping data separate from other companies' data
- Ensuring that data are not corrupted by other companies' data.
- Ensuring that data are held in secure storage on appropriately licensed software
- Ensuring that data are held on appropriate hardware that is physically and technically secured

Staff security
- Appropriate security checking of all authorized personnel
- Using only validated contract staff to maintain physical or technical security and access
- Periodically checking that authorized personnel are following designated procedures
- Ensuring that new staff sign protocol and procedural documentation

Backups and disaster recovery
- Keeping all data appropriately backed up
- Having appropriate disaster recovery plans and recovery procedures in place
- Periodically testing all disaster recovery plans
- Documenting disaster recovery procedures and ensuring that valid recovery contracts are in place

Hardware

- Ensuring that all hardware is maintained in an appropriate secure location
- Ensuring that correct power, air-conditioning, and fire prevention are available with hardware.
- Providing a validated hardware list to the customer
- Allowing the customer to inspect and query the hardware used
- Conforming to any legislative or procedural requirements for physical equipment maintenance
- Ensuring that data are removed in a secure manner from redundant, broken, or otherwise damaged equipment
- Providing a log of the procedures for removing data from equipment
- Ensuring that equipment is swept before it leaves the supplier's premises

Security documentation

- Providing physical and technical access logs to the customer
- Providing procedures for ensuring that no physical or technical breach of security occurs
- Providing reports on any security breach together with remedial action taken
- Documenting all security procedures including reporting procedures for breach of security

Intellectual property

Intellectual property (IP) rights are also of major concern to client and supplier. These refer to the rights that have been given to people over the creations of their minds: literary, musical, or artistic works; inventions; symbols; names; images; and so forth. The key forms of IP are patents, copyrights, trademarks, and trade secrets. Intellectual property shares many of the characteristics of physical property, and thus is treated as an asset that can become the object of different forms of transactions (buying, selling, licensing, and so on).

IP protection and enforcement mechanisms differ by country. For this reason, offshoring arrangements can become particularly complicated in managing IP issues. In addition, courts in different parts of the world operate under different laws and regulations and often give conflicting judgments. In these judgments there is regularly evidence of bias that is associated with the country in which each company domiciles (courts tend to favor companies residing in their respective countries). Along these lines, companies (from both the customer's and the supplier's side) should be particularly careful because the absence of suitable contractual safeguards can put at risk the firm's rights to its own intellectual property.

Baldia (2007) has suggested that IP concerns are particularly important in the case of KPO and that IP ownership, IP violation, and issues related to confidentiality and privacy must be carefully addressed in every KPO venture. According to Baldia, in any KPO venture, a customer must:

1. Perform careful legal due diligence on national and local IP regulations
2. Examine the legal issues that arise in relation to the specific KPO arrangement
3. Take appropriate action (measures and safeguards) to protect the firm from losing its IP rights

Compliance

Both the customer and the supplier need to ensure that they operate in compliance with the wider legal framework. For example, with regard to data protection, the sourcing partners will need to ensure that they comply with their respective obligations under the Data Protection Act (DPA, 1998) and that they follow its principles (based on Lewis, 2006):

1. Personal data shall be processed fairly and lawfully
2. Personal data shall be obtained only for one or more specified and lawful purposes and shall not be further processed in any manner incompatible with that purpose or those purposes
3. Personal data shall be adequate, relevant, and not excessive in relation to the purpose or purposes for which they are processed
4. Personal data shall be accurate and, where necessary, kept up-to-date
5. Personal data processed for any purpose or purposes shall not be kept for longer than is necessary for that purpose or those purposes
6. Personal data shall be processed in accordance with the rights of data subjects under the DPA
7. Appropriate technical and organizational measures shall be taken against unauthorized or unlawful processing of personal data and against accidental loss or destruction of, or damage to, personal data
8. Personal data shall not be transferred to a country or territory outside the European Economic Area unless that country or territory ensures an adequate level of protection for the rights and freedoms of data subjects in relation to the processing of the personal data

Another example of a wider regulation with significant legal implications for sourcing arrangements (more specifically outsourcing arrangements in the financial sector) is the Markets in Financial Instruments Directive (MIFID), an EU directive that came into force in November 2007. The principal objective of MIFID has been to harmonize the operations of the financial sector throughout the European Community. MIFID was intended to replace the Investment Service Directive and, unlike its predecessor, has been explicit in addressing outsourcing governance within the financial industry. More specifically, MIFID outlined the obligations of each party in relation to the outsourcing relationship and identified detailed rules on the steps that firms need to take to comply with these rules.

On this basis, MIFID had significant governance implications for existing and future IT outsourcing relationships. Firms currently in IT outsourcing relationships need to address the MIFID regulatory requirements and take appropriate action for renewal, renegotiation, or change of existing contracts. Firms intending to enter into new IT outsourcing relationships need to focus on issues of governance.

The contract: relationships and performance

A key mechanism for dealing with legal issues that arise in the supplier–client relationship is the contract. In essence, the contract sets a framework for the sourcing relationship by defining objectives and responsibilities, as well as the processes and procedures to be followed by the partners. Although it plays a fundamental role in the management and governance of the sourcing relationship, it cannot encapsulate all the contingencies that may occur. For this reason, although the role of the contract is critical in the creation of legal boundaries between the partners, the management of the venture goes beyond the legal reach of the contract to rely on the actual relationship between the sourcing partners.

An illustrative landmark case of contract, relationship, and performance issues is provided by the BSkyB versus EDS judgment in January 2010. In February 2000, Sky announced its £50 million project to create a world-class customer relationship management system at its contact centers in Scotland. EDS was selected as the software supplier and systems integrator in July 2000. A contract was signed in November 2000 setting out EDS's obligations as systems integrator. Early delays and problems led to the parties' amending their original contract in July 2001 to give EDS more favorable terms. However, poor performance continued. Sky eventually removed EDS and assumed the role of systems integrator in March 2002.

The system was finally completed by Sky in March 2006 at an estimated cost of £265 million.

Sky sought compensation from EDS, ultimately leading to Sky's issuing court proceedings against EDS in August 2004 for multiple claims, including fraudulent and negligent misrepresentation and breach of contract. Sky alleged that as a result of EDS's wrongful conduct, it was fraudulently induced to award the contract to EDS. But for the misrepresentations by EDS, Sky argued, it would have contracted with one of the other bidders who would have successfully implemented the project earlier and at a lower cost overall.

The court held that EDS did not carry out a "proper exercise of planning, sequencing and resourcing" to determine whether it could comply with the time frame. The court also found EDS liable in the tort of deceit, because misrepresentation as to the time it would take to deliver the system had been made by the managing director of the relevant division of EDS, who knew it was false. For EDS, one of the consequences of being found liable for fraudulent misrepresentation was that the contractual cap of £30 million on its liabilities in relation to the project was no longer effective. As a result EDS was likely to have to pay damages in excess of £200 million. As an additional claim, Sky alleged that EDS made further misrepresentations prior to the parties' agreeing to amend the contract in mid-2001. Sky claimed that EDS falsely represented that it "had a program plan that was achievable and the product of proper analysis and re-planning." Sky argued that the plan was unrealistic and was not based on proper investigation and planning. The court accepted Sky's argument and held EDS liable for negligent misstatement. The court also found that, having amended the original contract, EDS "failed properly to resource the project," did not adhere to contractual deadlines, and ultimately made minimal progress.

For clients, the case is a highly useful reminder of the need to vet suppliers' claims carefully, assess risks comprehensively, and pursue contract breaches more vigorously. Cullen et al. (2005) would argue that the adoption of a thorough life cycle approach to outsourcing would mean that cases such as BSkyB versus EDS would rarely get to court owing to the application of effective management processes The case reminds suppliers of their duty of care in bid preparation and submission and suggests the importance of such practices as internal peer review and capability checks and motivating and incentivizing sales teams appropriately. In this case, the role of systems integrator also needed more careful delineation. A key point from the case is the need to take extra care when drafting limitation clauses in IT contracts and settlement agreements, both of which were found to be partially ineffective in this case.

Summary

This chapter has reviewed various aspects of the relationship between a vendor and its client. It is about making this partnership work, and it really does takes much more than just action. Although the selection process of a partner is critical, no less important is the development of the retained organization to ensure that the client focuses on what is critical in this outsourcing arrangement. Meanwhile, as in marriage, understanding the legal implications, in case things go wrong, remains an abiding necessity.

Relevant teaching cases

Jaiswal, V., and Levina, N. (2008). "JIT Full Circle Outsourcing." In A. L. Albertin and O. P. Sanchez (eds.), *IT Outsourcing: Impacts, Dilemmas, Debates and Real Cases.* São Paulo, Brazil: Editora FGV.

PART III

Managing Sourcing Relationships

CHAPTER 7

The IT outsourcing life cycle and the transition phase

Although the multibillion-dollar outsourcing industry is flourishing, a number of outsourcing arrangements have been underperforming, and some have even been terminated. Poor management and governance of the outsourcing relationship have been often cited as the primary reasons for less successful outsourcing contracts. Before we investigate the management and the governance of outsourcing relationships, which will be further discussed in Chapter 8, it is important to understand the key stages of the outsourcing process, as well as the key practices that can be applied at each stage.

This chapter discusses the IT outsourcing life cycle. In doing so, it provides a checklist of key activities that a client organization needs to fulfill to prepare and properly execute an outsourcing relationship. The chapter also elaborates on the key requirements for designing and executing the transition phase. We therefore focus on the following aspects:

- The key stages of the ITO life cycle
- The most effective practices available for clients to cope with challenges throughout the entire ITO life cycle
- The key requirements for executing the transition phase

Key stages of the IT outsourcing life cycle

One of the most comprehensive models of the outsourcing life cycle has been provided by Cullen, Seddon, and Willcocks (2005). The model, shown in Table 7.1, consists of four phases: architect, engage, operate, and regenerate. These phases are composed of nine building blocks. In the outsourcing life cycle, each phase and its constituent building blocks pave way for the next phase. Thus, the effectiveness of each building block depends on the preceding ones, with the last phase initiating the next-generation outsourcing strategy and life cycle.

Table 7.1 The outsourcing life cycle model

Outsourcing phase	Building block	Goal	Key outputs
Architect	1. Investigation	Veracity, not ideology	Gather insights Test expectations Collect market intelligence Peer assessment
	2. Target	Appropriate services identified	Outsourcing model or mode Target services identification Profiles
	3. Strategy	Informed, not speculative, strategies	Rollout Strategic "rules" Program Skills Communications strategy Business case rules and base case Feasibility and impact analysis
	4. Design	Well-designed future state	Blueprint Scorecard Draft service-level agreements Draft price model Draft contract Relationship Retained organization Contract management function
Engage	5. Selection	Best value for money	Competitive stages Evaluation team Selection strategy and criteria Bid package Bid facilitation Evaluation Due diligence
	6. Negotiation	Complete, efficient contract	Negotiation strategy Negotiation team Effective negotiations
Operate	7. Transition	Efficient mobilization	Final plans Transition team Managed staff Knowledge retention and transfer Transfers Governance structures setup Engineering Acceptance
	8. Management	Results	Relationship Reporting Meetings Administration and records Risk management Issues, variations, and disputes Continuous improvement Evaluations
Regenerate	9. Refresh	Refreshed strategy	Next-generation options Outcomes and lessons Options: business case and strategy

Source: Cullen, Seddon, and Willcocks (2005)

Architect phase

The architect phase comprises the first four building blocks – investigate, target, strategize, and design – and thus lays foundations for the outsourcing venture.

The primary goal of the first building block namely the *investigation* is to identify the goals. The key activities for the company are to gather insights from experts and experienced organizations, determine and test goals and expectations, collect information on market conditions and potential suppliers, and investigate similar decisions and peer organizations. For example, a state government agency might investigate the sourcing decisions and strategies of two similar state government agencies, a federal agency, and two companies from the private sector. The company might also try to gather market insights and understand the implications of different sourcing tactics for its operations. This approach would enable it to develop its thinking on its outsourcing strategy.

The second building block is *target*. Its primary purpose is for organizations to identify the areas in which outsourcing can be beneficial to their operations. The key activities for the company in this second building block are matching goals to an appropriate outsourcing model, identifying objective criteria suitable for service providers, and defining the scope of outsourcing. For example, during the initial discussions concerning which activities to outsource, all of the executives of an international airline company supported the argument that the part of the business that was within their control was absolutely core and thus should remain in-house. Later, when consultants came in, the company created a set of objective criteria relating to the long- and short-term benefits to be pursued through outsourcing, as well as relating to the barriers to outsourcing a specific activity. On the basis of these criteria, they identified the processes that were the best candidates for outsourcing.

The third building block is *strategy*. Its primary goal is to conduct the planning that will enable effective decision making during the rest of the life cycle. The key activities for the company are deciding on the rollout approach (e.g., big bang or phased), determining key rules guiding the outsourcing relationship, designing the detailed life cycle program, identifying and sourcing the life cycle skills, preparing the life cycle communications strategy, preparing the business case rules and the base case, and assessing the feasibility, risk, and impact of the outsourcing on the organization. A poorly prepared outsourcing strategy can result in a number of time-consuming and costly mistakes. As an example, the handover period for the outsourcing team of a telecommunications company was delayed by three months because the company did not have a clear plan concerning employee transfer to the vendor. As a result, neither the client organization nor its chosen supplier had the necessary staff to conduct normal service delivery during this period.

The fourth building block is *design*. Its primary goal is to wrap up the architect phase and define the planned configuration of the deal. The key activities for the company are preparing the commercial and operating blueprint; developing balanced score metrics; drafting the service agreement and the price and contract framework; and designing the interparty relationship (structure, roles, authorities, and so forth), the retained organization, and the governance function. The lack of an appropriate design of the outsourcing relationship may result in poor performance for both the vendor and the client. As an example, an international airline had created a handshake agreement with a call center supplier because the two organizations had effectively cooperated in the past. Their cooperation was considered a strategic partnership, and for this reason, both parties believed that they needed only a high-level memorandum of understanding (MOU) for this agreement. Years later, the airline company found that it was being overcharged and that the overbilling resulted from the fact that there were no detailed descriptions of service delivery and pricing.

Engage phase

During the engage phase, the client chooses one or more suppliers to carry out the work and negotiates the contract. The fifth and the sixth building blocks are central to the activities carried out during this phase.

The fifth building block is *selection*. Its primary purpose is to choose the most appropriate vendor. The key activities for the company are planning in detail the content of the outsourced work, identifying the most appropriate evaluation team, determining the most appropriate evaluating criteria, requesting information from bidders for each bid, applying interactive evaluation techniques, selecting the supplier based on value for money, and conducting the five due diligence processes on the final list of potential suppliers (company, price, solution, contract, and customer reference). Consider an example of a bank that generated an extensive call for expression of interest (EOI) in an open tender process but did not develop a clear approach to evaluate the bids it would receive. The company received 14 bids and realized that it would need a structured evaluation methodology to select its supplier. After developing its methodology of evaluation, the company discovered that its EOI had elicited only 30 percent of the information it needed to choose a supplier.

The sixth building block is *negotiation*. Its goal is to complete the contract. The key activities for the client are preparing for negotiations and conducting effective negotiations. Some good tactics followed during this stage include preparation of service-level agreements (SLAs), the pricing framework, and the contract before choosing a supplier; requisition to the bidders to give exact wording changes and specifications they wish to negotiate; and clarification and a detailed explanation of the issues to be negotiated. Results of our research indicate that companies that followed these tactics were able to complete the negotiations in a couple of weeks in contrast to companies that lacked a thorough plan of negotiations and took months to complete the negotiations.

Operate phase

During the operate phase, the outsourcing deal is executed. The seventh and the eighth building blocks are key to this phase.

The seventh building block is *transition*. Its goal is to effectively and smoothly go through the change process in which the client hands services over to the supplier. The key activities for the company are completing the project plans, including resourcing the transition process (the required number of employees, nature of expertise, type of equipment, and infrastructure, for example); managing the impact on staff (whose jobs will be affected and how); managing the staff transfers; managing knowledge retention and transfer; implementing the contract (service delivery on behalf of the supplier according to what has been agreed, knowledge input and payment on behalf of the client, and so on); engineering work flows; establishing communication channels; conducting acceptance and close-out (making sure that both parties are satisfied with the terms of the venture and that the agreement is operational); and performing a post-implementation review of issues that cropped up during the of transition.

Some of the tactics that have been proved to be beneficial for the transition of employees include offering financial and career advice to the affected staff, including staff in the development of the supplier evaluation criteria, and involving staff in the supplier selection process. As an example of the successful transition of IT staff, an insurance company worked very closely with its supplier on how most of its 70 IT staff would willingly transfer to the supplier. The contract verified that the employment conditions at the supplier's organization would be the same as in the insurance company. Furthermore, the transferred staff would be employed by the supplier organization for at least two years. The two parties also tried to agree on a plan that would win the hearts and minds of the transferred employees. The supplier would make presentations to familiarize the employees with its operations. The staff would receive branded material such as hats, mouse pads, and T-shirts and training sessions, as well as an opportunity for individual conversations with the insurance company chief information officers. Key issues during the phase of transition are discussed later in this chapter.

The eighth building block is *management.* Its primary goal is managing the outsourcing relationship. The key activities for the company are investing in the relationship, monitoring the relationship, using diligent documentation and administration, engaging in risk management exercises, addressing disputes, developing continuous improvement procedures, and evaluating the relationship between supplier and client.

Regenerate phase

Finally, in the regenerate phase, the options for the next-generation outsourcing contract and relationship are assessed. The ninth building block , namely *refresh,* provides a set of activities that assist the client in deciding whether to engage in additional contracts with this particular supplier. The key activities for the company are assessing contract outcomes and the lessons learnt and assessment future requirements.

As an example, a university tried to evaluate whether the benefits pursued through its five-year outsourcing deal had been achieved. Toward the end of this deal, the university chancellor conducted an assessment in order to decide on its future outsourcing plans. Several issues had arisen over the course of this period: there were no monitoring reports, and the people who had been involved in the original outsourcing negotiations were not longer at the university. In addition, the current stakeholders had different views on the objectives of the outsourcing venture than had those who were originally involved. Consequently, it was difficult to determine the intended benefits of the outsourcing initiative as well as the extent to which they had been achieved. The contract manager therefore identified the actual achievements and how they had been accomplished:

1. The extent to which the supplier had performed in a satisfactory way. This is because the supplier was given responsibility for a process or

a function (not just a task) and thus it was more efficient to measure business outcomes through key performance indicators.
2. Supplier motivation through rewards.
3. Reduction of incidents due to the allocation of responsibilities between the parties in a clear and explicit manner.

The next life cycle round

Following this final phase, the life cycle begins a new round. According to the decision of either retendering, renegotiating, or backsourcing the work, the outsourcing life cycle will be repeated. If the outsourcing configuration differs significantly from the previous engagement, all stages of the cycle may need to be repeated. If the work is retendered with only minor changes, the organization may begin with vendor selection. If the firm decides to backsource the work, beginning with the transition phase would be appropriate. And if the company is renegotiating the same scope of work but looking for an improved deal, it starts from the design stage and then moves to the negotiation stage.

An alternative model of the outsourcing life cycle (Figure 7.1) provided by the US General Accounting Office (2001) identifies seven main outsourcing phases as well as the major practices associated with each phase:

Phase 1: Determine the sourcing strategy: During this phase, client organizations determine whether it is more efficient to keep a function in-house or source it to an external vendor. Table 7.2 lists the key practices associated with this phase. As an example, General Motors (GM) initiated an outsourcing relationship with EDS and hired a corporate CIO to set the

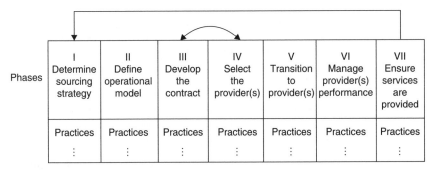

Figure 7.1 U.S. General Accounting Office outsourcing life cycle

Source: Based on General Accounting Office (2001)

Table 7.2 Phase 1 of the outsourcing life cycle: determine the sourcing strategy

Phase	Key practices
Determine the sourcing strategy	Examine how IT will support business processes when evaluating sourcing strategies.
	Use third-party assistance with experience in a variety of sourcing arrangements when formulating a sourcing strategy.
	Incorporate lessons learnt from peer organizations that have engaged in similar sourcing decisions.
	Estimate the impact of the sourcing decision on the internal organization as well as on enterprise alliances and relationships.
	Consider optimizing IT and business processes before deciding on a sourcing strategy.
	Benchmark and baseline the productivity of internal services prior to making the final sourcing decision.
	Consider starting with a representative service or selective set of services to outsource; balance against economies of scale.
	Identify the business reasons for outsourcing IT.
	Identify the reasons for outsourcing IT that can improve the organization's ability to use and manage technology.

Source: Based on General Accounting Office (2001)

vision and strategy of this the venture. The CIO maintained that IT should be integrated into corporate strategy. As a result of the tighter integration between corporate and strategic planning, GM was better able to adapt to changing market conditions.

Phase 2: Define the operational model: During this phase, the client firm formalizes the executive leadership, the composition of the teams, and the operating relationship with the vendor. The operational model enables the client to compare the performance of the relationship against the original objectives. Table 7.3 illustrates the key practices applied during this phase. For example, at DuPont the corporate CIO is at the head of the structure that manages outsourcing relationships and receives input from a collective leadership team composed of senior IT leaders across the company. The management structure also includes business unit CIOs and functional IT management groups that service each of the company's business units. This management structure aims to address issues regarding IT outsourcing while generating consensus between DuPont and its outsourcing providers.

Phase 3: Develop the contract: During this phase, the legal terms of the outsourcing relationship are being established. The contract, ideally intended to protect the interests of all parties and prevent opportunism, sets out the obligations and expectations of each party. Table 7.4 illustrates

Table 7.3 Phase 2 of the outsourcing life cycle: define the operational model

	Key Practices
Define the operational model	Establish executive leadership for IT to facilitate the outsourcing initiative.
	Make sure that the IT and business objectives are aligned.
	Manage provider performance, including auditing provider performance data.
	Define strategic objectives, and consider the creation of a position responsible for strategic sourcing decisions.
	Create and define the contract management structure with operational points of contact and managers.
	Have the provider establish an on-site support team to serve as liaison between client and provider.
	Educate the provider about the client business environment and goals.
	Select or develop standard tools for managing the relationship (e.g., performance scorecards, an enterprise resources management system).
	Use third-party assistance to take advantage of expertise from a variety of outsourcing arrangements in defining the operational model (i.e., defining roles and responsibilities).
	Understand the organizational structure of the provider, and identify who is empowered to make decisions.

Source: Based on General Accounting Office (2001)

Table 7.4 Phase 3 of the outsourcing life cycle: develop the contract

	Key Practices
Develop the contract	Base performance requirements on business outcomes.
	Include measures that reflect end user satisfaction as well as technical IT performance.
	Review and update performance requirements periodically.
	Require the provider to meet minimum performance in each category of service.
	Require the provider to achieve escalating performance standards at agreed-on intervals.
	Incorporate sufficient flexibility so that minimum acceptable performance can be adjusted as conditions change, the provider becomes more adept at satisfying customer demands, and improvement goals are achieved.
	Use SLAs to articulate all aspects of performance, including management, processes, and requirements.
	Specify circumstances under which the provider is excused from performance levels mandated by master service agreements.

Source: Based on General Accounting Office (2001)

the key practices in this phase. As an example, GM uses a master services agreement (MSA) to structure its outsourcing arrangements with each of its primary vendors. During negotiations, it uses a third-party consultancy and identifies some initial measures of performance that all three parties (GM, each of the vendors, and the consultant) have to agree on. The measures of performance are reviewed monthly and adjusted as needed. The contract is closely monitored and is periodically calibrated to elevate performance levels.

Phase 4: Select the provider: During this phase, the client firm finds one or more providers to help it reach its outsourcing objectives and chooses between them. Table 7.5 sets out the key practices in this phase. For example, J.P. Morgan chose to select a team of providers – three leading IT service providers – and asked them to identify partners for providing efficient service delivery. The rationale was that a single vendor could not provide the range of the services that it needed and that maintaining a network of partners could efficiently accommodate fluctuations in its demands for service.

Phase 5: Transition to the provider: During this phase the client organization transfers responsibility for the IT functions to one or more providers.

Table 7.5 Phase 4 of the outsourcing life cycle: select the provider

	Key Practices
Select the provider	Conduct research on the state of the market, vendors, and technology before defining vendor selection criteria.
	Identify and evaluate various sourcing solutions (e.g., single vendor, multivendor, alliance).
	Define a process for selecting vendors to be providers (e.g., issuing a request for proposals and prequalifying vendors).
	Define vendor selection and evaluation (acceptance) criteria at the outset (e.g., cultural fit, skill set, industry knowledge, proposed transition plan, past performance, and reputation).
	When issuing a request for proposals, identify services with expected performance levels, and define the client and provider roles and responsibilities.
	Use third-party assistance with expertise in a variety of outsourcing arrangements when selecting providers, including developing the request for proposals.
	Conduct due diligence activities to verify vendor capabilities before signing the contract (e.g., conduct past performance and reference checks as part of the evaluation).
	Make final vendor selections after contract negotiation.

Source: Based on General Accounting Office (2001)

This phase involves a number of contingencies, and for this reason, a transition plan can make the transfer of the IT function relatively smoother. Table 7.6 illustrates the key practices in this phase. As an example, J.P. Morgan decided to transfer 1,500 people (including existing contractors) to its new service providers. This process was planned jointly by all parties but was managed by J.P. Morgan. A management committee composed of J.P. Morgan senior executives and all provider companies was put in place to ensure that employees were transferred in a way that would result in minimal service disruption.

Phase 6: Manage the provider's performance: During this phase, the client organizations make sure that the vendor is meeting performance requirements. Table 7.7 identifies the key practices in this phase. As an example, GM closely monitors the performance of its vendors through frequent meetings. During these meetings, GM and its vendors discuss issues regarding quality and level of service as well as any problems that have surfaced. The aim of these meetings is to ensure that both companies have a common understanding of the required service. In addition, at a steering committee meeting every week, program managers discuss any problems and perform strategic planning. Frequent interactions with end users also deepen the relationship between end user needs and service delivery.

Table 7.6 Phase 5 of the outsourcing life cycle: transition to the provider

	Key Practices
Transition to the provider	Communicate a clear transition process to all key players from both the client and provider organizations.
	Handle resistance to change with meetings between upper management and employees..
	Establish the client transition team with representatives from across the organization to facilitate the transition.
	Create client–provider transition teams to address short-term transition tasks as required.
	Encourage transition of staff to provider, where appropriate, using bonuses, stock options, and other appropriate methods.
	Develop employee-retention programs, and offer bonuses to keep key people, where appropriate.
	Document key information to preserve organizational knowledge in the event that one or more providers change.
	Use change management strategies to help client employees deal with the transition.

Source: Based on General Accounting Office (2001)

Table 7.7 Phase 6 of the outsourcing life cycle: manage the provider's performance

	Key practices
Manage the provider's performance	Consider incentives to motivate the provider to exceed performance requirements.
	Use penalties to motivate the provider to meet performance requirements.
	Periodically undertake studies to assess how the provider's performance compares with the value being delivered to similar clients and the extent to which the provider's performance is improving over time (e.g., validate cost assumptions for multiyear contracts).
	Schedule periodic working-level meetings with both the end user groups and the provider to review the provider's performance.
	Conduct executive-level oversight meetings with the provider's senior management to review the provider's performance.
	Distribute performance data to stakeholders.
	Reserve audit rights on provider-supplied performance data.
	Ensure that the provider measures and reports on performance.
	Work with the provider to redefine service levels as appropriate.
	Sample performance data frequently enough to perform trend analysis and permit extrapolation based on historical data.
	Allow employees, and possibly stakeholders, to rate provider on a regular basis using, for example, scorecards and quarterly report cards.

Source: Based on General Accounting Office (2001)

Table 7.8 Phase 7 of the outsourcing life cycle: ensure the services are provided

	Key Practices
Ensure the services are provided	Monitor the provider's work to anticipate issues for resolution.
	Conduct periodic meetings to resolve issues jointly with the provider.
	Document and maintain organizational knowledge.
	Make sure the provider uses the standard tools and processes defined as part of the operational model.
	Use provider performance data to continuously improve processes.
	Pursue improvement based on customer satisfaction surveys.
	Have the provider ensure that adequate and appropriate resources are available to perform the services.
	Ensure that an appropriately empowered individual from the client organization oversees the work.
	Set realistic time frames that the provider agrees to.

Source: Based on General Accounting Office (2001)

Phase 7: Ensure the services are provided: During this final stage, the client firms make sure that services are provided as agreed and that end user needs are met. Table 7.8 identifies the key practices in this phase. It is important to note that there can be an overlap between this phase of the outsourcing relationship and the previous one (managing the relationship); both phases in essence are related to making sure that the venture is being implemented in a way that will generate efficient service delivery. A good illustration of the types of issues that companies deal with during this phase is the case of a major telecommunications company. The company aimed to ensure that it paid competitive rates and therefore closely monitored the fees that it paid its vendors for a certain service particularly keeping in mind the marketplace rates for that service. This process led to a continual reassessment and renewal of the fees, which allowed the company to save money in line with the industry-wide price reductions.

A comparison of the life cycle models

The two life cycle models presented follow a similar pattern regarding the stages of the venture while identifying best practices to address key outsourcing challenges: which activities should be outsourced and how, how vendor selection should take place, how the outsourcing relationship should be managed, and so on. However, the model that Cullen et al. (2005) developed appears to pay more attention to the final stage of evaluation and refreshment of the venture. In other words, it appears to be focusing on the options that the client firm can pursue (backsourcing, renegotiating, or retendering) and provides illustrations of the different routes that organizations may follow according to this decision. For this reason, we believe that the Cullen et al. model might be better suited for relatively short-term ventures, where issues concerning the regeneration of the venture are more frequent and relatively more prominent.

Managing the transition stage: key issues and best practices

The transition stage in outsourcing is a time of intense change during which the client and supplier are setting up the governance structure of the relationship and the client is gradually handing over the service to the supplier. Clearly this is one of the crucial stages in the relationship and therefore needs close examination.

The transition process often officially begins when the contract goes into effect and ends on a specified date or at the signing of a transition acceptance form (confirming that all aspects of the arrangement are fully operational). Regardless of the official start and end dates, the transition actually begins much earlier and ends much later, and if it is not managed properly, it may not end at all. We have witnessed all too many deals where "transition" becomes a permanent state.

Cullen and Willcocks (2003) identify these key objectives of the transition:

- Both parties are in a position to fulfill their obligations and complete specific transition actions as laid out in the contract and the SLA.
- A smooth transfer of the staff to the supplier (if applicable) and their integration into the supplier's organization, systems, and culture.
- A smooth transfer of the assets and obligations to the supplier (if applicable), including licenses and warranties.
- A smooth transfer of the third-party contracts to the supplier (if applicable), including maintenance and service subcontracts.
- Continuity of services during the transition.
- All service levels defined in the SLA will be measured and reported as required.
- Integration of essential business processes between the supplier's and the organization's systems.

Prior to embarking on the transition, the following should already be in place:

- *Transition plan:* The customer's needs were outlined in the market package, and the supplier prepared a detailed response in the bid.
- *Disruption-minimization strategy:* The customer's needs were outlined in the market package, and the supplier prepared a detailed response in the bid.
- *Communication strategy:* The strategy was developed in the very early days of the IT outsourcing life cycle.
- *Staffing arrangements:* Transfer conditions, redundancy, and redeployment processes are in place.
- *Management function:* The retained organization and contract management function has been designed.
- *Mobilized resources:* Training has been conducted and responsibilities have been reallocated to get the transition teams and operational teams prepared.

The old ways of working will no longer be appropriate under an outsourcing arrangement. A piece of the organization has effectively been removed. New work flows, communications, paper flows, and sign-offs are required within the organization to ensure united and efficient interaction with the supplier. New relationships will need to be quickly formed, and people accustomed to a certain way of operating will now need to operate in a completely different manner. Accordingly, a number of tasks need to be performed to set up the ongoing operations, including these major ones:

- *Transfer of assets, people, contracts, information, and projects that the supplier will be responsible for in the future:* In many cases, these transfers require dedicated teams made up of individuals from both parties because these areas of the former business were not designed to be easily transported to another organization.
- *Staff transition:* It is a common misconception that in ITO arrangements, the majority of the organization's IT staff is transferred to the supplier. Although this may be true for the very large deals that receive a great deal of media attention and can involve the transfer of hundreds, if not thousands, of employees, this is not the usual case.
- *Understanding the emotional impact on staff:* Regardless of the transition option the organization adopts, all IT personnel will be affected by the ITO arrangement: those who stay, those who transfer, and those who are laid off. Many organizations fail to realize that outsourcing can be a tumultuous change and always has an emotional impact on employees. This "people side" may be difficult to hear or see at first, but it can progress into the loudest problem that the outsourcing project may face if it is not managed well. Sometimes employees (occasionally in conjunction with their union) not only refuse to work but deliberately sabotage the outsourcing process. It is not surprising, then, that some of the larger suppliers have invested quite a lot of time and effort in getting their transition policies and practices well honed. In organizational change management terms, staff who will be affected are known as *change targets*. Organizations need to know the different behaviors that change targets may demonstrate so it can effectively manage any negative behaviors such as anger and depression that can be quite destructive. The model in Figure 7.2 shows the behavioral stages that employees are likely to pass through before they accept the reality of any major change. Most people pass through each of these emotions, though not necessarily in this order, and they may pass through some emotions more than once. To help staff come to terms with the impact – career impact or even

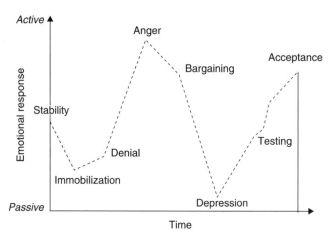

Figure 7.2 The emotional response to organizational change

self-esteem impact – organizations have offered career counseling, out-placement, financial planning, and personal counseling.

Managing the transition project

The steps outlined in this section document an approach for a large-scale transition. For smaller or less complex transitions, not all steps may not be needed. For example, a small transition may not need a full team to be responsible for the project, but there will be a need to ensure that someone is accountable.

Cullen and Willcocks (2003) suggest four major areas to focus on in transition projects.

Resourcing strategy

The types of roles an organization should consider for a transition project are shown in Table 7.9. These roles may not be carried out by just one person. Depending on the size of transition, it may be that one person has more than one role or that more than one person undertakes the same role. The formation of the transition team does not necessarily require the creation of a new team. If appropriate, it could be an existing team whose scope covers the transition. Depending on the initiative, it may be appropriate to break down the teams by division or process. Transition role descriptions are rarely sufficient for understanding and preparing

Table 7.9 Transition roles

Role	Description
Steering committee or a joint reference panel	Guide the project and provide strategic input to the implementation process.
	Facilitate timely decision making and resolve issues that the transition team has identified.
	Monitor the quality of key deliverables.
	Provide a forum for communicating progress and achievement of project milestones.
Transition program leader	Manage all the transition activities across all the divisions to ensure consistency.
	Report to the steering committee.
Transition project team leaders	Manage the transition for a specific service, geography, or customer group.
Human resource (HR) representatives	Provide HR-specific advice.
	Coordinate the HR initiatives and services to staff.
	Assist in setting up the retained organization.
Business representatives	Provide specific advice for business units.
	Coordinate business unit transition activities.
	Liaise with business unit line management.
	Test and accept business unit data migration and proper operational functioning.
Technical representatives	Provide technical advice.
	Coordinate technical transition activities.
	Liaise with the supplier's technicians.
	Test and accept technical migration, configuration, and proper operational functioning.
Communications representatives	Provide communication about the advice of the change leadership
	Develop communications messages and media.
	Liaise with the supplier's communications representative.
	Manage the feedback loop.
Administration resource	Coordinate logistical support.
	Create and manage control files.

thoroughly for the transition, particularly because at least two parties will be working together. For this reason, Cullen and Willcocks (2003) recommend developing a responsibility matrix for transition deliverables that are tracked until completion. The size and extent of the change will largely determine how long a transition will take. When determining the time frame, the organization will need to take into account its own unique factors: for example, the amount of consultation required, the speed of decision making, and the availability and competence of line management. However, most transition projects can be accomplished with one or two months designing the transition and then about three to six months to carry out and close out the project.

Risk assessment

By their very nature, transitions are fraught with a variety of risks – for example:

- *Project risks*: Resources skills and availability, lack of commitment from management, disparate levels of concern and priority between the parties, insufficient time and resources allocated, other organizational initiatives that may have a timing impact or require resources that are taken away from the transition project, conflict in coordinating between parties
- *Communication risks:* Mixed or conflicting messages put out by the parties, rumors that drive perceptions, adverse media
- *Employee risks:* Employee-union action, low morale, loss of motivation, loss of key personnel, disgruntled personnel
- *Operations risks:* Disruptions to normal operations and service continuity, data or systems conversion failure, missing documentation
- *Assets risks:* Wrong assets moved, assets go missing, assets not in the condition specified in the market package, missing documentation including third-party contracts and licensing agreements
- *Retained organization risks*: Impact of organizational change that was not adequately identified and addressed, required skills unavailable in the organization or in the recruitment market

Accordingly, it is important that the areas of potential hazard are identified, the consequences estimated, and strategies developed to mitigate risk. (Willcocks and Lacity, 2001, devote a chapter of their book to this subject, together with case studies.)

Communications

It is important for the transition team to communicate in an accurate and timely manner. Transition is a time of considerable anxiety for staff, and communication is one of the most important ways to of minimize uncertainty and anxiety. The transition team needs to identify their key stakeholders and develop a plan to keep them informed. The objective is to provide consistent messages across the organization, so this includes keeping line management informed as well. The amount of effort that will be required should not be underestimated. Staff under stress need to hear the message several times and through different media (e.g., group, face to face, written). Another key part of the communications strategy is to set the expectations of the customers or users of the service. It is important for the organization to work with the supplier on the communications rollout such that the supplier has the full opportunity to "sell" themselves and the arrangement to the users and understand any expectation gaps.

Close-out and acceptance

It is quite common to have some form of acceptance criteria that allows an evaluation and approval process to ensure that the transition has been successfully completed; it may even be in the form of a formal acceptance certificate. This is particularly important where there is a separate transition fee payable to the supplier.

Even without this formality around the completion of the transition, most organizations find it useful to conduct a post-implementation review, if only to comply with best practice project management principles. A more important reason is that the organization will undoubtedly go through similar events in the future. Even after over a decade of publications on the learning organization, learning from the experience and communicating that learning is an all-too-frequent, and costly, omission in outsourcing.

Messaging during transition

Given the importance of communications strategy and messaging during transition, it is worth looking at these areas in more detail. NeoIT (2005) suggested the following steps for dealing with communication challenges during the transition phase of global sourcing initiatives:

1. *Select the right communication vehicles:* Examples include company newsletters, individual meetings, company-wide meetings, and the press and other media.
2. *Develop key internal messages*: Often it is relatively difficult to communicate precise information with regard to the venture and its outcomes.

However, even the communication of alternative scenarios, possible ranges, estimates, and probabilities can be useful. Communication should be iterative and evolving, beginning with relatively uncertain information and progressing toward more solid content. Organizations that have been successful at communicating their global sourcing initiative have employed some of the following practices:

a. *Resist communication that says nothing:* Communicating without saying anything concrete creates rumors and uncertainty. Empty communication decreases levels of trust and confidence in the leading team and creates resistance to implementation efforts. The content of communication efforts should aim to address the concerns of all stakeholders, internal and external, and keep them well informed.

b. *It is better not to persuade:* The more a company tries to persuade people at the lower levels of the hierarchy with regard to the credibility and reliability of its decisions, the more untrustworthy it seems. Opinion leaders can play a mediating role between the business leaders of an organization and these employees. The challenge for the organization is to ensure that opinion leaders have some recommendations to make, that they can communicate alternative scenarios and outcomes, and that they can advise their colleagues on how to deal with the subsequent changes. For example, in an insurance company, the CIO played the role of opinion leader and advised staff members who would be transferred to the vendor's site on their professional and financial concerns.

c. *Painting a positive story does not always help:* If a positive story raises employee expectations that are not met, employee morale falls, and the implementation faces serious challenges. As an example, an organization may communicate to its staff that some of them will be transferred to the vendor's site with very favorable employment conditions. If this does not happen, employees will lose their trust, will resist implementation efforts, and, most important, will develop feelings of anxiety and uncertainty that will inhibit their productivity.

3. *Engage in frequent communication:* Successful organizations typically communicate on employees' issues related to the initiative after the completion of each critical phase in the process. The frequency of communication should be based upon the level of uncertainty associated with the global sourcing venture.

4. *Identify the senders and receivers:* Organizations need to ensure effective message delivery. For this reason, they should clearly identify the

senders and receivers of messages. Senders of internal communications may include the CEO, human resource managers, line managers, and business unit heads. Senders of external communications may include the CEO, the corporate communications department, or the public relations department. With regard to receivers, internal receivers are mainly the company's employees at different levels of the organization, and external receivers are customers, vendors, financial analysts, the media, and the overall community. Mapping each set of senders to the appropriate receivers along with the right message is critical for successful communication of information.

5. *Develop an effective external communications plan:* In the minds of many people, offshoring is associated with taking work out of a country. Along these lines, people tend to believe that companies engaged in offshoring initiatives are trying to achieve financial benefits at the expense of their national workforce. Therefore, major global sourcing initiatives are highly likely to be faced with negative publicity. To mitigate this image-tarnishing effect, organizations need to develop a communication strategy that will send the sort of message that maintains a positive image of the company. E-Loan was very effective in managing its external communications strategy regarding its offshore venture in India. The chief privacy officer of the company explained the rationale behind their offshore initiative: "Essentially, as we close our business day in the US, India begins theirs. This 24-hour processing capability enables us to fund loans one to two days faster – in ten days versus eleven to twelve days – than if they were processed entirely in the US." He noted further that customers were given the opportunity to decide whether they wanted the entire transaction to be processed domestically or overseas. The effort of the company to communicate its philosophy with regard to its offshore venture was particularly effective in convincing its customers about its intentions. The chief privacy officer explained, "Currently 87 percent of our customers are selecting the overseas option. ... While we believed that disclosing the program, providing a choice, and explaining a time benefit would be appreciated by consumers, we didn't think the numbers would be as high as they have been from the start. However, the results of our program support the idea that when you make the effort to explain the 'what', 'where,' and 'why' to consumers, they are comfortable with it." An effective communication strategy can help a firm avoid negative publicity and criticism, while maintaining its positive corporate image.

Risk management issues

While the issues of knowledge transfer and communications are among the most prevalent ones during the phase of transition in sourcing ventures, IGate (2004) suggests a more wide-ranging set of risk management strategies:

1. *Put key contract terms into practice:* While outsourcing, clients and suppliers spend much time in the design of the contract, and it appears that in most cases after the contract is signed, clients and suppliers revert to contract and to some of the risk-mitigating practices only when something has gone terribly wrong. As a result, risk-mitigating practices that are in the contract are never put into practice or have been used only when it is already too late.

2. *Use scenario-based predictive modeling to identify and mitigate risk:* In most outsourcing relationships, the partners do not undertake a vigilant identification of risks related to the project. This is not only because identifying risks can be a costly and time-consuming process, but also because it is almost impossible to predict all contingencies related to the relationship. For this reason, the client and supplier must agree on a systematic approach to mitigate risks that are critical to the success of the relationship.

3. *Use monitoring and testing to detect unaddressed risks early:* Since addressing all risks and contingencies during the outsourcing relationship is almost impossible, it is important to monitor the health of the relationship on an ongoing basis. Keeping close track of key performance metrics can help detect risks early by picking up deviations beyond acceptable ranges and analyzing their source.

4. *Make the plan fit the transition for people, not vice versa:* Though many of the risks that are identified during scenario planning can be mitigated, risks relating to people are harder to mitigate. Such risks tend to be more unpredictable and may crop up for various reasons. For example, the time lines in the transition plans should take into account not only the time needed for the technical aspect of the transition, but also the special issues associated with making the transition of the people as smooth as possible. Knowing how people have responded in similar situations and what motivates people to accomplish a task on time may assist in mitigating people-related risks during transition.

5. *Build flexibility into the system to address common risks:* Establishing change management processes that come into effect only when things go wrong is not enough. The entire transition process should be designed

to absorb some of the problems. Without this absorption capacity or flexibility built into the process, even a small contingency can have a dramatic influence on the entire transition plan. Consequently transition plans must be flexible enough and designed to accommodate changes to a certain extent.

6. *Have a broad plan to address potential contingencies:* If the previous practices are put in place, the outsourcing relationship will be flexible enough to absorb a certain number of changes. However, some changes may have more dramatic results, and for this reason a contingency plan (even a broad one) should be put in place. Examples of such contingencies could be natural or man-made disasters and dramatic shifts in the markets.

Summary

The outsourcing life cycle framework provides a step-by-step guide to integrating the strategic and the operational levels of outsourcing objectives and results. The transition phase, the starting point of most outsourcing relationships, requires special attention. Failing to properly design and execute this phase will likely result in additional challenges for client and vendor as the relationship matures. In this regard, this chapter provides the most effective practices for transition and the entire outsourcing life cycle.

CHAPTER 8

Governance of outsourcing projects

Although the outsourcing industry has demonstrated impressive growth during the past few years, some outsourcing relationships have yielded poor results, and some have even been terminated early. Both the professional press and academic publications have identified poor governance as the primary factor leading to these results. In this chapter, we therefore focus on understanding governance issues related to outsourcing projects and the practices that could support formal structures. In particular, we review the following issues:

- The governing structures for outsourcing ventures
- The roles involved in governing outsourcing projects
- The most effective governance practices for outsourcing projects

Governance of outsourcing projects

Governance refers to the processes and structures that ensure the alignment of strategies and objectives of the parties involved. In most cases, these processes and structures will facilitate the alignment of the client's objectives and strategies with the vendor's delivery system. However, governing structures and processes may also include aligning the goals and strategies of the client, intermediaries, and providers in multisourcing settings. Clearly, as outsourcing projects become complex, with multiple vendors, multiple sourcing arrangements, and multiple geographical locations, the governing structures also need to be designed so that they offer a wide range of opportunities to govern the relationships under various contexts and settings.

The set of tasks involved in governance structures is managerial in nature. Most books and consultants identify the following elements as critical for a healthy governing structure: the outsourcing organizational structure, the communication channels, the control and monitoring frameworks, and the performance metrics. Both vendor and client should agree on the mechanisms put in place as governing structures. More important, both parties should also devise problem-solving mechanisms in case of breakdowns in these governing structures and processes.

The literature highlights some aspects of governing structures that require special attention regardless of the settings or geographical location of the outsourcing project. First, communication channels between the client and the vendor should be smooth and effective at all times. Second, trust and building rapport between the vendor and the client are essential for achieving healthy and effective collaborations. And an effective and reliable reporting system should be maintained throughout the life cycle of the outsourcing project.

Governing the outsourcing project can be an expensive activity. For this reason, clients consider the size of the project as one assessment criterion in their decision regarding the scope and complexity of the governing structure. Evidence suggests that outsourcing projects with a budget of $50,000 or less are rarely supported with a governing structure. Nevertheless, most outsourcing projects have some elements of the governing structures – for example, an account manager – to ensure coordination of activities and monitoring of results from the client's side.

A key element in governing the outsourcing project is the service-level agreement (SLA), a legal document that details the services contracted to a vendor. It also defines aspects regarding the delivery of these services, such as at what quality the services will be delivered and through what channels, using what methods. The SLA also provides a detailed account of the conditions under which service can be disrupted. Effective SLAs accommodate changes in the method and mode of delivery subject to changes in market conditions or the client's strategic intent. However, such changes may put heavy burden on the vendor when attempting to meet client's needs. Therefore, we advise vendors and clients to build some flexibility into SLAs, along with assessing the impact on the vendor should client needs change.

SLAs are monitored on a dashboard – not as a simplistic indication of whether the vendor has met the basic requirements but as a representation of achieving the business goals behind each SLA. For this reason, the dashboard is a balanced scorecard regarding business-oriented objectives. A simple example is an SLA of a hosting service in which the vendor is required to provide support at all times. This SLA will provide a detailed account of the specific elements relating to this service, the expected service quality, and the downtime allowed for each region. The dashboard will provide a general indication of whether these conditions have been met. A green light on the dashboard means that the hosting service is provided without interruption. A red light signifies that one or more of the conditions has not been met, and therefore the service has been interrupted. In this situation, the client and the vendor must resolve this problem.

Roles involved in governing outsourcing projects

Setting up roles for the governing structures is often the responsibility of the vendor, and most large vendors have developed robust methodologies to govern complex outsourcing projects. The main governing body is the global office, which often consists of numerous units that deal with project management (also known as the project management office), quality assurance (quality assurance office), and infrastructure (the infrastructure office). The global office also consists of the business unit officers who are responsible for each relationship based on their functional or geographical area. For example, TCS set up a global office for its contract with ABN AMRO Bank that accommodated business unit officers for the Netherlands business unit (a geographical area) as well as for the private client unit (a functional area). The client should set up a project management office at the global level to coordinate activities and liaise with the vendor's global office. In global outsourcing projects, these roles are replicated at each geographical location. It is also common for the vendor to establish local offices near the client's site.

Figure 8.1 illustrates a governing structure typical of what most large vendors propose to clients for offshore outsourcing projects. This structure

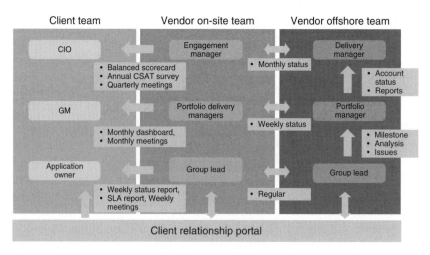

Figure 8.1 Governing structure for a large vendor

shows parallel roles between client personnel, on-site vendor personnel, and offshore vendor personnel. It also emphasizes the need to have corresponding roles at various levels. For the application maintenance and development, there is a need for corresponding roles that can liaise and coordinate work regardless of their physical location. At the portfolio level, there is a need for middle managers to align business objectives regarding ongoing maintenance and possible future development. A general manager from the client side is usually responsible for managing and coordinating such efforts. At the strategic level, both clients and vendors should assign senior managers to strategic roles. The client chief information officer should ensure that the client's objectives are met by the vendor and that the client is providing the support needed to meet these objectives by the vendor. The vendor on-site engagement manager (OEM) and the offshore delivery manager should assume equivalent responsibility on behalf of the vendor to meet client's expectations.

Most effective governance practices for offshore outsourcing projects

Companies can devise governing plans and set up governing structures designed to provide ideal conditions for successful offshore outsourcing projects. However, this does not guarantee the success of such projects. Therefore, sensing what might not work and applying effective practices that are suitable for these particular settings could improve the impact that the governing structures we have described would have on offshore outsourcing projects. According to their empirical work, Rottman and Lacity (2006) identified the most effective governing practices for offshore outsourcing projects:

1. *Develop the infrastructure*: Clients tend to underestimate the difficulty of integrating supplier employees based offshore into the work processes of their companies. Although various sorts of security concerns, human resource issues, and management matters must be addressed before the launch of a project, a special focus should be directed toward infrastructural issues. With regard to these issues, the project manager of one client company noted, "It really took us a long time to figure out how to make it [the onboarding process] run smoothly. ... Since the suppliers needed access to systems from various business units and IT sectors, we had to cross organizational boundaries and create new protocols and rights profiles. However, without these processes, the suppliers sit idle waiting for us to build a tunnel in the VPN [virtual private network]. We should have had

all these processes in place much earlier than we did" (Rottman and Lacity, 2006: 8). Consequently, it is important for the client company to facilitate the integration of offshore supplier employees by anticipating and managing infrastructural challenges before the initiation of the cooperation.

2. *Elevate your own organization's capability maturity model certification to close the process gap between you and your supplier*: Capability maturity model (CMM) certification aims to foster the use of processes that standardize, predict, and improve IT software development. More specifically, it defines five levels of software development maturity (level 1 is the lowest) and identifies the sets of processes that need to be in place to achieve each level. A number of clients suggest that the best way to extract value from the supplier's CMM processes is for the client to become CMM certified. The director of application development of a transportation company noted, "A real problem we had was our CMM level 1.5 guys talking to the vendor's level 5 guys. So together, we have worked out a plan with our vendor to help bring our CMM levels up. When we do, it will be a benefit to both of us; our specifications will be better and so the vendor can use them more efficiently" (Rottman and Lacity, 2006: 18). Along these lines, bringing the client's CMM levels up contributes to the process of communication between the two parties, improves requirements specification, and facilitates efficiency in software development.

3. *Bring in a CMM expert with no domain expertise to flush out ambiguities in requirements*: In many instances, drawing up the specification of the client's requirements is a long and costly process. A major issue is that clients and suppliers may interpret the requirements differently. To reduce the iterations during the requirements specification stage, an Indian supplier pursued a unique solution. The vendor brought in a CMM level 5 expert to the client's site. Intentionally, the chosen expert had no expertise in the client's business. This forced him to get into the process of clarifying ambiguities in the client's requirements thus reducing the number of iterations for specification issues.

4. *Negotiate a flexible CMM*: Clients want to use only those CMM processes that will add value to their operations. As the project manager of one financial firm noted: "You ask for one button to be moved and the supplier has to first do a 20-page impact analysis – we are paying for all this documentation we do not need" (Rottman and Lacity, 2006: 17). Suppliers recognize that their clients are not satisfied with the idea of following CMM patterns to their very last detail so that the supplier maintains the reliability of its CMM processes. The managing director of an Indian supplier noted, "My clients are telling me: you do what you have to do to pass your audits, but

I can't afford all of this documentation. So we have developed a 'flexible CMM' model that maintains the processes necessary for high quality but keeps the customer-facing documentation and overheads to a minimum. Our customers have reacted favorably and our internal processes are still CMM 5" (Rottman and Lacity, 2006). Consequently, sourcing partners have to find a balance between the client's desire for flexibility and minimum hassle and the supplier's need to maintain the integrity of its operations

5. *Use an on-site engagement manager*: Studies suggest that on-site engagement managers contribute to the success of offshoring relationships. People in this role are familiar with the offshore supplier's culture, working style, and internal processes and thus are able to smooth the transition phase and contribute to the quality of the service provided. However, it is important for on-site engagement managers to be included in the staffing and cost structure model. For example, Biotech, a major biotechnology firm that was working with an Indian vendor, realized that it had to staff the project differently. A technical leader noted: "If this project were to be staffed by domestic contractors, we would have added two just new contractors. However, since we were new to offshoring, we priced in an OEM to interface between the business sponsors and the two offshore developers. We realized that all project cost savings were lost, but the OEM helped us improve our processes, interviewed and managed the developers, and was responsible for status updates" (Rottman and Lacity, 2006). Although OEMs carry a significant cost, they can benefit the venture in many ways and lead to cost savings in the long run.

6. *Give offshore suppliers domain-specific training to protect quality and lower development costs*: Although domain-specific training may dramatically increase transaction costs, clients need to understand that these costs protect quality and lower development costs in the long run. The reason is that the supplier becomes more knowledgeable about the client's business and processes and consequently more productive. The client has to make sure that trained employees remain on the account for a certain period of time, or the supplier should reimburse training costs.

7. *Develop governance metrics*: The need for governance tools and measures that consider costs, quality, time, risk, and rewards has been widely recognized by clients as a fundamental way to ensure outsourcing value. The metrics used as governance tools as well as their specifications should be determined by the strategy and vision of the organization. Examples of metrics are "percentage of supplier business," which measures how much of the supplier's revenues come from the client organization; the "comparative efficiency metric," which assesses the relative productivity of in-house

staff relative to offshore employees; and the "bottom-line metric," which assesses the impact of the outsourcing relationship on the client's business. A particular metric may have different meanings for different organizations depending on their business strategy and philosophy. For example, for some clients, the expectation is that the metric "percentage of supplier business" will be high, providing a strong motivation for the supplier to deliver better service, while other organizations may want this metric to be low because they do not want their suppliers to be overly dependent on their business for revenue generation.

Another view on how to strengthen the foundation provided by the governing structures described suggests that clients and vendors should focus on developing their relationship (Liker and Choi, 2004). Among the most effective practices to improve governance of outsourcing (and other) project are as follows:

Conduct joint improvement activities
- Exchange best practices with suppliers.
- Initiate continuous improvement projects at the suppliers' facilities.
- Set up supplier study groups.

Share information intensively but selectively
- Set times, places, and agendas for meetings.
- Use rigid formats for sharing information.
- Insist on accurate data collection.
- Share information in a structured fashion.

Develop suppliers' technical capabilities
- Build suppliers' problem-solving skills.
- Develop a common lexicon.
- Hone core suppliers' innovation capabilities.

Supervise your suppliers
- Send monthly report cards to core suppliers.
- Provide immediate and constant feedback.
- Involve senior managers in solving problems.

Turn supplier rivalry into opportunity
- Source each component from two or three vendors.
- Create compatible production philosophies and systems.
- Set up joint ventures with existing suppliers to transfer knowledge and maintain control.

Understand how your suppliers work

- Learn about your suppliers' businesses.
- Go to your suppliers' locations to see how they work.
- Respect your suppliers' capabilities.
- Commit to prosperity for both of you.

Ross and Beath (2005) support this view and argue that in developing relationships as part of the governing processes, clients and vendors should work out the difference between their expectations and the actual offering. They call finding a middle way between a client's expectations and the vendor's offering "the sweet spot." Table 8.1 summarizes the sources of the differences between clients and vendors and offers some sweet spots for both parties to build and renew their relationship.

Mani et al. (2006) have argued that insufficient attention to governance is the main reason that some BPO projects fail to deliver value. They identify three key dimensions that shape the nature of governance structures required for BPO:

1. The interdependence of a process with other processes, which refers to the extent that a business process works independently or affects or is affected by other processes.

Table 8.1 Client expectations, vendor offerings, and the sweet spot

	Client expectations	Sweet spot	Vendor offerings
Transaction relationship	Best practice Variable capacity Management focus on core competencies	Low-maintenance relationship Reasonable margins Innovation to ensure process improvements	Standard best practice process components Economics of scale Distinctive assets
Cosourcing alliance	Cost savings Access to expertise on demand	Variable project staffing Leverage offshore Disciplined project management	Labor arbitrage Project management expertise Expertise on specialized technologies
Strategic partnerships	Cost savings Variable capacity Management focus on core competencies	Second-choice provider moving up value chain	Capability to deliver a broad range of specialized series Integration expertise Disciplined practices Economies of scale

Source: Based on Ross and Beath (2005)

2. Process complexity, which refers to how difficult it is to understand the specifics of a process and to measure its output.
3. The strategic importance of a process to an enterprise, which refers to the extent that a process has an impact upon its competitiveness.

Mani et al. (2006) explained that these three key dimensions of the outsourced process should determine the type of an outsourcing contract, the management of the relationship, and the technical capabilities, which they refer to as key BPO governance capabilities. Table 8.2 summarizes guidelines for determining the necessary BPO governance capabilities.

Table 8.2 Guidelines for determining BPO governance capabilities

Governance capabilities	Governance guideline
Outsourcing contract	The BPO contract should take into account uncertainties regarding the outsourced process. If uncertainties regarding the process are high, it can be difficult to build comprehensive contingencies into the contract. Therefore, as uncertainty increases, the client must shift emphasis from controlling uncertainty through performance contracts to managing it through relational contracts.
	Independent processes whose requirements can easily be described can easily be disaggregated from other client processes. They should be owned and managed by the providers with the relevant process expertise. However, if the outsourced process shares interdependencies with other client processes, the requirements are more difficult to define. Furthermore, there are fewer opportunities for the provider to benefit from economies of scale. Thus, the outsourced process needs to be jointly owned.
Relationship management	Effective relationship management helps bridge cultural gaps between companies and fosters a collaborative working approach in BPO. The more strategic the outsourced process is, the greater is the need for more collaboration and the more comprehensive the approach to relationship management needs to be.
	The BPO relationship must strike a balance between coordination and control. The higher the process complexity and strategic importance, the more the emphasis needs to be on coordination and less on control.
Technical capabilities	Technical capabilities are measured by the scope and intensity of the use of IT and the sophistication of the coordination systems. These capabilities must be aligned with the contract type and the depth of relationship management. BPO relationships that need high technical support are those that require collaboration and transparency, have a strategic agenda, and aim to improve enterprise competitiveness.

Source: Based on Mani et al. (2006)

For example, Merrill Lynch outsourced the restructuring of its wealth management work station platform – a case of transformational BPO that involved high levels of process interdependence, complexity, and strategic importance. More specifically, there was a high process interdependence because the new platform would have links among client management systems, call centers, and online service management. Furthermore, the new platform would be particularly complex because it would accommodate 130 applications. Its importance to the organization was highly strategic as the new platform would facilitate the prioritization of work, something that was expected to benefit the company significantly. In particular, the new platform would enable the company's financial advisors to focus on the major clients while diverting the rest to the company's call centers or Web site.

In alignment with the high levels of process interdependence, complexity, and strategic importance, Merrill Lynch tried to develop a relational contract emphasizing the joint ownership of the outsourced process as well as the partnering nature of the venture that would enable the BPO initiative to be adapted to changing business needs. Furthermore, it developed a partnering model of operations that involved frequent communication and information exchanges from lower to top management levels. In terms of technical capabilities, the BPO venture was highly challenging and demanded intense client–supplier collaboration.

As an example of transactional BPO, Qatar Airways outsourced its revenue accounting and recovery processes to Kale Consultants in India. The outsourced system was low in terms of process interdependence, complexity, and strategic importance. More specifically, the revenue accounting and recovery process could be disaggregated from the firm's value network, which made it independent. Furthermore, it was a straightforward process with a low level of complexity. In terms of its significance to the competitiveness of the firm, it was considered a strategically peripheral corporate function.

The low levels of independence, complexity, and strategic significance of the outsourced process were combined with low BPO governance capabilities. In other words, the company signed a clearly defined performance-based contract with its supplier. The management of the relationship relied on SLAs. Furthermore, Qatar Airways did not need to make any technological investments. The new system interfaces required only the exchange of transactional data such as manual tickets, coupons, and billing data.

Table 8.3 summarizes the BPO governance models of Merrill Lynch and Qatar Airways, as well as their attributes.

Table 8.3 Characteristics of two governance models

Governance model	Process requirements	Governance capabilities
Transformational BPO	High interdependence	Contract: Relational contract emphasizes joint ownership of the outsourced business process.
	High complexity	Relationship management: Partnering model marked by relational emphasis on coordination and high levels of information exchange, joint action, and commitment between the client and provider.
	High strategic importance	Technological capabilities: High technological capabilities.
Transactional BPO	Low interdependence	Contract: Arm's-length performance contract emphasizes transfer of ownership of the outsourced process to the provider.
	Low complexity	Relationship management: Relationship marked by emphasis on control and low levels of information exchange, joint action, and commitment between the client and provider.
	Low strategic importance	Technological capabilities: Low technological capabilities.

Source: Based on Mani et al. (2006)

On this basis, according to the findings by Mani et al. (2006), BPO processes characterized by high interdependence and complexity and of high strategic significance should be combined with high governance capabilities (transformational BPO). Processes that are of low interdependence, complexity, and strategic significance should be combined with low governance capabilities (transactional BPO). Misalignment of governance capabilities relative to these process dimensions would yield poor results.

Summary

This chapter focused on the governing structures and processes in various outsourcing settings. It first emphasized the formal approach of governing structures and the traditional way to setting up roles and communication channels, and then examined the relational aspects of governing outsourcing projects. Clearly, investing in both formal governing structures and informal relational mechanisms improves the results expected from governing outsourcing projects.

Relevant teaching case

Jaiswal, V., and Levina, N. (2008). "JIT Full Circle Outsourcing." In A. L. Albertin and O. P. Sanchez (eds.), *IT Outsourcing: Impacts, Dilemmas, Debates and Real Cases.* São Paulo: Editora FGV.

CHAPTER 9

Managing globally distributed teams

Globally distributed work is an integral part of offshore outsourcing. Offshoring and offshore outsourcing often imply that client and supplier teams need to work together in a globally distributed fashion. In such cases, some teams will be based onshore, at either the client's site or the supplier's onshore site, and others will be based offshore. *Globally distributed projects* are those that consist of two or more teams working together from different geographical locations to accomplish project goals. These teams face major challenges on various fronts, including cultural differences, language barriers, national traditions, values, and norms of behavior. Therefore, this chapter focuses on the following topics:

- The challenges that distributed teams face
- The methodologies for globally distributed teams
- Coordination, collaboration and communications in globally distributed teams
- Socialization and the role of face-to-face meetings in globally distributed teams
- The role of a client in distributed
- The role of the client in distributed collaboration

Challenges that globally distributed teams face

Research on the management of globally distributed teams has tended to focus on issues related to the geographical dispersal of work. Because of the constraints associated with globally distributed work, such as distance, time zones, and cultural differences, traditional coordination and control mechanisms tend to be less effective in globally distributed projects. Distance reduces the intensity of communications – in particular, when people experience problems with media that cannot substitute for face-to-face communications. Cultural differences expressed in different languages, values, working and communication habits, and implicit assumptions are believed to be embedded in the collective knowledge of a specific culture and thus may cause misunderstandings and conflicts. Time zone differences reduce opportunities for real-time collaboration, as response time increases considerably when working hours at remote locations do not overlap. Therefore, receiving an answer to a simple question may take far longer than in colocated projects.

Globally distributed teams, including offshore–onshore teams, have reported problems and breakdowns in various areas – for example:

- The breakdown of traditional coordination and control mechanisms.
- Loss of communication richness (Cramton and Webber, 2005), limited opportunities for interactions, and leaner communication media (Espinosa et al., 2007).
- Lack of understanding of the counterpart's context and lack of communication norms in coordinating distributed teams. In particular, the risk factors in offshore outsourcing scenarios are client–vendor communication (e.g., miscommunication of the original set of requirements, language barriers, and poor change management controls), the client's internal management issues (e.g., lack of top management commitment, inadequate user involvement, lack of offshore project management know-how, poor management of end user expectations, and failure to consider all costs), and vendor capabilities (e.g., lack of business and technical know-how by the offshore team).
- Language barriers (Sarker and Sahay, 2003).
- Misunderstandings caused by cultural differences, such as different conversational styles and different subjective interpretations (Lee-Kelley and Sankey, 2008).
- Dissonance or conflict, such as task or interpersonal conflict (Lee-Kelley and Sankey, 2008).
- Loss of team cohesion and motivation to collaborate, such as decreased morale and lack of trust.
- Asymmetry in distribution of information among sites (Carmel, 1999).
- Difficulty collaborating because of different skill sets and training methods, various tools, technologies, and IT infrastructures (Sarker and Sahay, 2004).
- Lack of informal interpersonal communications (Cramton and Webber, 2005).
- Difficulties working across time zones (Lee-Kelley and Sankey, 2008).
- Delays in distributed collaborative work processes. This is often described in terms of unproductive waits for the other side to respond with clarifications or feedback, which can be the result of time zone differences but

may also be because of different interpretations of priorities, especially when local and global priorities are not the same.

Studies have described some of these challenges in depth. For example, Oshri et al. (2007b) describe how Baan, a software development firm based in the Netherlands that offshored software development to India in the late 1990s, struggled to develop successful collaboration between the Dutch and the Indian teams. One problem area that the Indian counterparts described was the lack of ownership of the product, which affected the Indian team caused by the difficulty in perceiving themselves as part of the Baan global team. The Indian engineers kept referring to their Dutch counterparts as "them" and portrayed the relationships as if these were between a client and a vendor.

In another study, Kotlarsky et al. (2007) described the challenges regarding knowledge sharing between onshore and offshore teams involved in component-based development. In this study, the authors showed that while the common wisdom regarding distributed component-based development suggests that each site should take responsibility for a particular component, in reality, as illustrated by TCS, the Indian IT service provider, success stories are based on a development methodology that encourages the joint development of a component by more than one site. As a result of such methodology, remote sites, such as TCS's on-site team in Zurich and their offshore team in Mumbai, developed collaborative methodologies that quickened the development process and produced highly reusable components.

A study by Kotlarsky, van Fenema, and Willcocks (2008) illustrated the challenges in codeveloping software across remote sites. In this study, the emphasis is on the transfer of work packages between on-site and offshore teams. Although generally there has been a growing dependency on the codification of knowledge and therefore the transfer of documentation back and forth between on-site and offshore teams during the various software development stages, Kotlarsky and associates showed that codification of knowledge is not sufficient for successful collaboration. Successful teams, such as at SAP, the German software warehouse, have combined informal and formal mechanisms to support collaborative software development.

Clearly globally distributed teams face a number of challenges. In particular, offshore and on-site teams may experience these challenges to a greater extent because of the cultural and time zone differences and the effects of the local context in relation to global priorities. Nevertheless, many teams have introduced and implemented methodologies and tools to help cope with such challenges, the topic we now turn to.

Methodologies for globally distributed teams

Consider again the case in which software was developed by a globally distributed team located in both the Netherlands and India. Historically, software systems have been developed following a waterfall approach, which prescribes a number of phases to follow in a sequential manner: requirements analysis and specifications, conceptual design, coding and testing, as illustrated in Figure 9.1.

Other methodologies for software development facilitate concurrent development based on organizing tasks in an overlapping (parallel) mode or for contract-driven software (developed for a specific customer, as opposed to off-the-shelf, sometimes customizable software systems) methodologies that aim to increase user participation in the development process, such as joint application development, rapid application development, and prototyping. The choice of which development methodology to follow has implications for the way work will be divided and integrated across the various sites. In particular, organizing sequentially dependent tasks to be conducted in parallel changes the way tasks are coordinated and controlled. For example, overlap between tasks means that developers cannot check the output from preceding tasks and compare this to standards, and therefore need to rely on interpersonal communications. In a globally distributed environment, work is divided between teams and individuals at multiple geographically dispersed locations, and thus coordination and integration of work need to be done across these remote locations. This results in the delay of work completion time because distributed tasks appear to take longer to complete compared to similar tasks that are colocated. More recently, there has been growing evidence that agile software development practices seem to be effective in reducing the delays associated with inter-site communication and coordination.

In fact, many of the methodologies developed for globally distributed software development teams concern the coordination challenges that these teams face. These methodologies therefore are known as inter-site coordination methodologies. We now describe some of these methodologies in depth.

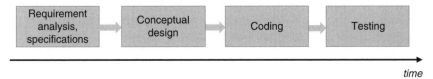

Figure 9.1 Waterfall approach: traditional software development life cycle

Inter-site coordination, collaboration, and communications for globally distributed teams

Solutions have been developed for software development that is carried out in a distributed manner in three key areas: (1) division of work, by which the coordination and integration of work conducted at remote locations can be made easier; (2) coordination solutions for distributed environments, and (3) communication patterns aiming to make inter-site coordination more efficient through planning systematic communication between remote counterparts and establishing rules of communications.

Division of work

Typically strategies to divide work between remote locations are such that their main objective is to reduce the need for inter-site coordination and communications. These are therefore the most commonly mentioned strategies for the division of work in globally distributed teams in the specific context of software development:

• *Phase/process step,* when globally dispersed sites engage in different phases of a project in a sequential manner. This means that work is handed over to a remote site after completing certain process steps. For example, requirement analysis may take place in a front office located in New York, after which specifications are transferred to Dublin for the conceptual design and then coding will be carried out in Mumbai. Figure 9.2, which we refer to as scenario A, illustrates this strategy.

• *Product structure (product module),* when each product module or feature is developed at a single site. This approach allows different sites to work on different modules in parallel. Figure 9.3 illustrates such a scenario (scenario B), when a system is divided into modules (typically different product functions) and each module is allocated to a different site. For example, while the requirement analysis is carried out in London, the specifications, design, coding, and testing of the three key modules of a complex system are carried out in Ireland, India, and Russia, respectively. We wish to emphasize that structured, well-defined tasks are more suitable to be allocated by phase/process step, while unstructured, loosely defined tasks are more appropriate to be allocated by product structure (product module).

• *Minimizing requirements for cross-site communication and synchronization,* which, however, works only for particular types of product

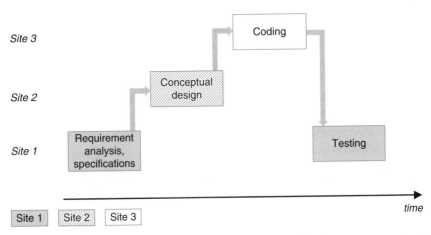

Figure 9.2 Scenario A: globally distributed software development organized by phase/process step

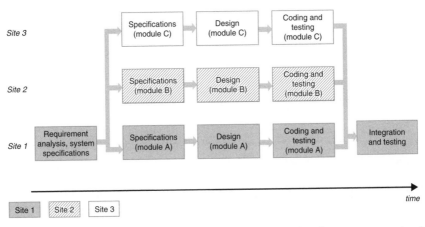

Figure 9.3 Scenario B: globally distributed software development organized by product structure or product module

architectures. The philosophy behind this practice is that "tightly coupled work items that require frequent co-ordination and synchronization should be performed within one site" (Mockus and Weiss, 2001: 30). Figure 9.4 illustrates such a scenario (scenario C) in which some tasks require frequent coordination. In this example, requirements analysis and specification, conceptual design and integration, and testing are conducted at one site, and only well-defined tasks (coding and testing of different modules) are conducted at two locations in parallel.

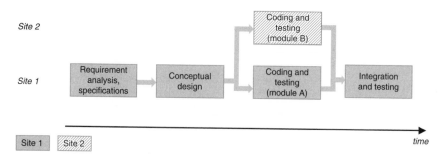

Figure 9.4 Scenario C: globally distributed software development organized by minimizing requirements for cross-site communication and synchronization

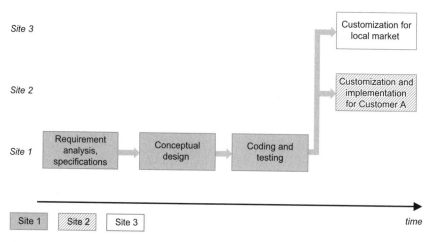

Figure 9.5 Scenario D: globally distributed software development organized based on product customization

• *Product customization*, so that one site develops the product and other sites perform customization, that is, changes such as adding features and enhancements for specific customers. In this case, the sites that customize the product are geographically near the customer. Figure 9.5 illustrates this scenario (scenario D), in which a system is developed in one location (site 1) and other globally dispersed sites customize the system for specific customers (site 2) or for local markets (site 3).

• *Division of work across time zones*, where a task is passed from one person to the next person, located in a different time zone, at the end of a workday to reduce project completion time and improve resource utilization through 24-hour development (Jalote and Jain, 2006).

Clearly, offshoring projects that work with onshore teams have a range of work division practices to rely on in making a decision regarding where to place activity X and how such a decision will affect the mode of collaboration between onshore and offshore teams.

Coordination mechanisms

Offshoring and offshore outsourcing projects also face coordination challenges. Experience has resulted in a number of strategies that can help such teams cope with these challenges – for example:

- An explicit, documented, and formalized project process. Standardizing and documenting the development methodology, distributing it across sites, and storing it in a shared repository; educating all team members about the chosen methodologies. A recent study we conducted at Capgemini showed that front office teams based in the Netherlands were facing major challenges collaborating with back office teams, which were based in India, because approaches to development methodologies were not standardized.
- Promoting task-related interaction by encouraging interdependence and reliance on one another among the members of distributed teams. Our study at TCS has shown that this practice is particularly successful between on-site and offshore teams.
- Providing approaches that can coordinate distributed software development tasks, such as integration-centric engineering processes, which aim at managing crucial dependencies in distributed software development projects (Taxén, 2006).
- Adopting a more structured project management approach. Ghosh and Varghese (2004) propose a project management framework based on process restructuring that can be used efficiently for managing and tracking the distributed development of large-scale projects.
- Encouraging visits to remote sites and face-to-face meetings (Malhotra and Majchrzak, 2005). In a study we conducted at SAP, TCS, and LeCroy, we noticed that while face-to-face-meetings are important, it is far more important to build a socializing system within which remote teams renew social ties and resocialize after a kick-off meeting and after each project meeting. In this regard, remote teams need to renorm and reestablish a shared team identity (Oshri, Kotlarsky et al., 2008).
- Establishing liaisons between remote locations.
- Creating transparency in project goals and the company vision.

- Identifying different modes of task assignment mechanisms: self-assignment, assigning to others, and consulting with others (Crowston et al., 2007).
- Building awareness of the work conducted at remote sites by making project plans accessible over the Web and awareness of who is doing what by creating a Web page for each team member with personal information.
- Sharing the local context with the global team by providing information about local working hours and holidays.
- These coordination practices will help remote teams avoid the pitfalls often associated with distributed work. Agreeing on communication styles and setting up communication protocols is another important area in the management of globally distributed team.

Communication practices

Extensive research has been conducted on communication patterns that could have a positive or negative effect on collaboration between remote counterparts. In particular, these practices can lead to successful collaboration among globally distributed teams:

- Scheduling phone and videoconference meetings between remote counterparts, including managers and team members.
- Establishing communication protocols that cover the ground rules and expectations concerning communications. In our research, we observed that SAP held team-building meetings between German and Indian counterparts during which some of the discussions were dedicated to the remote teams' agreeing and accepting certain communication protocols.
- Providing appropriate training and access to collaborative tools and communication technologies.
- Being clear and patient in communications because not all counterparts can comprehend and communicate in English
- Investing in language and cultural training. For example, New York–based LeCroy has invested in language training of Geneva-based engineers (Kotlarsky and Oshri, 2005).

Clearly global firms are becoming more aware of the need to develop communication skills as one enabling factor of successful collaboration. The range of practices available is growing, and we have dedicated our discussion to the more commonly applied practices. However, another critical element in supporting globally distributed work is the tools and technologies implemented and used by remote teams.

Tools and technologies for globally distributed teams

Numerous tools and technologies have been introduced to overcome the challenges we have examined. The main tools and methodologies applied in globally distributed contexts are a powerful information and communication technology (ICT) infrastructure that allows the transfer of data at high speed, generic collaborative technologies enabling remote colleagues to connect and communicate, and software engineering tools that support software development activities conducted in parallel at remote locations.

ICT infrastructure

A reliable and high-bandwidth ICT infrastructure is required to ensure connectivity among remote sites. ICT facilitates the process of boundary crossing to overcome the challenges presented by geographically remote and culturally diverse team members. ICT can help to mitigate the negative impact of intercultural miscommunication and support decision making in distributed environments.

Collaborative technology

Among the many collaborative technologies for global teams are:

- Teleconferencing, often combined with e-meetings
- Virtual whiteboards that allow document sharing
- E-mail
- Online chat (instant messaging)
- Voice over Internet protocol (VoIP)
- Videoconferencing
- Internet and intranet
- Group calendars
- Discussion lists
- Electronic meeting systems

Collaborative technologies recommended for global teams can be classified according to time and space dimensions. One could consider these collaborative technologies based on the following four categories: same place, same time, in which collaborative technologies are for colocated group decision support; same place, different time, in which work flow systems are used; same time, different place, in which telephone and chatting technologies are mainly applied; and different place, different time, of which bulletin boards are one example.

A more extensive classification of collaborative technologies is presented in Table 9.1. In this framework, there is a distinction among several types of collaborative technology that support the different needs of globally distributed teams in different time and place settings.

Table 9.1 Types of collaboration technology

	Setting		
	Different place, different time (offline): support between encounters	**Different place, same time (online): support for electronic encounters**	**Same place, same time: support for face-to-face meetings**
Communication systems: Aim to make communications among people who are not colocated easy, cheap, and fast	Email Voice message Text Fax	Phone / Voice-over-IP Video Multi-point video / audio-conferencing systems Online chat	
Information-sharing systems: Aim to make the storage and retrieval of large amounts of information quick, easy, reliable, and inexpensive	Document sharing systems Portals and web-based databases and repositories for searching remote information sources	Screen sharing applications Podcasting	Presentation systems
Collaboration systems: Aim to improve teamwork by providing document sharing and coauthoring facilities	Coediting systems	Shared whiteboard Computer-assisted design	Group decision support systems
Coordination systems: Aim to coordinate distributed teamwork by coordinating work processes	Synchronizers: Group calendar Shared project planning Shared work flow system Web-based scheduling / voting (e.g., Doodle poll)	Awareness or notification systems (e.g., active batch)	Command-and-control center support systems
Social encounter systems: Aim to facilitate unplanned interactions	Social media (e.g., Facebook, blogs, twitter)	Virtual spaces Virtual worlds	

Source: Adapted from Huis, Andriessen, and Soekijad (2002), modified by the authors to include modern technologies

Tools that support software engineering

In addition to collaborative technologies that are generic to a great extent, a number of tools specific to software development are central to supporting globally distributed software development teams. The most commonly suggested tools are as follows:

- Configuration and version management tools
- Source management system
- Document management system
- Replicated databases and repositories
- CASE tools that support the modeling and visibility of design
- Integrated development environment tool sets such as editor, compiler, and debugger

These tools ensure consistency in the product and development environment across dispersed locations, such as front office and back office teams. In fact, there are more possibilities for improving collaborative work provided by collaborative engineering tools by adding generic collaborative tools, such as e-mail, instant messaging, screen sharing, and a configuration management tool to the tools reported above.

Socialization and the role of face-to-face meetings in globally distributed teams

Though the concept of globally distributed projects implies that team members work over distance, typically some of them do have an opportunity to meet in person. Studies that have focused on social aspects in globally distributed projects have suggested that firms should promote and hold face-to-face (F2F) meetings to tighten interpersonal ties among remote counterparts in an attempt to improve collaborative work (Oshri et al. 2007b). Indeed, creating and renewing social ties between remote counterparts may open additional channels, supplementary to the technical solutions proposed, through which collaborative work can be improved. Using F2F meetings to advance social ties in globally distributed teams may also improve the formation these teams as members get to know each other during meetings, learn about cultural differences among members of the team, discuss and agree on ways to resolve tensions, set up procedures to coordinate work activities, and start working together toward the successful completion of a project.

We have observed that supporting interpersonal contacts between remote counterparts throughout the project life cycle is rather challenging to managers. So far, the emphasis in practice and research has been on F2F meetings that serve as a stage for bonding, socializing, and creating social ties among remote counterparts. Nonetheless, F2F meetings alone may not create the conditions through which interpersonal ties such as trust and rapport can be created and renewed. F2F meetings tend to be short and often last only a couple of days. The agendas for these meetings often revolve around project and technical issues that need to be resolved, leaving little space for socialization and one-on-one meetings. The emerging challenges in creating social ties among members of globally distributed teams are as follows:

- F2F meetings are short and tend to offer only limited social space that accommodates cultural differences.
- Most time spent in F2F meetings is dedicated to project procedures and technical issues, that is, they are formal to a large extent.
- F2F meetings are selective in the sense that not all counterparts are invited to these meetings.
- Short and infrequent F2F meetings offer sporadic interpersonal interactions between remote counterparts, which restrict the buildup of interpersonal relationships.
- ICT offers limited opportunities for personal contact and social space as compared to F2F meetings.

While F2F meetings assist in acquainting counterparts of globally distributed teams with each other and addressing project and technical issues, these meetings, being sporadic, short, selective, and formal to a great extent, do not support the long-term buildup and renewal of interpersonal ties between dispersed counterparts very well. Therefore managers of globally distributed teams need to pay attention not only to planning the actual F2F meetings but also to the activities that can be carried out over distance before and after these meetings to help make the most of the meetings and to help establish social ties in global teams. Table 9.2 summarizes activities that we recommend to implement before, during, and after F2F meetings at individual, team, and organizational levels.

F2F meetings activities provide insights into the way that managers of global teams can supplement collaborative tools and methodologies with human-related activities to ensure strong social ties among remote counterparts. We suggest that firms can move on from the traditional focus on F2F meetings as the main vehicle through which interpersonal ties are created,

Table 9.2 Individual, team, and organizational activities supporting social ties

	Before F2F meeting (introduction stage)	During F2F meeting (build up stage)	After F2F meeting (renewal stage)
Individual	Increase awareness of communication styles	Create space for one-on-one interactions	Ensure real-time communication channels
	Offer language courses	Provide a sense of importance to each member to the team	Ensure mixed audio and visual cues
	Offer short visits of individuals to remote locations	Adjust communication styles	Offer short visits to remote locations
			Offer temporary colocation
Team	Introduce new team members	Conduct kick-off meeting	Facilitate reflection sessions
	Increase awareness of team composition	Discuss differences between national and organizational cultures	Facilitate roundtable discussions
	Increase awareness of communication protocol	Offer space for multiple interactions among counterparts	Facilitate progress meetings
	Appoint a contact person for each remote team	Offer team-building exercises	Conduct virtual F2F meetings
	Set up mini-teams	Organize social events	Offer F2F meetings
	Offer virtual F2F meetings	Discuss organizational structure	
Organizational	Distribute newsletters	Support sharing of information from F2F meetings (e.g., photos)	Encourage direct communication channels
	Create and offer shared cyberspaces		
Tools	Phone/teleconference, VoIP, e-mail, collaborative technologies, shared knowledge repositories and shared databases, videoconference, online chat, intranet, Internet, social media, virtual spaces		

and invest in before-and-after F2F meeting activities. In this respect, managers should consider the full life cycle of social ties when planning and executing collaborative work among remote sites.

The life cycle of social ties consists of three stages: introduction, buildup, and renewal (as shown in Figure 9.6). Each step represents an array of activities (presented in Table 9.2) that a globally distributed team may apply in order to move from the introduction stage to building up of social ties, and finally to the renewal phase in which social ties are renewed through various activities during and after F2F meetings (Oshri et al., 2007b).

Managers should assess at which stage the dispersed team is before embarking on the introduction of specific activities. For example, dispersed

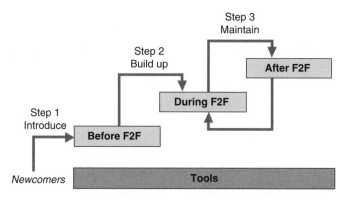

Figure 9.6 The life cycle of social ties in globally distributed teams

teams that are at the introduction stage, such as the SAP team we investigated that included members located in Walldorf (Germany), Bangalore (India), and Palo Alto (US) that had no prior experience of working together, require activities that foster social ties; these are different from activities for teams at the renewal stage, such as the LeCroy team, whose members from New York (US) and Geneva (Switzerland) had a long history of working together over distance on various projects (Oshri et al., 2007b).

As the project progresses and remote counterparts get to know each other, establish interpersonal ties, and develop a collaborative mode of working together, renewing these social ties may require only a subset of the activities offered in Table 9.2. In this regard, the activities in Table 9.2 are not a recipe for building and renewing social ties but rather represent a set of possibilities available to managers who are seeking to strengthen social ties among team members. Each team and each team member differs in the way they bond with others. The manager's responsibility is to choose the most appropriate activity at the right time to ensure that social ties are renewed and the collaborative work strengthened.

From a social ties perspective, we have observed that globally distributed teams need to "renorm" from time to time as newcomers join and change the dynamics of interpersonal ties within dispersed teams; in addition, disagreement and miscommunications can arise even in later stages of a project because of a lack of F2F interactions that resulted in fading interpersonal ties. For this reason, we recommend that managers consider renorming dispersed teams and renewing social ties through bonding activities, such as short visits or F2F meetings. These activities, we have learned, should be offered not only in the early stages of team development but also later, because social ties may loosen over time and affect collaborative work.

The role of the client in distributed collaboration

So far, this discussion of distributed collaboration has mainly focused on the vendors and companies that adopted a global teams approach as part of the captive mode of working (e.g., by carrying out global projects with team members from different sites of the same company). We have noted that vendors and other global companies should introduce and use cutting-edge methodologies, practices, tools, and technologies to ensure that software solutions can be jointly developed by remote team members. In offshore outsourcing arrangements, the client is part of this distributed collaboration and can improve the degree of collaboration between the vendor's on-site and offshore teams. For example, the client can work with the vendor to ensure that there are no knowledge or expertise asymmetries between on-site and offshore teams. In such a case, the client can ask the vendor's offshore team to "play back" the information the offshore team has acquired from the on-site team. However, such involvement is not always welcomed by clients, in particular if the client perceives the outsourcing contract as transactional in nature. Therefore, we highlight two propositions for the client that could improve collaboration amongst the client, on-site teams, and offshore teams and also improve the value delivered to the client from the outsourcing contract:

Proposition 1: Clients must understand the benefits they will receive from a vendor's collaborative system. In the precontract stage, clients need to obtain a detailed statement, in financial terms as far as possible, of the benefits to themselves of their provider's collaboration practices. These benefits could include a speedier improvement in service performance, faster availability of expertise at lower rates, and the provider's commitment to a higher level of innovation in processes, services, and technologies, resulting in observable performance improvements. Such benefits must be agreed on, documented, and signed off on in the contract, with money or credits going to the client where they do not materialize.

Proposition 2: Clients must understand the costs of a provider's collaboration system. Generally these costs involve helping the provider coordinate service delivery by making the client's and vendor's staff available for knowledge transfer activities through methods such as seminars, interviews, and offshore visits. Clients should agree to these costs contractually. They should also understand and agree contractually to the net benefits they will receive versus the net benefits the provider will receive. As we have observed, when there is a large difference between the two, the disadvantaged party's commitment to delivering on the collaboration strategy falls off.

Summary

Offshore, nearshore, and onshore teams have become part of globally distributed teams. For this reason, such teams should consider how they operate to ensure successful collaboration. Previous chapters have focused on key aspects of managing outsourcing relationships without analyzing the specific context within which such collaborations take place. This chapter has considered the unique challenges that global teams face and strategies to improve their collaboration.

CHAPTER 10

Innovation through sourcing

There are many reasons that companies of various sizes see the benefit of outsourcing particular aspects of innovation, here defined generally for a business context as deploying new and creative ways of achieving productivity or top line growth (Coulter and Fersht, 2010). Quinn (2000) has listed reasons that include limited resources and capabilities within the organization, a shortage of specialist talent, management of multiple risks, attracting talent in the company's nonspecialized areas, and getting to market faster. So how can companies innovate through all the various ways of sourcing available? Often they have an ad hoc approach to innovation, or what Linder, Jarvenpaa, and Davenport (2003) call a transactional approach. This approach, however, often fails to leverage organizational learning and may also result in an unintended loss of knowledge. An ad hoc approach cannot create a culture in which external contributions are accepted or welcomed. Moreover, it is difficult to measure innovative processes and outcomes when companies innovate on an ad hoc basis.

In this chapter we look at how organizations go about sourcing innovations more productively. This sets the context for our major, more restricted focus on whether, and, if so, how, IT and business process innovations can be achieved through using external ITO and BPO service providers. The chapter starts by detailing the debate around whether innovation can be outsourced and, if so, under what conditions. We then look at the case for internal control and the research on how outsourcing innovation can be managed. The chapter then describes our own research-derived approach to collaborating to innovate, which we position as the next phase in the evolution of the ITO and BPO agenda. Therefore, this chapter focuses on the following topics:

- The debate about innovation in outsourcing
- Tapping into the sources of innovation in outsourcing
- Rationale and management of outsourcing innovation
- Collaborating for innovation in outsourcing
- Best practices for innovation in outsourcing

The outsourcing innovation debate

Over the past 20 years of ITO, BPO, and offshoring, the record on innovation through suppliers has been one of many disappointments and false starts. In practice, clients and suppliers have found it difficult to draw up contracts that lead to innovation. Suppliers have created and tried to use innovation centers, and clients have created innovation funds or have set up multisourcing arrangements in which they hoped that greater collaboration and competition might lead to greater innovation. But time and again, such well-intended efforts have not yielded significant innovation. All too often, the promise of innovation has been too small a part of the overall contract and, moreover, has tended to be negotiated out of outsourcing contracts as both parties seek to reduce their risk and investment exposure (Lacity and Willcocks, 2001; Willcocks and Lacity, 2006). More recently, Coulter and Fersht (2010) have suggested that an additional limitation for ITO and BPO alike lies with outsourcing providers that historically have been organized around the industry verticals of their clients. They argue that suppliers need to develop a new organizational model from their experiences of servicing multiple industries that bypasses an industry vertical's inherent resistance to collaborate and creates an environment of willing collaborators.

Certainly there is plenty of evidence that if an innovation agenda is to be productive, a lot needs to change from the way things are done now. The case study evidence of Willcocks et al. (2011), looking at over 1,200 outsourcing arrangements, is supported by a range of surveys. For example, a PA Consulting 2009 survey found innovation sidelined in favor of quick cost improvements – perhaps understandable in an economic downturn. A 2009 Forrester Research survey found that 38 percent of IT outsourcing customers cited a lack of innovation or continuous improvement as their biggest challenge with vendors. But even before the downturn, IT analysts were registering considerable skepticism amongst clients about suppliers' innovation pitches (Overby, 2007; Savvas, 2007). More recently, looking at BPO, Fersht (2010) surveyed 588 senior decision makers in client, supplier, and advisory organizations. While 43 percent of clients viewed innovation as a critical element in BPO, more than half of all BPO buyers were disappointed with their current state of innovation. Customer care, recruitment, payroll, and management reporting were noticeably failing to meet clients' expectations. Buyers saw their major impediments as ineffective change management and un-empowered internal governance teams. The report concluded that the BPO innovation gap represented a huge opportunity for clients and suppliers alike, if only they could act on it.

There has been a long-standing debate around whether innovation is too important and too challenging to be outsourced. This has been brought into focus by Cramm (2010) who suggests that with extensive outsourcing, companies lose the ability to innovate IT. Moreover, successful outsourcing requires strong internal leadership. How can an organization attract, retain, and develop leaders who are savvy about IT in an environment where many of the development assignments are outsourced? She also sees three practices working against innovation from long-term client–supplier relationships: (1) outsourcing one contract at a time, and thereby ending up with myriad relationships that are broad and relatively shallow; (2) an attitude of managing scope to manage profit that precludes the supplier from adding value or investing beyond the original scope of the contract; and (3) silos in large outsourcing companies that make it difficult to coordinate resources to optimize benefits to the client. Overby (2010) suggests that problem instead lies more with clients' critical mistakes in attempting to procure innovation from external suppliers. She cites three such errors: clients do not know what they want (a failure to define innovation in the context of corporate objectives), choose the wrong providers (they do not adequately examine the provider's culture, history, suite of services, and innovation track record), and do not set up effective innovation metrics (therefore avoiding traditional IT metrics; in addition, most service-level agreement regimes and pricing models deter innovation).

The case for internal control

All this would suggest that before looking to the market for innovations, companies should first consider whether innovating through outsourcing is a strategy. As Chesbrough and Teece (1996) and Chesbrough, Vanhaverbeke, and West (2006) point out, the virtues have sometimes been oversold. Companies that place a great deal of emphasis on external sourcing while neglecting to nurture and guard their own capabilities may be taking many risks. One approach, therefore, is to build an internal capability to innovate. This is particularly important in firms that are highly dependent on innovation for market leadership. Westerman and Curley (2008) provide a useful example here of building IT-enabled innovation capabilities at Intel. Their study charts how, from 2003, Intel adopted a staged approach and built a global network of IT innovation centers, together with a virtual innovation center that acts as a focal point for making new innovation tools and activities available throughout the company. They suggest seven lessons:

1. Take the lead in innovation. Do not wait to be asked.
2. Build momentum early, and use it to expand scope.
3. Measure and publicize progress.
4. Culture is not a prerequisite; it can be changed to be more innovative.
5. Build an enabling environment and infrastructure for innovation.
6. Do not innovate alone: obtain external people and funding.
7. Gain and maintain executive support.

Chesbrough and Teece (1996) distinguish two types of innovation: autonomous and systemic. *Autonomous* innovation can be pursued independently from other innovations, whereas the benefit of *systemic* innovation can be realized only in conjunction with related, complementary innovations. The two types of innovation call for different organizational strategies. Autonomous innovation can be very well managed in decentralized virtual networks, while systemic innovation requires a high level of information sharing and the capabilities to coordinate adjustments throughout an entire product system. Such capabilities of coordination and integration are usually available within a well-managed organization rather than a loosely connected network.

IBM is a good example. In the early 1980s, IBM had an open architecture based on standards and components that were widely available. This architecture enabled IBM to take advantage of third-party development of software applications and hardware accessory products. It also relied on the market to distribute the product. As a result, IBM greatly reduced its costs to bring a PC to market and outperformed Apple, the market pioneer at that time. However, IBM has since lost its advantage as other competitors have tapped into the same sources in the market, over which IBM has little control. Moreover, most of the profits from the PC architecture have migrated upstream to the supplier of the microprocessor (Intel) and the operating system (Microsoft). IBM's experience shows that key development activities that depend on one another must be conducted in-house to capture the rewards from long-term R&D investments.

A company that cultivates and strengthens its unique competencies and capabilities is also able to maintain the position of a dominant player in a network, and thus to drive and coordinate systemic innovation. As Chesbrough and Teece (1996) observed, the most successful companies withhold dominant control in a network. For example, Toyota was much larger than its suppliers and was the largest customer of most of them. As a result, it could compel those suppliers to make radical changes in their business practices.

Tapping into innovation sources

Where companies make the decision to leverage externally sourced innovation, they should establish deliberate, consistently available channels to match their strategic requirements. Once established, these channels can be used as needs arise. Linder, Jarvenpaa, and Davenport (2003) identify five types of external innovation channels:

1. *Building innovation on the market*: One source of innovation that companies can turn to are universities and private research labs. Another way to tap into innovation on the market is through strategic procurement, that is, by seeking differentiated products or innovative processes from suppliers.
2. *Investing in innovators:* Companies can take equity positions in organizations focused on small or emerging markets. This often helps to resolve the innovator's dilemma that arises when established firms resist innovation that might undermine their existing offerings. By investing in an equity partnership, a company can participate in and nurture an emerging market.
3. *Cosourcing:* Companies sometimes band together to share the costs of innovation, for example, to address regulatory requirements that affect them all. Some high-tech firms sponsor professors in universities who work in promising areas and share any intellectual property that is produced. Joint venture is another way to cosource innovation.
4. *Community sourcing:* This refers to innovation produced by loosely connected communities of sophisticated users. One successful example is the open source software industry. Another is eBay, which uses community-based innovation extensively to identify new sales categories and expand its capabilities.
5. *Resourcing:* Companies can support their research staff by contracting with external suppliers for on-demand talent and innovative new tools. For example, DuPont Crop Protection hires high-quality researchers in India, Russia, and China who are paid much less than their counterparts in the US. Aventis S.A. identifies cutting-edge technologies in the market and brings them in-house to support product development.

Outsourcing innovation: rationale and management

A plethora of studies and commentators have supported the notion of increasingly working and innovating with external parties in order to compete effectively in the global economy. Hagel and Seely Brown (2008) point to the importance of new forms of connection and coordination and the value of offshoring. Prahalad and Ramaswamy (2004) see cocreating value with customers as among the best future competitive plays. Davenport, Leibold, and Voelpel (2006) argue that globalization, aided by rapid technological innovation, has changed the basis of competition. It is no longer a company's ownership of capabilities that matters, but rather its ability to control and make the most of critical capabilities, whether or not they reside on the firm's balance sheet. A new strategic mind-set is required that supports coshaping value innovation and open innovation processes.

To put flesh on this rationale, Stanko, Bohlmann, and Calentone (2009) usefully researched the sourcing habits and innovative performance (patents produced) of 359 companies. The most successful companies used outsourcing in four circumstances:

- When a company needed to add lots of new knowledge to innovate – for example, figuring out how to work with an unfamiliar chemical compound to develop a new line of pharmaceuticals.
- In the early stages of a project, when there are many technical hurdles to overcome and the outcome is far from certain.
- When intellectual property is not well protected in the industry. In this situation, since new ideas spread quickly, it may not be possible to differentiate products with innovations. Therefore, businesses turn to outsourcing to limit spending;
- When a company has a great deal of experience with outsourcing. The costs and benefits of outsourcing are more certain for experienced firms, and they can better manage the situation to produce effective results.

Quinn (2000) has been a strong advocate of outsourcing innovation in areas such as early-stage research product development and introduction and the technology chain, and cites examples from Cisco Systems, Dell, Ford, pharmaceutical companies, and outsourcing business processes such as advertising, maintenance, logistics, worldwide accounting, software development, and operations. Quinn points to ten keys to preparing and managing successful outsourced innovation:

1. *Commit to exciting goals:* Shared commitment to common goals inspires internal and external people to work together. This requires common interests and mutually agreed targets.

2. *Make sure your partners benefit from the partnership:* While companies should focus on their core capabilities to achieve best-in-world performance, outsourcing their noncore areas of activity to suppliers provides an opportunity for the vendor to innovate and build on their best-in-world expertise.

3. *Create internal masters of the process who can help find and develop the most talented outsourcing partners:* Process masters are usually inquisitive and gregarious people with excellent specialist skills. They identify, benchmark, and track best-in-class capabilities for the company's processes.

4. *Develop open, interactive software models*: These models provide a constantly updated, accessible, visual, and multidimensional view of the system to which any innovation must adhere and the performance that the innovation must surpass. They also provide software hooks and define interfaces that enable external designers to innovate independently. As a result, participants in different time zones or work cycles can perform precisely and asynchronously, thereby increasing the speed and precision of innovation.

5. *Establish figures of merit*; Figures of merit, that is, exciting performance targets, would induce innovators to rethink existing approaches and come up with something genuinely new. Studies show that virtually all of the top innovative companies (including Sony, Hewlett-Packard, Intel, Motorola, DuPont, and Vanguard Securities) have used figures of merit. Their company leaders would project known trend performance in the industry and set performance targets from 30 to 500 percent higher.

6. *Concentrate on what needs to be accomplished, not on how to get there:* Imposing detailed control of processes constrains innovators. Buyers should understand that true innovations are not linear but complex and chaotic, often entailing spurts, frustrations, and sudden insights. Buyers should closely engage with the innovators through continuous interactive tests and feedback and make sure that the partner understands the customer's needs. Moreover, it is advisable to keep a number of innovative outsource partners participating and competing with each other for as long as possible.

7. *Use software to coordinate the players:* Software provides a common language, a measurement system, and a set of rules that facilitate human communications and capture and preserve knowledge that is precise, detailed, and easily transferable. With sophisticated electronic modeling and visual presentations, companies are able to perform joint reviews with their outsourcers. Such capabilities enable collaboration to move beyond colocated teams. Collaboration can take place among geographically distributed and independent entities that may not work under the command of a single authority.

8. *Share gains from surpassing targets:* It is important that both parties agree on specific performance targets that are fair, few in number, easy to understand, and readily usable by the people doing the work. Sometimes the outcomes of innovation are well beyond initial targets. Under such circumstances, it is unrealistic to expect that suppliers pass all gains from innovations to the buyer. Instead, buyers should use value pricing and share gains with the innovators to sustain jointly shared innovation incentives.

9. *Implement a three-point system of information exchange and project execution:* A three-point system consists of three contact points: top-level managers to oversee the innovation relationship, middle-level managers who are champions on both sides, and the people who develop inventions. Interactions at these contact points help ensure that the tacit knowledge about problems and processes gets transferred when needed and that the best vendor talent and sufficient urgency are applied to the project.

10. *Set up incentive systems and provide open, compatible information*: At the heart of successful innovation is a common open information capability that places all participants on the same footing in discussions. In general, companies that are successful at innovating have porous organizations developed around the three contact points. Such arrangements enable maximum information exchange. A flat organizational structure also reduces the inefficiencies that can arise from the need for endless approvals and communications delays. It also provides individuals with higher levels of responsibility and flexibility.

Outsourcing: developing a collaborate-to-innovate agenda

It has become obvious that traditional ITO and BPO outsourcing contracting and relationships will not lead to significant innovation. Willcocks and

Craig (2009) reviewed the literature and carried out their own research on innovation sourcing practices in 41 organizations. They concluded that outsourcing has evolved through three phases between 1989 and 2009: contract administration, contract management, and supplier management. The next phase in outsourcing, already observable among a small minority of outsourcing arrangements, is a move toward greater collaborative innovation. Their research points to how organizations can achieve greater innovation through closer collaboration. We use their work to frame the rest of the chapter.

Definitions

A start into this subject is to provide definitions of collaboration and innovation useful for the type of outsourcing under review.

Collaboration

Collaboration is a cooperative arrangement in which two or more parties work jointly in a common enterprise toward a shared goal. In the context of business relationships, the word *collaboration* signals close partnering behaviors developed over and for the long term, distinguished by high trust, flexibility, reciprocity risk sharing, and the investment of resources and time if high performance on individual and shared goals is to be achieved (Kern and Willcocks, 2001).

All outsourcing requires a relationship to succeed. But what kind of relationship works? This depends on the activities being outsourced. Commodity services such as accounts payable processing, mainframe processing, and specialized repeatable processes like credit checks and unique technology services can be accomplished with relatively hands-off, contract-based relationships between a client and its suppliers. Deeper, more trust-based relationships are required if external resources are to be used for more sophisticated risk-bearing and critical services like large-scale IT development projects, business process changes, and technology innovations. Collaboration sees value-added relationships as a norm, with clients looking for business ideas, innovation, and environmental scanning from their suppliers and a much greater focus on business rather than just technical outcomes. Collaboration in a strategic sourcing context, then, is proactive in working together and risk sharing in flexible integrated ways to achieve high performance on larger, mutually rewarding commercial goals.

Innovation

The clients in Willcocks and Craig's (2009) study described innovation as "doing things differently for the better" and "the ability to wake up one morning and realize there is a different and better way of doing something ... then combining that with an ability to deliver." Essentially innovation is the introduction of something new that creates value for the organization that adopts it (Westerman and Curley, 2008). The general innovation literature talks of product, process, and organizational innovations, referring to new products or services, new ways of doing things, and new ways of organizing and managing people. Innovations are also characterized as incremental (a small series of changes), radical (a large, transformative change), or revolutionary (game changing) (Davenport et al., 2006; Westland, 2008). For our purposes, we turn to Weeks and Feeny (2008) and use their client-focused definitions. They see three types of innovation:

1. *IT operational:* Technology and IT organizational, work, and personnel changes that do not affect firm-specific business processes such as new e-mail platforms, new operating systems, IT infrastructure remodeling, and new IT staffing arrangements.
2. *Business process:* This innovation changes the way the business operates in some important ways. In his study of the BAE Systems–CSC deal, Weeks (2004) found one such successful implementation: the development of a product data management system for the Astute submarine program. This helped to add computer-aided technology to the production process by documenting all of the parts and essential manufacturing information used in the design and production of the final submarine.
3. *Strategic:* These innovations significantly enhance the firm's product and service offerings for existing customers or enable the firm to enter new markets. As one example, in Asia Pacific, Willcocks and Craig (2009) found the Crown Casino introducing technology to automate (and thus speed up) the roulette and thus increase revenues from high rollers.

Given these definitions, Willcocks et al. (2011) point to a new performance agenda for outsourcing practitioners to aim at over the next five years. The messages of their findings, shown in Figure 10.1, can be summarized as follows:

1. In outsourcing, the collaborative capabilities of all parties determine the type and degree of innovation possible. Only deep collaboration makes large business process and strategic innovations feasible.

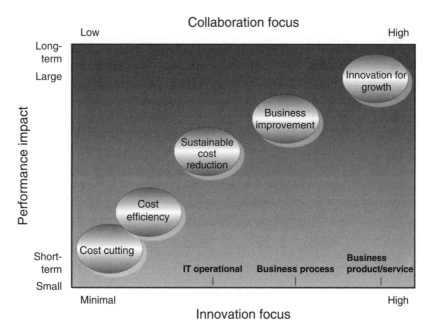

Figure 10.1 The new performance agenda

Source: Willcocks et al. (2011)

2. Without an innovation focus, outsourcing can achieve cost cutting mostly of a one-off kind or, at best, cost efficiency – that is, similar service at lower cost.

3. Focusing on innovations in IT operations achieves larger, sustainable cost reductions.

4. The real performance impacts over time come from business process and business product and service innovations. Business process innovations create sustainable business improvements in areas much bigger than IT operations alone – a bigger target and innovation with a broad impact. Business product and service innovations can support firms' revenue and profit growth targets.

5. Innovation is risky. Collaborative innovation finds ways of sharing and offsetting risk. It also galvanizes behavior toward lowering risk and achieving shared goals.

The KPN case study that follows, drawn from Willcocks et al. (2011), illustrates these propositions in action in a real business situation.

Case Study

KPN: CHALLENGING VENDORS FOR INNOVATION

KPN provides high-quality telephone, Internet, and television services and products and is an all-around provider of ICT services. Consumers in the Netherlands use fixed and mobile telephony, Internet, and TV from KPN. Business customers use an entire array of innovative and reliable services that include everything from telephony, Internet, and data traffic and management all the way through to the management of information and communication technology (ICT) services. In Germany, Belgium, and elsewhere in Western Europe, the services of the KPN group consist mainly of mobile telephony. KPN made a profit of €2.5 billion in 2007 on annual sales of €12.6 billion.

Between 2009 and 2010, the Netherlands business underwent a radical transformation. The All-IP network announced in March 2005 moved into its final phase with the implementation of a new access network. In addition, KPN will pursue a radical simplification of its business at the front end in retail segments and at the back end in network operations. The significant cost reductions that will be generated by this simplification will be used for reinvestment in revenue growth and will lead to improving margins.

Hans Wijns is the senior vice president for innovation at KPN. For Wijns, the maturing of the global outsourcing services market has made it possible to do very large jobs and take large steps in innovation: "You can't outsource innovation. Our responsibility is for time to market, for business development for innovation; we must have the architects. We don't outsource our vision. But we really do believe that innovation can only be done if we use a lot of capacity outside of the company. I really believe that we have to use the knowledge and the power from places like India."

Wijns saw the client as responsible for making the innovation plan for the next few years. He felt that a lot of sector-based innovation no longer succeeds and that KPN would have to find trans-sector innovation in the future. Requirements had to be very clear, and this started at board level. The first step was the strategy to market, and the next was the architecture: "As an example, we

▶

▶ put the designing teams from the several suppliers together in one building and in five months together they built the new IT solution. Designing, building, and testing their own part are the responsibilities of each supplier; we have the integration function and the architecture."

KPN uses a lot of innovation power from its network of suppliers, and not just IT: "We are only the facilitator. We bring together those technologies in IT and in our network and take the products to the customers. We are not the most innovative party. We have to challenge the suppliers for innovation." He stressed that KPN wanted to collaborate and not just manage contracts. A client that only manages the contract has much more difficulty working with several suppliers: "If they are competitive, then we have a special meeting and say this behavior is unacceptable; you have to work together. Collaboration only happens if there is a higher-level goal for everyone. We put in the necessary incentives for them to put their best people on it and they can't succeed without the help of the other suppliers."

The sourcing strategy therefore is long-term relationships with several partners that are focused on quality and delivery. KPN did not want to outsource everything to one party and essentially say, "Okay, we are not involved any more." The board wanted to be involved in its own destiny. "I think that we have to cocreate."

For KPN, innovation is related to what it brings in for the business. In outsourcing the network, cost cutting is not the main goal. Wijns summed up: "We are looking to suppliers that can help us in transformation and not only in the existing network. It has to be a combination of cutting costs and innovation together."

This case study highlights the following learning points for innovation:

- Do not outsource innovation, but make an innovation plan.
- Trans-sector innovation will be the way forward.
- Use the innovation power from your network of suppliers.
- Suppliers need to collaborate with each other.
- Collaboration happens only if there is a higher-level goal for everyone.
- There is a need to cocreate.

Collaborative innovation framework

As a result of their research into innovation in outsourcing arrangements, Willcocks and Craig (2009) developed a framework of effective collaborative innovation: e-leading, contracting, organizing, and behaving. Of these, they suggest that leadership is primary (see Figure 10.2). Leadership shapes and conditions the environment in which requisite contracting, organizing, and behaving can occur. The right kind of contract supports collaborating and is an incentive for the right behavior. The right kind of organization supports teaming among the parties and, through the right behaviors, enables high performance.

Phase 1: leadership for collaborative innovation

Heifetz and Linsky (2004) make an important distinction between technical and adaptive work. Technical problems are rarely trivial, but what makes them technical is that the solution, in the form of specialist know-how, techniques, and routine processes, already exists within the organization's (or a supplier's) repertoire. Managers can delegate such work to specialists and monitor the outcomes (see Table 10.1).

By contrast, leadership deals with adaptive challenges. In fact, Heifetz and Linsky (2004) define leadership as shaping and mobilizing adaptive

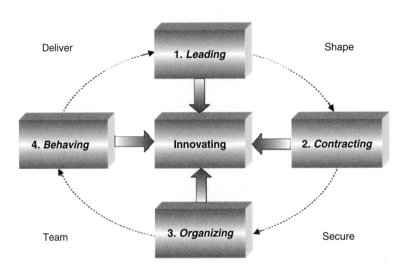

Figure 10.2 The process of collaborative innovation
Source: Willcocks and Graig (2009)

Table 10.1 Technical, adaptive, and innovative work in outsourcing

Issue	Technical approach	Techno-adaptive approach	Adaptive or innovative approach
Problem definition	Clear	Clear	Unclear; requires learning
Solution and implementation	Clear	Requires learning	Requires much learning for all parties
Primary responsibility	Specialists	Specialists and user; participatory	User with specialists; multifunctional teams
Type of problem solving	Technical	Techno-adaptive	Adaptive and innovative
Contract with external services	Outsource	Time materials, resource based	Shared risk and reward; outcomes based
Objective	Efficient use of existing technical know-how	Effective implementation of existing solution in new setting	Effective business solution
Primary leadership	Specialist	Collaborative	Business sponsor champion

work, that is, engaging people to make progress on the adaptive problems they face. For Heifetz and Linsky, the hardest and most valuable task of leadership is advancing goals and designing strategy that promote adaptive work. An adaptive challenge is a particular problem, often difficult to specify precisely, where the gap between values and aspirations, on the one hand, and circumstances, on the other, cannot be closed by the application of current technical know-how and routine behavior. Adaptive challenges require experiments, discoveries, and adjustments from many parts of an organization. When is it an adaptive challenge? When people's hearts and minds have to change; when all technical fixes fail; when conflict persists despite all remedial action; when a crisis arises, indicating that an adaptive challenge has been festering. As we have seen, modern outsourcing is full of adaptive challenges and work that cry out for leadership and learning strategies. And innovation is essentially an adaptive challenge.

As Willcocks et al. (2011) argue, the CEO and senior executives, including the CIO, lead in outsourcing first by shaping its context:

- Formulating and monitoring the sourcing strategy that fits with dynamically changing strategic and operational business needs over the next five years.
- Ensuring that the organization can buy in an informed way through understanding the external services market, supplier strategies,

capabilities and weaknesses, and what a good deal with each supplier would look like.

- Shaping relationships and putting in place a process for managing outsourcing across the life cycle of a deal.
- Shaping the conditions for a contract that delivers what is expected and needed without sustaining hidden or switching costs.
- Developing and sustaining a post-contract management capability that retains control of its own destiny and leverages supplier capabilities and performance to mutual advantage.
- Facilitating the maturing of business managers' ability to manage and own it as a strategic resource, including stepping up to roles as sponsors and champions of major IT-enabled business projects.

Case studies of collaborative innovation are invariably saturated with leadership challenges and responses. Consider the 1999–2006 $600 million human resource (HR) outsourcing deal between BP and Exult that Willcocks and Lacity (2006) described. Here the complexity of taking over an established HR function covering 56,000 employees, and centralizing and standardizing the service, was greatly underestimated. Moreover, the supplier was a start-up, and the premise that its superior technical Web expertise would take BP's HR to a new level greatly underplayed the risks and adaptive challenges. Much leadership at all levels within BP and the supplier was needed over four years to put this deal on an even keel. Even so, Exult lost the rebid for this contract.

Leadership begins in the boardroom with the CEO and other key executives. In their study, Earl and Feeny (2000) found that the CEOs who leveraged IT the best had a vision that IT could transform their business and demonstrated their belief by their own actions. This CEO transformation agenda is also what is needed to achieve innovation with outsourcing collaborators. It also needs a top management team process designed to achieve new things, the relevant CXO (e.g., IT, HR, procurement) as a member of the top team, and a CXO tied to and capable of delivering on an innovation agenda.

Gooding (2002) carried out highly pertinent research on the CIO's contribution to business innovation. His findings, summarized in Figure 10.3, apply equally to other CXOs interested in shaping their organization's innovation agenda. Gooding found the major attributes were being a business visionary, a member of the inner circle, a communicator of direction, an external and internal networker, a purposeful change agent, a holistic implementation champion, and a creator of agile IT. What emerges is how

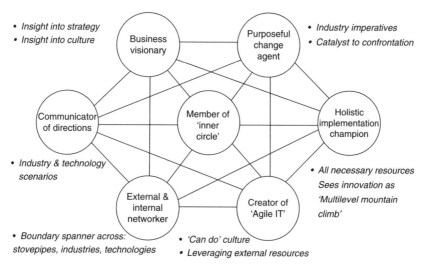

Figure 10.3 CIO business innovation framework

Source: Adapted from Gooding (2003)

fundamentally engaged senior executives need to be, and in multiple ways, if an organization is to shape and move on its own innovation agenda

Phase 2: contracting for collaborative innovation

Leadership, then, creates the environment for innovation. In earlier IT outsourcing deals, especially the long-term strategic alliances signed in the 1990s (e.g., EDS–Xerox, IBM–Lend Lease, BAE–CSC, UBS–Perot Systems), innovation invariably was cited as something the customer expected and the supplier could and would deliver. In study after study, however, Willcocks and Lacity (2009) found that such innovation was not forthcoming and that even large innovation funds rarely produced lasting, important innovations. The same applied to many joint venture and equity share initiatives designed partly to stimulate innovation. They disappointed invariably because they were mere add-ons in mainly fee-for-service deals where both clients and suppliers prioritize service and cost issues well above innovation issues. What, then, is the way forward?

In practice, according to Lacity and Willcocks (2009), senior executives have four main approaches to achieving innovation, each with a distinctive knowledge objective and approach (see Figure 10.4).

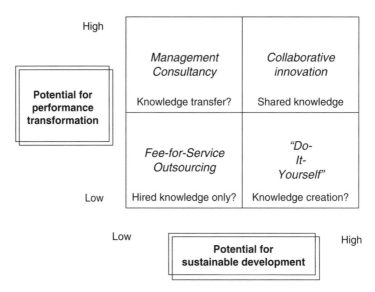

Figure 10.4 Options for back office innovation

Source: Lacity and Willcocks (2009)

Of these four, Do-It-Yourself scores highly on retaining control and keeping the value of transformation within the company. But to succeed, it requires both funding and appropriate skills, either of which may be lacking. It is also the option most likely to encounter internal resistance if senior management does not give a clear signal of its importance.

The Management Consultancy route brings in external energy, gives a clear signal of commitment to major change by bringing in outsiders, and reduces political resistance. The most significant risks are cost escalation, lack of sustainability, and little knowledge transfer.

Fee-for-Service Outsourcing, whether ITO or BPO, can see limited, usually one-off, innovations through reforming inherited back office management practices, streamlining business processes, and fresh investment in new technology, but even where these are forthcoming, the available research shows that the innovation zeal is rarely sustained. The contract is structured around cost and service issues and does not give the supplier an incentive to innovate. There is an overreliance on the supplier to innovate in business areas where innovation should be primarily an in-house concern. The supplier focuses on selling extra services to make further margins and also gets embedded in solving today's pressing crises and operational problems. The employer does not develop or employ people capable of innovating. The customer loses interest in joint boards and often downplays the in-house responsibility to leverage the relationship further.

Some form of Collaborative Innovation is required if sustained, significant IT or back office and business innovations are to be achieved. The greater the innovation ambition, the more this is likely to have a risk–reward component in the contracting arrangement. Collaborative innovation may also take the form of a formal joint venture as in Xchanging's back office deal with the London Insurance Market in 2001 (and ongoing). In that case a jointly resourced and owned third entity was created to deliver service and innovation to the client. Competencies of the third entity, including the transformational capabilities of reengineering, technology exploitation, leadership, customer development, program management, sourcing, and behavior management, are detailed in Chapter 6. However, the approach to innovation has been incremental rather than a big bang.

There could be real dangers in relying on the supplier for technical and business innovation, even where this has been explicitly contracted for. This can be most dramatically observed in examples of transformation outsourcing where transformation is treated largely as a supplier responsibility. Transformation, as the word suggests, can rarely be merely a technical matter and invariably involves behavioral, organizational, social, and political issues. Nor is it easy to define precisely the outcomes – what work is to be carried out, by whom, and how. This means that transformation is about learning, experimentation, and bringing many different forms of know-how together to deal with adaptive challenges. It requires primary leadership and learning by the client organization.

These considerations probably help explain some of the extreme difficulties that the Sainsbury–Accenture IT and logistics transformation outsourcing program experienced. The $ 3.25 billion deal was signed in 2000. By late 2004, the deal had been renegotiated twice, and Sainsbury had announced a 2004–5 write-off of $254 million of IT assets and a further write-off of automated depot and supply chain IT. In October 2005, Sainsbury announced that it was terminating the Accenture relationship and bringing IT back in-house. In practice, the transformation was driven essentially by the supplier, more along management consultancy lines, and the massive adaptive challenges received insufficient leadership attention.

Phase 3: organizing and teaming: the process of innovation

Willcocks and Craig (2009) summarize much of the available learning on the role of organizing and teaming for innovation. Their framework is shown in Table 10.2.

Table 10.2 The leadership challenge: technical versus adaptive work

Challenge	Type of Work	Done By
Technical	Apply current know-how techniques and processes	Specialists
Adaptive	Learn new ways	The people with the problems

Let us revisit the very useful distinction between technical and adaptive work. Technical work requiring the application of existing specialist know-how and techniques can be outsourced relatively safely, assuming competent specialists can be hired. The more that work becomes adaptive, the more leadership is required, and the more that multiple stakeholders need to be engaged with defining the problem and working together on arriving at and implementing a solution. Adaptive challenges represent situations where problems and solutions are unclear, a multifunctional team is needed, learning is vital, innovation is usually necessary, and a general business goal rather than precise metrics points the way forward. The role of leadership is to maintain direction and shape the context and process by which all this can happen. Moreover, the more radical and business focused the innovation required is, the more the leadership role should be played primarily by the client.

In practice, in-house leadership is vital to large-scale IT and back office innovation and transformation because these inherently comprise predominantly adaptive challenges for the organization. But even fee-for-service outsourcing has some adaptive challenges mixed in with, and often mistaken for, technical challenges. For example, tried-and-tested technology introduced into a new client environment bears on existing technical and social systems and presents adaptive challenges. The specialist will need to collaborate with business users and in-house IT people to get it to work. Willcocks, Petherbridge, and Olson (2002) found this time and again in implementing enterprise resource planning and HR systems, for example. In many respects, the techno-adaptive challenges in outsourcing are the most difficult to deal with because they are the most difficult to define and understand in the first place, unlike situations requiring the technical, or adaptive or innovative, approaches outlined in Table 10.2.

Table 10.2. makes clear that teaming across organizational boundaries and functional silos is vital for adaptive and innovative work. All the respondent organizations looking for innovation that Willcocks and Craig cited (2009) had this understanding and were putting it into practice. Two of their examples follow. The first is from Andrew Wolstenholme,

Heathrow Terminal 5 construction director in 2009 (Willcocks and Craig, 2009: 23):

> *We got sufficient leverage and sufficient buy-in and understanding from all the senior executives in the supply chain to say we are prepared to sign up to this. This is about behaviours. This is about how we work together in this unit that we call integrated teams and it appears that you are going to take off our shoulders the traditional commercial risk that we'd otherwise be carrying. In response to that, we need to give you our best people and we need to make sure their reputation is high. This is a very different sort of commercial leverage.*

The second example is from Tom Lamming, in 2009 the vice president of transformation at Telstra who oversaw the IT-enabling component of its $A13 billion transformation program. He commented: "We have 12 strategic technology suppliers... I think a lot about the people and the chemistry and it's not about uniformity and unilateral decision making. We have multiple suppliers, and it's about the ability to team and work together for the outcome."

In the case study earlier in this chapter, KPN also saw the client as responsible for making the innovation plan, but also felt that KPN had to find trans-sector innovation in the future (see the point made earlier in the chapter by Coulter and Fersht, 2010). Requirements had to be very clear and this started at board level. But in building the architecture and achieving delivery, multiple suppliers were needed. In practice, KPN used a lot of innovation power from its network of suppliers.

Phase 4: behavior change: key to innovation payoff

Leadership, creative contracting, and organizing and teaming in new ways build the way to the fundamental behavior changes needed to undertake collaborative innovation. The partnering behaviors required for innovation are summarized in Figure 10.5.

Willcocks et al. (2011) argue that the behaviors represented on the left side of Figure 10.5 are very limiting in terms of what can be achieved by either the client or the supplier. They are essentially tied to an adversarial game, with no third corner to move to. Unfortunately, recessionary conditions often pressure organizations to regress to this default position. Behavior change can come about as a result of a crisis, but lasting collaborative innovation is shaped in the context of prior work on leadership,

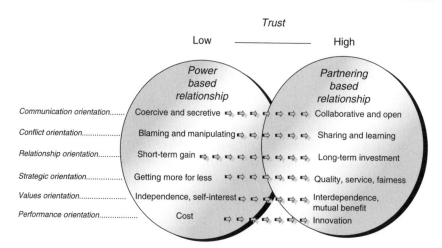

Figure 10.5 power- and partnering-based relationships

Source: Adapted from Willcocks et al. (2011)

contracting, and organizing, which creates rising levels of trust, teaming, and performance.

As Figure 10.5 illustrates, trust is a key component in partnering. Willcocks and Lacity (2009) note that there is no such thing as instant trust in outsourcing. It is built over time through demonstrable performance.

Weeks and Feeny (2008) have developed a useful three-pronged model of trust that reflects the complexities of the outsourcing environment. *Personal trust* refers to the confidence one has that another person will work for the good of the relationship based on his or her integrity and adherence to moral norms. The high uncertainty associated with innovation adds another dimension to this, but all the case histories in this book show how high personal trust means that all parties will accept responsibility for risks that do not work out rather than pointing fingers or deflecting blame. *Competence-based trust* exists when one party has confidence that the other will successfully deliver allocated tasks and responsibilities. This may well include innovation. Successful completion of projects and achievement of joint goals enhance competence-based trust, while operational failures will degrade it. *Motivational trust* refers to where both parties believe the rewards and penalties they experience are geared toward the achievement of joint goals – a win-win situation. As Willcocks and Craig (2009) found in their research, bonus structures and risk–reward sharing mechanisms are elements used to build this type of trust in collaborative innovation efforts. Weeks and Feeny (2008) found that, ultimately, all three types of trust have to be present across all parties for success. The evidence from Willcocks and Craig (2009) suggests that this is true whether the goal is IT operational, business process, or strategic innovation.

Weeks and Feeny (2008) provide an additional significant insight. Against conventional wisdom, they found that effective relationships with high levels of trust also possessed high levels of measurement specificity, defined as the level of detail at which activity is monitored as prescribed in the outsourcing contract and any supplementary arrangements. These measurement mechanisms served several purposes. First, detailed attention to service levels and costs gave the firms a clear idea of where to target innovation efforts. Second, the firms were able to monitor costs and benefits of innovation activities more effectively. Measurement also demonstrated to the parties that the trust in each other was well placed, thus reinforcing future collaboration efforts.

Summary

This chapter makes clear that changing business needs, recession, the globalizing and technologizing of the supply of business services, and the much greater use of outsourcing are challenges that will require many more organizations to make a step-change from outsourcing management to collaborative leadership if governance, control, flexibility, innovation, and superior business outcomes are to be outsourcing's consequences.

It emerges that innovation using the external services market is increasingly realistic as both clients and suppliers are maturing in their ability to go beyond traditional outsourcing relationships and build the collaborative arrangements necessary for innovating. But innovation with large-scale, long-term impact requires deep collaboration within clients, and with and across their external suppliers. Without this, innovation, and the consequent high performance, cannot be delivered. Thus, collaborating to innovate requires a change in objectives pursued, relationships with suppliers, and how work and innovation are conducted.

Leadership shapes the context for collaboration, innovation, and high performance and is primary. New forms of contracting are required for collaborative innovation to succeed. Such contracts share risk and reward in ways that incentivize innovation, collaboration, and high performance to achieve common goals. Organizing for innovation requires more comanaged governance structures and greater multifunctional teaming across the organizations and people responsible for delivering results. Teaming now requires the ability to collaborate within a client organization, between client and supplier and between suppliers in multivendor environments. Leading, contracting, and organizing in these ways incent behavior and enable collective delivery of superior business performance. High trust is a key component and shaper of the collaborative, open, learning, adaptive, flexible, and interdependent behaviors required.

CHAPTER 11

Offshore captive centers

Introduction

Offshore captive centers are one of the sourcing models available to firms within the broad range of sourcing models. While most of the literature on outsourcing and offshoring has focused on a third-party sourcing arrangement, this chapter will solely examine the option of in-house, however, from an offshore or nearshore location. The key aspects examined in this chapter are:

- The history of the captive centers industry
- The strategies captive centers have pursued
- The trends and changes in the captive centers industry

Background

Throughout the past few decades, large multinational companies such as General Electric, Texas Instruments, and Motorola have established captive centers in various foreign countries, most notably in India.[2] Captive centers are wholly owned subsidiaries that provide services, in the form of back office activities, to the parent company from an offshore location. While traditionally they have kept most of their offshore tasks in-house, numerous information technology service providers that have emerged within the Indian marketplace have developed the capabilities to execute both simple and complex work projects – a few of the most recognizable companies being Tata Consultancy Services, Infosys, and Wipro. These companies can often provide services at a lower cost than their Western competitors.

---

2 For more about captive centre strategies see Oshri I. (2011). *Offshoring Strategies: Evolving Captive Centre Models*, MIT Press, Boston.

This development has enabled Western multinationals to consider alternatives in the way they implement their offshoring strategies. As just one example, in 2006, SAP Hosting Services in Bangalore outsourced several of its services to Tata Consultancy Services, also based in Bangalore. Many other companies have pursued an approach in which certain specific, often noncore, activities have been outsourced to local service providers, while core activities remain in-house (i.e., in a captive center). Other companies, such as Standard Chartered and Hewlett-Packard, have followed a different approach in which their captive centers provide services to both the parent company and external clients.

Other companies seem to have outgrown their offshore captive strategies. British Airways, for example, sold a majority stake of its captive center to a private equity firm, Warburg Pincus, in 2002. Apple went even further and shut down its development center in India in 2006.

The worldwide economic crisis beginning in 2008 has raised many questions about the continuing viability of captive center models in sourcing. The worldwide drop in demand for goods and services has significantly affected companies in all industries. Questions of efficacy have surfaced as major Fortune 250 companies divested their captive endeavors throughout late 2008 and 2009. In October 2008, Citi divested its BPO center in India to TCS, and in May 2009, it sold its Indian IT center to Wipro. Similarly, AXA sold its 600-person center to Capita Group in May 2009. Dell has also been a major contributor to the sell-off phenomenon. In October 2008, it sold its El Salvador support center to Stream Global Services; in March 2009, it sold its Pasay consumer tech support center to Teleperformance.

And this is just the tip of the iceberg. The year 2009 saw sales of captive centers in India by American Express, UBS, and AIG as well. Indeed, some commentators predict that captive centers are no long needed. David Rutchik of Pace Harmon, an outsourcing consultancy, believes that captive centers have become a drain on many companies: "The larger issue is that these captive centers are difficult to manage and quite a distraction from a company's core business. They haven't been the panacea they were expected to be." Rutchik cites several reasons for this. First, captive centers represent a large, fixed cost for companies. In times of recession, getting these captive centers off the books and gaining some much-needed capital from the sales offers a short-term benefit. Second, as Indian and other outsourcing providers have improved their capabilities over the last few years, Rutchik thinks that captive centers may no longer seem worth the effort: "It takes a lot of overhead and management attention to manage internal facilities... You're exposing yourself to a lot of administrative burden just to do back office type work in lower-cost locations."

However, in spite of these and other divestitures, the captive center model, according to the latest data by Everest Research Institute, has not collapsed. As of the fourth quarter of 2009, captive projects were in fact beginning to rebound. Everest reports that in the third quarter, there were 28 captive announcements compared to 40 in the fourth quarter, a 24-month high. Salil Dani, senior research analyst for Everest, states that although there were many divestitures of captive centers in 2009, more new captives were established than there were divestitures: 20 to 30 new captives announced per quarter compared to three to four divestitures. Dani cites risk and sensitivity preferences and regulatory considerations as main drivers of the captive model.

Everest Research also revealed other significant trends in both captive and third-party outsourcing models. India and the Philippines continue to account for 40 to 45 percent of new delivery centers for both captive and third-party entities. There were 35 new captive announcements and a marked increase in offshore activity in Brazil, China, India, and the Philippines, with 44 new delivery centers.

These developments bring to the fore significant challenges. First, how should a parent company strategically perceive its captive center in view of its allocation and use of resources? Second, what sets of capabilities should companies develop offshore to support the evolution of a captive center?

GLOBALSOFTWARE

GlobalSoftware, a leading software developer, planned to set up a product development center in India in the late 1990s. According to the codirector of the captive center, "India has excellent people and it provides many opportunities to grow fast."[1] When the captive center was established, the Internet boom was at its peak and IT companies were in need of talent and skills. Alain, the director of Process Improvement and Performance Management, recalls: "There was an arbitrage of costs and to certain extent some pressure to recruit the people."

In 1998 GlobalSoftware acquired IndiaTesting, a company that provided front office software for marketing and business operations. The acquired company already had a team of 70 experienced

---

1 Singapore Press Holdings Limited. (1999, August 13). Bangalore tech par signs on more investors. *Straits Times*. p. 1.

software professionals, who immediately started to work on the parent company's new "Sales Force Automation" project and were directly involved in testing and customization. Within a few years, the captive center was able to expand its activities. Testing was among the most important services because of its cost advantage and effectiveness. For cost reasons, the captive center also hired many young people coming straight out of colleges in India. They were three to four times cheaper than engineers from the home country, claimed the captive center manager of Business Research Extension. In 2002, the captive center employed 500 software developers and received investments of over $125 million from its parent company. By 2006, it had increased the capacity to over 3,000 staff, many of them software developers.

Despite all the success, both the captive center and the parent company had their worries. Top managers from the captive center felt that the full potential of the captive center had not materialized. In particular, managers thought that the software giant still considered its captive center as a back office that should perform low-level tasks cheaply. One aspect of this was that all product development decisions regarding products that were partly or fully developed by the captive center were still taken by the parent firm headquarters. This approach did not allow the captive center to make recommendations about the firm's product portfolio and about the development of product features within the existing product line.

From the parent company's perspective, the captive center's high staff attrition rate was a serious problem. This problem was not unique to GlobalSoftware – many Western companies in India as well as local IT vendors faced the same challenge. "If we have a high level of attrition," said Alain, "we do not get to build domain knowledge. And if we do not build domain knowledge, we do not get more responsibility from the parent firm, GlobalSoftware. If you have an attrition of 25 percent, every two years you virtually start from zero."

Addressing the high attrition challenge

In order to cope with the high attrition levels, the captive center sought to outsource some of the repetitive tasks performed in-house. These were some of the hosting services that provided technical support to both internal and external clients. The captive center also perceived the outsourcing of these services as an opportunity to divert talent from low-value to high-value activities. To accomplish this, the company entered a due diligence process with a service provider that was based nearby and which had had long-term relationships with the parent firm. The outsourcing project was of small scale, about $2 million per year, and it involved the transfer of knowledge and hosting services from the captive center to the vendor over a period of three months, after which the vendor would assume full responsibility of these services. In order to successfully accomplish this outsourcing project, the captive center and the vendor agreed on the governing structure, business processes and knowledge transfer mechanisms and procedures, and the timelines per each major milestone. As the vendor was one of the leading Indian vendors in this area of services, Alain felt that he was in good hands. After all, the vendor had undertaken so many similar contracts that providing the captive center with such services should not be a major challenge. Furthermore, there was also the perception that since the client and the vendor were located nearby, any issue which might arise would be easy to handle over a face-to-face meeting. Having discussed these matters, GlobalSoftware and the vendor were ready to launch this outsourcing project.

By early 2006, not long after their collaboration had commenced, Alain was not satisfied with the vendor's performance. Things got worse later that year. Alain complained:

> *"We are so busy managing the vendor that at times it feels that we could have kept this activity in-house and would be better off. They never catch up with our introduction of new services. We trained their staff and yet we see that knowledge is not retained within their teams. We assumed that their employees, who are Indians, have the same perception as we have regarding quality and service standards. We were wrong!"*

The project manager from the vendor's side, who was also frustrated with the situation, gave a different picture:

> *"True, we suffer from a high level of attrition that affected our ability to retain knowledge. However, the client does not help with their continuous introduction of new services. They want far more than what we can deliver for such a small project. Yes, we have excellent methodologies to capture and retain knowledge*

and we also have service standards. But how can we justify applying these methodologies, procedures and techniques when it comes to such a small project?"

Alain was rethinking recent developments within the GlobalSoftware captive center. Although the outsourcing project was not going so well, he developed a good personal relationship with the vendor's relationship manager. He was hoping that the relationship with the vendor could be improved and that soon the performance would also get better. But what should they do? He was hoping to free up resources who could focus on high value activities and instead his workforce was now tied up in vendor management activities. Furthermore, he was wondering whether this outsourcing contract is changing the original purpose of setting up the captive center? If so, how did this strategy fit into GlobalSoftware's overall strategy?

Research shows that between 1990 and 2009, Global Fortune 250 companies established 367 captive centers worldwide. These 367 captive centers were owned by 137 companies (54.8 percent). Furthermore, 77 of these companies own more than one captive center. Thirty percent of these captive centers have changed their strategy over time, mainly from providing services to the parent firm to servicing external clients, outsourcing to local vendors, or in some cases, being divested, moved, or terminated.

We also argue that offshore captive center strategies tend to evolve based on the strategic intent of the parent company and conditions in the destination country. Therefore, offshore captive centers will gain momentum only as multinationals seek to reap the value of their initial investment in an offshore operation (and in some cases, minimize losses).

A historical perspective on offshoring and captive centers

Offshoring has emerged as a major trend in international business. Over the past decade, the issue of whether to offshore business processes has become one of the most vigorously debated topics in management. Decisions concerning offshoring are rooted in much larger strategic business concerns. Generally companies consider offshoring when they face decreasing profit margins stemming from competitive pressures or are interested in accelerating their value chain activities. Considering this choice is a strategic reaction for companies confronting rising costs and fiercer competition.

The roots of offshoring lie in the mercantilism and imperialism of the seventeenth century. The East India Company first established its own factories in India, recognizing the cost-effectiveness, flexibility, and viability of having a company foothold in the targeted trade country. The idea of establishing company-owned factories in host countries quickly swept commercial trade endeavors and expanded to such industries as sugar and rum processing and trade. Thus, the concept of offshoring has been around for centuries. In the modern day, this has become more visible since US multinationals began to offshore labor-intensive manufacturing processes to low-cost developing countries such as Mexico and Panama.

One significant new development within the concept of offshoring began in the mid-1990s. Companies such as Citicorp and American Express set up offshore facilities to carry out enterprise-wide activities, such as converting data from one medium to another (e.g., converting paper documents to digital data in corporate databases). Since then, significant technological developments, such as telecom bandwidth, satellite technology, and the Internet, have eliminated distance issues, enabling information to be sent around the world in seconds at marginal costs. Overall, a high degree of global collaboration has been evident since these developments in the 1990s.

In *The World Is Flat*, Thomas Friedman describes how a Web-enabled global playing field has been created as a result of the convergence of ten flattening factors, among them the introduction of search engines and work flow applications and the growing tendency to outsource and offshore work. These factors offer a real-time platform for collaboration and knowledge sharing to almost anyone on the globe. Following these developments, information technology requirements such as software maintenance and development could be carried out at lower cost in countries such as Israel, Singapore, India, the Philippines, and China.

In the late 1990s, numerous companies worldwide anticipated major IT problems at the turn of the millennium, dubbed the Y2K problems, for which significant numbers of programmers were required. Reliable, trained programmers were unavailable in local markets such as the United States in the numbers required to address the potential issues the new millennium presented. India had the resources available to adjust software to correct potential Y2K problems envisioned by the business community. One issue arose concerning the quality of the IT services provided in

India: Would Indian companies compare to the expertise offered by programmers and software companies in the home country? The Center for eBusiness at MIT found that projects developed in India only had 10 percent more bugs than comparable projects in the United States. Furthermore, Indian software development teams quickly began using quality assurance programs such as Six Sigma and capability maturity model integration (CMMI) approaches to quality management issues, which made their processes more reliable and equivalent to those of Western software development teams. Although this fact had become apparent to several businesses, more and more companies witnessed the high quality of IT services that Indian companies offered, and soon other activities such as call centers, accounting services, payroll administration, debt collection, and even clinical research were transferred offshore to India. Although most of the jobs transferred offshore were considered dead-end types of jobs in countries such as the United States, they offered relatively high pay to the offshore communities and were viewed with respect.

When companies consider the strategies available with respect to offshore work, they basically look at two options. One is to offshore the desired activities and processes while still maintaining them in-house through the captive center: wholly owned facilities with the purpose of processing activities that were previously done in a company's back office in the domestic country. Alternatively, they can outsource the activities and processes to an external service provider located offshore. Most companies initiate the process of offshoring by choosing one of these two options. Companies have steadily increased the volume of work outsourced to external service providers located offshore, and a large number have also set up captive centers in offshore locations to maintain internal control of the business process.

Most captive centers are set up for one or more of the following three major reasons: to reduce costs, access skilled and qualified personnel, or expand and enter new markets. Indeed, captive centers have delivered value through cost savings, increased productivity and quality, and innovation. One highly visible example of successful captive center offshoring activity is demonstrated by Dell's Indian captive center, which developed process innovations that were later diffused worldwide to other Dell factories.

Some companies began their offshoring experience pursuing both options. For many large multinationals, offshoring some specific operations was seen as an ordinary development, as the CEO of Siemens explained: "Offshoring is a funny thing for an international company. Where is your shore? My shore is as much in India and China as it is in Germany or the US."

Multinationals have set up captive centers in various countries and regions, including India, China, Central Europe, and Latin America. India has nevertheless become the dominant location for captive centers in the world. Since the beginning of this century, the number of captive centers in India has grown rapidly: Among the Forbes 2000 companies, 44 had captive centers in India in 2000, 71 in 2003, and 110 in 2006. Everest Research Group found that large North American and European firms offshored about $9 billion worth of IT and business process outsourcing work to captive center facilities in India in 2006.

Among the most important factors affecting companies in their decision to set up captive centers in India are the country's vast human capital, the sophisticated level of education, and the relatively low language barrier. Indeed, the Indian captive market employs over 200,000 employees and accounts for 30 percent of the Indian offshore services market.

The economies of offshoring are clear. A programmer in the United States, for example, earns around $100,000 a year in comparison to a programmer with the same qualifications and skills in India, who earns $30,000 or less (2008 figures). Farrell found that US companies saved a significant amount of money when offshoring to India. She states that American companies save 58 cents on every dollar spent on jobs moved to India, with the main saving coming from the significant disparity in wages. Additional savings stem from bundling activities in one location, which results in a gain from economies of scale. Moreover the shortage of qualified labor in the Western world is another main driver of the increasing number of companies that offshore business and other IT-related processes.

The technology boom in the 1990s, coupled with the Y2K effect on computer systems, resulted in a significant increase in programmer wages in Western countries. This strained budgets and forced companies to search for alternatives abroad in India, China, and countries in eastern Europe. Technological advancement and availability has been one of the main drivers of service offshoring worldwide. These technological developments made the dispersal of business activities across the globe over the past decade possible. The rapid development in telecommunications and related areas, such as the Internet, is another facilitating factor.

According to recent research by Oshri and Kotlarsky (2009), access to skills is the most important motivator affecting the decision to offshore IT and business processes, followed by costs saving as the second driver. The results of our survey represent the shift in executives' mind-set regarding offshoring. It is about accessing skills and expertise not available in-house rather than only achieving reductions on the IT cost-base. Offshoring is also about opportunities and not just exploitation. However, we acknowledge that in some business processes, cutting costs will continue to be the main driver, such as with call center operations.

Research also suggests that a large percentage of businesses that are currently offshoring certain activities are also planning new projects abroad in the near future. Call center activities are one of the projects frequently cited as an area for new implementation. This phenomenon is surprising because of growing evidence that some large firms, even those from the Fortune Global list, have closed their captive call centers because of customer dissatisfaction. Many of these companies have already moved their call center operations back to their home country.

Setting up a captive unit in an offshore location is not free of challenges and involves more than simply hiring employees, renting a building, and installing hardware. Considering the competitive nature of the offshoring market and high employee turnover, a significant investment is required to obtain high-quality human resource professionals and processes, software development process optimization, state-of-the-art training facilities, engagement management expertise, and service management expertise.

Many other challenges arise through the adoption and implementation of captive centers. For example, some firms have struggled with ever increasing costs, employee attrition, and the lack of integration and management support. Some experts suggest that the nature and purpose of captive centers must evolve for them to be successful; for example WNS, previously owned by British Airways, has evolved from a basic captive providing services to a parent firm to a larger center that now provides services to international customers as well. Small-sized captive centers are often hard to maintain because they offer little long-term career growth to employees, resulting in a high level of attrition. Such negative impacts on captive centers have led firms to explore a wider range of strategic options that are available offshore.

GLOBALAIRLINE

In 1996, Nicolas, the now former managing director of GlobalAirline, one of the biggest European airlines, received a warning alarm: if the company wanted to survive, it had to get in shape soon. Profits had declined and the cost-base of passenger processing activities had been rising. Nicolas put together a task force that included the general manager of the engineering department. His task was to analyze cost savings. He noticed that passenger revenue accounting demanded high-volume, low-skilled work that could be moved to a cheaper off-shore location. The passenger revenue accounting unit then had over 600 full-time staff. Though GlobalAirline was familiar with offshore outsourcing, it had not outsourced passenger revenue accounting because it "was the blood of the organization" and had to be kept under control, according to Nicolas.

In August 1996, GlobalAirline decided to establish a wholly owned captive center in India, to bring down costs while keeping control. The captive center was to be run as an independent profit center. India was chosen because the airline had direct flights from the headquarters location. GlobalAirline saw India's infrastructure as developed, which allowed for a relatively easy data transfer process. Culture was not perceived as a problem: the company was already familiar with the local markets and many of the cultural aspects in India. Indian workers were fluent in English and in addition the Indian government provided significant tax breaks among many other benefits.

The captive center was set up under an airline subdivision responsible for providing services and systems to external clients. A general manager who had experience of customer services, sales, and marketing in foreign countries was sent to India to set up the captive center. Shortly after its establishment, the captive center started to offer additional services such as customer relations. "Again, this was a high-volume activity, requiring a very quick turn-around," said Nicolas. "The prime reason for moving customer relations to the captive center was that it was becoming very expensive as a department to run – it needed many extra staff."

As a wholly owned subsidiary, the captive center was not named after GlobalAirline. Its staff were employees of the captive center, not of GlobalAirline, to prevent union problems. A wholly owned subsidiary also had the flexibility to reach third-party clients. Nicolas said: "It became easier for me to make deals. If the captive center had had the parent company's name, there would have been major restrictions."

The captive center started off with 60 employees in a commercial space that could accommodate 300 people. But it grew quickly. Nicolas remembered:

> *"I had a number of companies coming to ask me what we were up to and wanted to know more about our services. Following this, GlobalAirline's top management quickly agreed that the captive*

center should offer services to third parties because it could bring down costs."

However, "there was a lot of skepticism among the middle managers back home about whether the Indian captive center would work," said Nicolas.

This skepticism was unjustified. The captive center successfully acquired third party clients within a short period of time, thanks to GlobalAirline's worldwide alliance programs. When the captive center was launched, the parent company had already formed an alliance with other airlines, which included a trading services program. One key aspect to any success was information security. Being a wholly owned subsidiary that did not carry the parent company's name helped the captive center to be less exposed to security breach attacks and made competitors less suspicious about confidentiality aspects when negotiating deals with the captive center.

Consequently, in November 1996, the captive center was already serving three external clients and was best known for supplying specialist computer skills such as ticketing and computer-based training. In 1998, the captive center broke even as expected and started to offer services to other businesses outside the airline industry, such as insurance. Nicolas said: "Again, the opportunity came partially through the parent company because one of the management directors was also on the executive board of an insurance company." By 2000, the captive center was offering services to nine other airlines and had revenues of $25 million a year.

Following the expansion of the GlobalAirline captive center and its range of services to third-party clients, the captive center management team sought ways to further develop the unit. At that point in time, the captive center employed 1,500 staff, of whom 65 percent were serving the parent company and 35 percent were providing services to third-party clients. In fact, the 35 percent focusing on external clients generated 45 percent of the captive center's total $11 million revenue.

Dave, the former captive center general manager, remembered that when he forwarded the five-year additional expansion plan to the management director of GlobalAirline, the director snapped: "What have you smoked? You have put forward a plan for 12,000 staff, which is about 30 percent extra headcounts for GlobalAirline." The board of the parent company stressed that they were running an airline, not an investment house, and therefore rejected the plan. However, as an external commentator observed: "The future strategy of the captive center requires investments to fully exploit its growing third party client base."[1] Capital was needed to develop skills relating to marketing and sales and building the scale of transactions within the captive center. A clash arose between the parent company and its captive center regarding the center's strategic direction. "It became obvious that the only way for the captive center to advance was to be sold off," Dave commented.

In 2001, GlobalAirline considered a takeover of its captive center by an investment house. The basis for the negotiations was that any agreement should "allow the future growth and development of the captive centre, with the airline company still retaining a significant stake in the business."[2] The negotiations took over 18 months. According to representatives from the captive center side, the airline did not want management overheads in India and was concerned with service quality and costs once the private equity firm assumed a majority stake of ownership. Losing key employees was another concern. The private equity firm wished to see the new captive center managed without the parent company's influence. It was prepared, therefore, to sack old employees and let its people run operations.

Finally, in 2002, a deal was struck. GlobalAirline announced the sale of 70 percent of its captive center equity stake.[3] GlobalAirline did not intend to be involved in management decisions relating to the captive center, now that its major stake was held by the private equity firm. However, it hoped to still improve the financial performance from this transaction when the eventual value of its 30 percent stake in the captive center would increase.

GlobalAirline chose the private equity firm for two reasons. "Money-wise they came with a good offer," Dave remarked, "and they had the right structure and culture to protect the interest of the airline, the captive center's principal customer." The takeover would also let the airline concentrate on its core business and let the captive center develop new businesses outside the airline industry.

---

1 Dow Jones International News. (2001, November 23). GlobalAirline Starts W. GlobalAirline stake sale talk. *Dow Jones International News*, p. 1.

2 Reuters News. (2001, October 23). GlobalAirline in talks for unit sell-off in India. *Reuters News*, p. 1.

3 Financial Times. (2002, April 4). Companies & finance UK – GlobalAirline sells business outsourcing arm to W. *Financial Times*, p. 1.

The private equity firm was interested in acquiring GlobalAirline's captive center because the captive had established a leading position in the BPO segment in India. "The basis of the captive center, its infrastructure, set-up, and management team, was very attractive," Dave added. GlobalAirline's positive reputation, strengthened by its ISO 9000 certification and Six Sigma model, also helped the private equity firm make this acquisition decision. According to the private equity firm, during the divesture the BPO sector worldwide was poised to witness tremendous growth, and the firm saw the buyout as a valuable investment in building a leading global organization. The CEO of the private equity firm confirmed: "With this captive center, we now have deep domain knowledge of the sector. We will let the new company grow organically as well as through acquisitions in the Indian BPO market." The new chairman of the captive center also thought that the captive center had a great potential to handle complex and varied business processes, as there was no other captive center in India with such large-scale and advanced domain knowledge.

After the acquisition, the private equity firm allotted a considerable sum of money to further develop the services provided by the captive center. The intention was that the captive center staff would increase to 10,000 full-time employees in the next five years. "We can grow organically at 50 percent a year to the foreseeable future," predicted the new captive center chairman.

Within its first year as an independent company the captive center revenue grew by 120 percent, and by 2005 the BPO firm reported $165 million in revenues. Supported by this rapid growth, the captive center went public in July 2006. It then faced new challenges. The Indian government applied different regulations to public BPOs and captive centers. Tax breaks for captive centers shrunk and in June 2006 the captive center was asked to repay service taxes to the government for the period 2003–2005. Meantime, however, the captive center had to satisfy its shareholders, who wanted a higher return on their investment each year.

Despite the difficulties, the IPO still allowed both GlobalAirline and the private equity a return on their investments. In 2008, according to Dave, only 10–12 percent of the $460 millions in revenues were being generated by the former parent company. The captive center was able to increase its capacity to over 18,000 employees, who were considered as core staff and no longer as back office workers. This attracted more talent to the captive center and supported the knowledge base developed offshore.

According to Dave, fast growth was possible because the private equity firm spent a great deal of money to "rebuild the communication infrastructure and bring in some very senior management plus their contacts and networks." Fast growth, however, did not come easily. Dave added: "The captive center had to fight for contracts after larger multinational players like IBM had entered India – there are few contracts left in the market not taken by the big companies."

Accounting for 40 percent, travel was still the strongest segment of the captive center's mainstream revenue. Banking, financial services, and insurance, however, together generated 40 percent of the revenue. The emerging segments of manufacturing, retail and consumer products supplied the remaining 20 percent of the revenue. According to the director of Investments and Alliances at GlobalAirline:

"The venture has turned out more successful than most of the airline leadership expected. There was no question that the airline made the right decision. The company has benefited from both its initial stake in what later became a successful commercial venture and also from the fact that its business processes are being done by a more efficient and viable entity."

But one might wonder: have GlobalAirline done the right thing? Perhaps they should have maintained ownership of the captive center, considering its success?

One area that requires more in-depth exploration is the question of why offshoring and outsourcing work for some firms but not others. The problem stems from the widely held view that offshoring is a universally applicable solution for reducing costs, creating flexibility, and broadening access to the required talent pool that is not currently available in the home country at a reasonable cost. Contrary to popular belief, offshoring is not a single strategic model applicable to every business need, intention, or process. Rather, it comprises a variety of models, each with its own risks and benefits to consider and address. Successful offshoring depends heavily on choosing the appropriate model to fit the specified business need as much as it does on a cost–benefit analysis of performing the same activities at home.

Captive center strategies

We have identified six fundamental types of captive centers (see Figure 11.1). The basic captive center focuses on providing services to the parent firm only, the shared captive center services external clients as well, the hybrid option refers to the case when a captive center outsources an offshored operation to a local vendor, the divested option encompasses the sale of part or all of the captive center by the parent firm, the migrated captive center suggests the relocation of the business unit to another location, and the terminated captive center represents the case in which the captive center was closed down.

Our research shows that the basic captive center has evolved into a hybrid, shared, or divested model. In our data set, we identified three evolutionary paths: basic-shared-divested, basic-hybrid, and basic-divested; however, one can envisage nearly any evolutionary path depicted in Figure 11.1. In some cases, the captive center will initiate its own evolutionary development (basic-hybrid); in other cases, especially those involving ownership changes, the parent firm will decide which path the captive unit will follow (basic-divest or basic-shared-divest). The terminated captive center and the migrated captive center do not offer an evolutionary path.

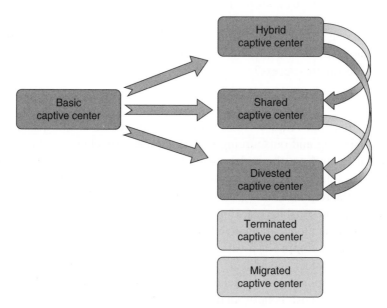

Figure 11.1 The six fundamental types of captive centers (Oshri, 2011)

Future trends in the captive industry

Today firms have allocated about $1.7 trillion to manage and process back office operations. With an annual growth of about 5 percent in outsourcing and offshoring and the emergence of new offshoring locations (estimated at about 125 countries around the globe) that are offering IT and business processes services, captive centers will continue to play a role in sourcing arrangements. We have identified seven trends for the present and future of captive centers.

1. More captive centers will be built by large firms looking to reduce costs and access skills that are not available in-house.
2. Central and eastern Europe will emerge as the most attractive location for European multinationals to set up captive centers in the next five years. Nearshoring, which is the sourcing of IT and business services to a relatively close country, will also be a strong trend in captive centers for North American multinationals.
3. Captive centers will continue to be sold for two main reasons: many captive centers (at the moment about 60 percent) will struggle to become or remain successful and therefore will drive their parent firms to look for a buyer. Captive centers that have built large scale or developed an area of specialization complementary to the commonly found expertise in the local vendor market will become attractive for an investment house or a local vendor and therefore will eventually be divested.
4. Large captive centers in maturing and mature outsourcing markets such as India will expand outsourcing offshore activities to local vendors in an effort to transform the captive center from a service and cost center into a profit and innovation center and free up talent to focus on value-adding activities.
5. Small- and medium-sized enterprises will explore ways to use existing captive center facilities as pools of expertise in order to reduce costs as well as access skills at a global level. This will accelerate the evolution of captive centers into the shared captive center model.
6. Many multinationals with captive centers will struggle to sell their offshore assets. These are mainly captive centers that failed to build up scale or develop a unique area of expertise that is complementary to the mainstream line of expertise commonly found in the local vendor market.
7. The captive center concept will move from the experimentation stage to the maturity stage, significantly reducing the number of captive center terminations.

WNS BUYS AVIVA'S CAPTIVE CENTERS

On July 10, 2008, Aviva announced that it would sell its five captive centers (Aviva Global Services), located in India, to WNS. With the sale, it signed a contract, extending over eight years, in which WNS would provide offshore services to Aviva.

Since 2004, Aviva had offshored its finance and accounting division to captive centers in India and Sri Lanka. Aviva set up these centers using the build-operate-transfer (BOT) model and worked with three BPO vendors: EXL, WNS, and 24/7. The essence of this model is that the client contracts with an offshore or nearshore vendor to execute an outsourcing arrangement whereby the vendor builds and operates the service center (a call center or any other business process) for an extended period of time. The client retains the right to take over the operation under certain conditions and certain financial arrangements. On July 3, 2007, Aviva announced that it was bringing back over 300 accounting professionals from WNS to Aviva Global Services as part of the BOT agreement, signaling its intention to take over the virtual captive center eventually.

A year later, however, Aviva announced that it was selling its offshore operations to WNS and signing a contract to receive BPO services worth $1 billion. According to Aviva, it selected WNS because of its proven operational performance and the fit between the cultures and values of both firms. Aviva also believed that WNS truly understood the insurance industry and that the BPO provider had demonstrated commitment and customer care.

The outsourced services include life and general insurance processing services covering policy administration and settlement, finance and accounting, customer care, and other support services. Aviva also indicated that by early 2009, 6,000 professionals would be transferred from Aviva Global Services to WNS, some of them transferred back only a year after they joined Aviva. It explained the reason for this strategic move as protection from rising inflation in India and fluctuating exchange rates.

WNS, which is facing increased competition in the BPO industry, benefited from its acquisition of Aviva Global Services. In 2009, the BPO provider's revenues increased by 17 percent, and it expanded its service offerings and market share.

Conclusion

In this chapter we examined the evolution of the captive center industry and how this evolutionary path resulted in the diversification of the concept into new strategies. Of particular interest are the growth strategy, shared captive center, which emphasize the potential in long-term investment in captive centers. At the same time, the hybrid model highlights the need to develop sourcing capabilities offshore, critical for the captive center's ability to both focus on higher-value activities and properly manage its supplier base.

Norwich Union: Managing strategic IT-based outsourcing projects
David Feeny and Leslie Willcocks

> The IBM solution is recommended because the higher risk of delivery is outweighed by the potential to provide Norwich Union with greater competitiveness in the Life and Pensions Market.
> — Roger Taylor, October 1994

> It should have been the perfect partnership.
> — Roger Taylor, June 1996

In December 1995, Philip Scott – general manager of the Life and Pensions (L&P) business of Norwich Union (NU) – presented to his colleagues on the Group Board a progress report on the implementation of L&P's business systems strategy (known as CLASS (Client Administrative Service Systems)). He was able to note a number of major achievements:

- Under the restructuring and reskilling plans instigated by Roger Taylor, L&P's Head of IT, staff numbers had reduced by 40 percent but productivity had more than doubled.
- The rollout of Image technology, part of the wider CLASS project, had been successfully completed ahead of schedule and Norwich Union was now believed to be the largest user of such technology in Europe.
- Development of L&P's client server/communications infrastructure had also made excellent progress and was similarly expected to reach completion ahead of schedule

However, another component of the CLASS project had experienced major difficulties. L&P's executive management now had little confidence that the attempt to replace existing policy management systems with a new generation based on IBM's Insurance Application Architecture (IAA) would succeed on anything like the planned timescale. Scott asked for and received his colleagues' agreement to exercise the escape clause within NU's contract with IBM. He informed IBM UK's chief executive, Barry Morgans, of NU's decision in a letter dated December 11, 1995.

As he reflected during the coming months, Scott became convinced that there was important potential learning from the successes and disappointments of the CLASS project for both NU and IBM. He asked Barry Morgans whether IBM and NU could cooperate in the creation of case study material which would enable this learning to be achieved.

Business background to the CLASS project

From its early origins in 1797, the Norwich Union Life Insurance Society became established as one of the three largest providers of life and pensions products to the UK market. (With premium income of more than £2 billion, UK Life and Pensions is the largest business of the Norwich Union Group. The group had more than £40 billion in assets under management in 1995. It includes a major UK General Insurance business, with 1995 premium income of £1,372 million, and smaller businesses operating in life and general insurance markets beyond the UK.) Its business history reflects the wider pattern of the industry, which for decades could be characterized by words such as "stable," "cautious," and "gentlemanly." Government rhetoric and legislative changes in the 1980s then prompted sudden extraordinary growth, fierce competition, and upheaval in distribution channels. NU's premium income from life and pensions quadrupled between 1985 and 1991. However, widespread allegations of industry misselling damaged consumer confidence which led to a difficult five-year period. In NU's case, UK premium income fell by nearly one-third in 1992, and in 1995 was still 24 percent below its 1991 peak.

Renewing the sales growth was not the only – or indeed the most pressing – problem which Philip Scott faced in July 1993, when he moved from being group finance director to general manager of UK Life and Pensions. During the heady years of market expansion, many new and complex products had been launched without sufficient regard for their administration needs over what might be decades of active life. As support systems creaked and staffing soared to fill the gap, the 1980s created a legacy of high costs and poor client service.[3] (L&P's products were sold to consumers primarily through thousands of independent financial advisers. Hence client service involved response to both these advisers and direct consumer contacts.) In Scott's view the business need was for transformational change, to achieve radically different levels of cost, service, and time to market. The L&P management team formally embraced the language of business transformation, and it was in this context that the CLASS project was conceived and adopted.

IT background to the CLASS project

While the businesses needed IT support for its transformational agenda, it was clear to Scott that the IT function itself was in need of urgent management attention. Until recently IT had been almost entirely centralized, operating as a support service across NU's constituent businesses. The familiar dissatisfactions with this sort of arrangement – high costs and lack of responsiveness – were being strongly voiced at the beginning of the 1990s, and a review by Coopers and Lybrand led to adoption in 1993 of a "federal" IT structure. L&P now became responsible for its own systems development needs, and more than 400 IT staff were transferred into the business. However, changes in organizational arrangements could only be a first step in the achievement of more effective IT support. Scott perceived that when he took over as general manager, "our IT was just not delivering, and the cost was going up exponentially." In January 1994 he brought in Roger Taylor and gave him "quite a simple brief... to double productivity in 12 months."

This was not the sort of brief to daunt the new IT Head, whose previous career included 13 widely travelled years in BP. "I'm not your typical technically driven IT man," explained Taylor. "I am essentially a businessman. My style has always been to hit the ground running, play things straight down the line, no politics, say it as it is. Basically I am a trouble-shooter." He quickly set up five major initiatives, four of which addressed the inherited operational problems:

- To improve relationships and create a business/IT partnership, support teams were set up, aligned to each department, to handle day-to-day activity and minor systems enhancements.
- To improve delivery track record, any development requiring more than six man-months of effort was transferred into a formal development team and subjected to "full project management disciplines."

- To eliminate demarcation and overmanning, the myriad existing job profiles and descriptions were scrapped and replaced by simplified professional and managerial profiles with a three-level structure.
- To enhance development productivity, a client-server environment was introduced, to largely replace NU's traditional mainframe orientation.

Building on the achievements of these initiatives, Taylor "downsized" the IT function by around 40 percent in January 1995, without loss of momentum. While total cost reduction was less dramatic (some contractors were employed to introduce new skills), the measures in place demonstrated that Taylor could claim to have largely fulfilled his initial brief.

The fifth initiative, which took place in parallel with all this activity, was to develop a forward systems strategy which was truly aligned to the needs and priorities of the business. By the mid-1994, a small group of Taylor's senior people put together a three-phase strategy designed to fundamentally change the systems support provided to the business.

The reskilling and repositioning drives represented by the first four initiatives comprised one component of Phase One of the strategy. In addition Phase One embraced a number of major new developments. The Continuum Company's Life 70 package would be replaced by a new "contract engine" to support the management of existing and future policy products. A "Client Repository" data warehouse would be created to enable customer-based rather than policy-based service. Call center and electronic data interchange (EDI) technologies would be introduced to transform the existing means of communications between customers, distribution channels, NU branch offices, and the center. In combination, these developments would provide the required breakthrough in L&P's ability to provide high-quality service at low cost for existing products, and to rapidly launch and support new products. Phase One also envisaged replacement of L&P's current finance and accounting systems by package-based products.

Outlined in more general terms was Phase Two of the strategy, starting in 1997, in which other existing legacy systems would be replaced. And a Phase Three would identify and address aspects of L&P's business that were currently unsupported by IT.

In agreeing to adopt the strategy, the L&P Board recognized that extensive use of external resources would be required to achieve the new development components of Phase One. The search began for suppliers who could work with NU to achieve these components on the aggressive timescale which the business required.

Selecting suppliers for the CLASS project

Although the general market for IT products and services is very large, the systems support needs of life and pensions businesses have long been recognized as specialized and demanding. This is particularly emphasized in the UK, whose financial services providers have led the large-scale introduction of complex and sophisticated unit-linked investment products. As a result, NU approached just three suppliers with initial requests for information: the Continuum company, IBM, and Oracle. Continuum in 1994 was the established specialist in the sector, and indeed held an almost monopoly position as provider of policy management systems for the life and pensions market. NU had been a major customer of Continuum since 1985, when they installed the Life 70 package as the "contract engine" to support L&P's first unit-linked products. Interestingly even in 1985, Life 70 was seen as an interim solution. From 1985 through to 1994, NU joined with other life companies in providing funds for the development of Continuum's target successor package, CCA2.

NU was also a major and long-established customer of IBM, but principally for that company's mainframe range of products. In 1994, IBM was going through its own process of transformation, adapting to the major changes which had occurred in hardware and software markets, and the emergence of a large and growing market for IT services. NU already had some involvement with the IBM business unit, which now focused on creating products for the insurance sector. In contrast to Continuum's package-based approach, this IBM unit was developing an insurance application architecture (IAA) that they believed could be the basis for rapid development of bespoke policy management systems. IBM also had a well-established position in imaging technology and was perceived to possess strong project management skills.

In evaluating responses to their request for information, NU found confirmation that both Continuum and IBM were obvious candidates as potential suppliers. While Oracle was a large and respected supplier of software to the general market, they were seen to lack the ability and inclination to provide the envisaged project leadership and were excluded from further discussions.

A formal Invitation to Tender (ITT) was issued by Taylor to Continuum and IBM on August 4, 1994. It ran to more than 200 pages and addressed the context and scope of L&P's requirements, the form of response to be provided and the proposed contractual terms. All Phase One developments from the business systems strategy were included, notably the provision of a new contract engine to replace Life 70, imaging technology and workflow management, client repository and call center capability, and outbound communications infrastructure. While it was made clear that significant numbers of NU staff would be provided to the development team, the ITT called for responses on a fixed price-basis with the supplier taking full responsibility for the complete project on a turnkey basis. (Suppliers could also volunteer alternatives to a fixed-price approach that "would facilitate greater opportunity for sharing the risks and rewards associated with a project of this scale.") Required completion dates were defined for each component of development, ranging from nine months for imaging/work flow management support, to 30 months for migration of all products to the new contract engine. Payment schedules would be linked to these completion dates, and therefore to the realization of business benefits by L&P. Initial responses to the ITT were required by August 30. After further discussions with NU staff, both suppliers made their final submissions on October 12.

In a number of respects, L&P Board members found there was little to choose between the two submissions. Both represented total external costs of around £30 millions, with no significant differential. Each supplier was seen to be well able to deliver three components of the solution – imaging/workflow management, client repository/call center, outbound communications – either directly or through use of agreed subcontractors. Discussion centered therefore on the requirement for a new contract engine, an area where neither bid was seen to be wholly convincing, but for quite different reasons.

Continuum's CCA2 was already seen to possess 60 percent of the functionality required, and the company undoubtedly possessed extensive experience, understanding, and skills in the insurance industry. On the other hand, after more than ten years of development of CCA2, the package still fell well short of NU's needs, and Continuum was known to be in some difficulty with meeting their commitments to other major insurance companies. L&P executives were also concerned that the outcome of a decision for Continuum might be a cumbersome all-embracing package that was closely controlled by the supplier. NU might face future disadvantages such as high ongoing supplier costs and lack of systems flexibility.

The IBM position was almost a mirror image. Its contract engine solution was based on a new approach: the use of IAA to rapidly drive out systems requirements and turn them into new code. Yet little was known of IAA, and IBM refused to provide details in order to protect its intellectual property. There were also strong concerns that IBM, lacking in-depth knowledge of the life and pensions industry, had seriously underestimated the size of the task. But if IBM did deliver, it was clear that NU would have taken a quantum leap forward and would be in a position of competitive advantage for years to come. There might even be new revenues for NU through operation of administrative services for other life companies. As one senior NU staffer colorfully described it, it was like a choice between an experienced but ageing lady of the night and an 18-year-old virgin.

Two further considerations weighed heavily in the minds of L&P executives and influenced the final outcome. First, they were all conscious that NU had provided Continuum with development funding for the past ten years, with little to show for it. Did Continuum deserve a new vote of confidence? Second, IBM was seen to be very highly motivated. Its insurance business unit was desperately keen to break into the market in a major way and saw the NU project as the available springboard. In addition, the IBM bid had the personal backing of Javaid Aziz, IBM UK's charismatic chief executive. Aziz was quoted as saying that "not winning the business at Norwich Union will hurt IBM. But winning and then not delivering it successfully will harm us enormously." L&P executives reasoned that while the IBM solution was high risk, the company had the technical and project management resources to get them out of trouble and the management commitment to deploy them when necessary. IBM became the preferred provider.

Contracting for the CLASS project

The task was now to achieve a satisfactory contract between NU and IBM for completion of what had become known as CLASS (Client Administrative Service Systems). A number of risks had been identified – and Insurance companies are alert to managing risks. The contract formalized IBM's responsibility for overall program leadership and delivery of all components within the fixed price submitted. Milestones were defined for each strand of development. The first major milestone in development of the new contract engine was that detailed requirements should be created and agreed with NU by September 1995. Payment schedules were detailed, with the first payment becoming due in January 1996 on completion of the image/workflow management system. There were provisions for liquidated damages to be paid on late completion of any deliverables.

In addition the contract contained a termination clause. NU had identified three related risks in the IBM solution: that IBM lacked experience in the life insurance industry, which might have led them to underestimate the complexity of NU's products and systems needs, which might in turn result in substantial project overrun. Taylor believed it could be mid-1995 before IBM understood the full scale of the project. He talked through with his colleagues a scenario in which they were nine months late in delivering the new contract engine. It was agreed that the contract should provide for reexamination of delivery schedules in the final quarter of 1995, after the detailed statement of requirements had become due. If the prognosis was for a delay exceeding six months, NU could cancel the entire contract without penalty (and before the first payment became due). NU would retain rights in the requirements specifications developed, and would be in a position to exercise a fallback option with either Continuum or Oracle.

These tough contract conditions, although agreed in principle by IBM before the October decision, took some weeks to negotiate in detail. A particular setback was the sudden resignation from IBM of Javaid Aziz. However, his successor as chief executive, Barry Morgans (formerly finance director for IBM UK), reaffirmed IBM's commitment. With negotiations complete, there was a formal contract signing ceremony in February 1995.

CLASS project set up

In parallel with the contract negotiations, IBM was working hard to set up their project team.

In November 1994, they appointed John Goble as program director. Goble was by background an accountant with more than 20 years of experience in IBM. He had been increasingly drawn into systems activity, and during the 1980s had been the business-side leader of a project to implement some common financial systems in IBM worldwide. For two years he then worked on a task force looking at the restructuring of the IBM UK organization. He had gone on to be the company's supply operations manager, overseeing the introduction of new systems and processes, which had resulted in radically improved business performance. Goble saw the CLASS project as an opportunity to help achieve for a major IBM customer the sort of systems-led change he had managed in IBM.

Goble's key technical manager, Kenny Lister, for the project was also identified in November 1994. Kenny Lister was a career IT professional with a dozen years in IBM. He had built his career within IBM's own internal systems department, following the familiar progression from programmer/analyst, through systems designer and group leader, to project manager. As IBM built its presence in the emerging IT services marketplace, Lister was one of those who had moved to work on projects for IBM customers. Within the CLASS project, Lister became responsible for almost all of the systems development work. The imaging technology component was set up as a separate subproject under IBM's David Gibbs who also reported directly to Goble.

NU's own direct involvement in the project was to be led by Peter Hardy, one of many senior managers whose whole career had been with the company. After training as an actuary, he now had 25 years of experience in the industry and a particular knowledge of policy administration. In the second half of the 1980s, he had project-managed the launch of NU's new series of pension products, and gone on to build and manage the 800-strong organization that supported the administration of those products. Hardy now had two roles within the CLASS project, to which he was assigned on a full-time basis. Reporting to Goble, he was involved in the logistics of setting up the overall project, and was specifically responsible for the supply of NU resources to the project – including the 20-plus senior business people who were to work full time with IBM on the development of the detailed business requirements. In his other role, reporting to L&P's client services director, Nick Smith, Hardy effectively signed off on behalf of Norwich Union the achievement of each phase of specifications.

Apart from Hardy, NU seconded three other managers to the project. With his combination of actuarial skills and work on the Life 70 System, Kevan Fogg was seen as NU's leading authority on policy management systems – one of the few who understood the full internal complexity of such systems. He and Dick Ong from the Finance Division were designated consultants to the project. In addition, Matt Fahy from Business Systems Division (BSD) took up a line management position, reporting to Goble and responsible for data migration and systems interface aspects of the project.

As project resourcing began to build up, the decision was made to bring the team together within an existing NU facility, Norvic House, a few minutes walk from NU's Head Office. All secondees to the project moved in, apart from the small group working on further development of IAA in Brussels. At the project's peak there were around 200 project staff in Norvic House, of whom about 120 were employed by IBM.

Governance represented the other strand of project setup. Philip Scott and Javaid Aziz (subsequently Barry Morgans) were designated executive sponsors of the project, with overall the responsibility of ensuring that each company met its commitments, and for arbitrating on critical issues. Nick Smith became the business sponsor. As L&P's client services director, he was the line executive most directly affected by the project and the obvious person to maintain its business focus through to achievement of benefits. The nature of Taylor's involvement in the project changed radically at this point. Whereas the Business Systems Division had been driving the initiative prior to contract, IBM now held full responsibility for CLASS development and implementation. Taylor took up responsibility for quality assurance of the project, a role for which he felt that he and his staff were better positioned than a third party could be. A steering group was formed, to meet monthly under Smith's chairmanship. In addition to Smith and Taylor, its members included two other L&P executives – Finance Director Geoff Shaw, and Sales and Marketing Director Tom Kelly. IBM was represented by one of Morgan's Directors, Stuart Rangeley-Wilson, as well as by Goble. Hardy acted as secretary to the meetings.

The CLASS project in action

By January 1995 all the key players were in place and the project was well underway. It was clear to everyone that they had embarked on a major and complex undertaking with challenging deadlines. But both NU and IBM stood to benefit hugely from the successful outcome, leapfrogging their respective competitors and establishing advantage for years ahead. And it was accepted that tight timescales should stimulate and bring the best out of all concerned. The only irritant at this stage for members of the project management team was that the finalization of contract details was prolonging a rather adversarial climate and diverting their attention from the task in front of them.

Unfortunately as soon as contractual negotiations were finally out of the way, the first signs of deeper problems began to emerge. In late February, IBM produced their "analysis stage plan" to produce detailed business requirement for the new contract engine, and Fogg and Hardy refused to sign it off. As far as they were concerned, the fact that IBM was scheduling such a "ludicrously small" amount of resource for the work confirmed their worst fears that IBM had seriously underestimated the scale of this part of the project. The argument about scale became the first of the four issues that dogged project progress over the coming months.

The relatively relaxed response of IBM to NU's concerns about the scale was largely explained by their position on the second issue, that is, the role of IAA. NU's staff were all accustomed to a traditional and time-consuming approach to generating detailed systems requirements. IBM's bid, on the other hand, had always been based on the belief that IAA could be used to very rapidly and efficiently drive out requirements in the course of structured workshops with users. IBM managers reminded their NU counterparts that IAA represented a radically different approach, a new mind-set which was the basis for their own confidence. But in practice, these reassurances failed to take root. User members of the project team reported to Hardy that the initial workshops were a very frustrating experience. They found the IAA-based approach very theoretical, generic, and high level. And when in March Fogg came back from a trip to the IAA development team in Brussels, he was less convinced than ever that the IBM approach was viable. The IAA debate was to prove a lengthy and crucial one.

Trying to resolve these first two issues, Lister pulled together a small working group of his most technically able people. His aim was to define for the contract engine development an overall methodology that commanded everybody's confidence. IAA would be a part of it, but not the whole of it. The need for some more traditional process decomposition work was now recognized. New estimates were made for the analysis stage plan.

At the steering group meeting held on April 21, Goble and Lister reported that the new analysis work was expected to require an additional 20 man-years of effort – with obvious major implications for the cost and timescales of the project. Steering group members reacted in a variety of ways:

- For IBM, Rangeley-Wilson wanted discussions to apportion costs of the unplanned work between IBM and NU. He also emphasized the importance of avoiding unnecessary complexity and suggested the steering group should have a role in containing user requirements. He was reminded that NU's position had not changed from that stated in the ITT. IBM would be expected to step up to its responsibilities.
- Taylor was concerned that the potential benefits of IAA should not be lost through the new approach. NU still required a consistent systems architecture and low-cost technical platform.
- Smith emphasized the need to reassure NU that IBM really had now identified a sound methodology for capturing the detailed business requirements. Lister was asked to demonstrate the proposed new process within the next two weeks.
- The meeting agreed that the priority was to ensure that the program was put back onto a firm footing through the current replanning exercise.

Further concerns surfaced in May with the quality assurance report submitted by Taylor and his team. While recognizing the excellent progress being made in some parts of the project – notably Image – the report included around 50 required action points. It was particularly critical in the project management area, highlighting the lack of clear project plans and the need for a more hands-on style of project management.

While various NU managers expressed it in different ways, it seemed clear that project management had by now become a third critical issue. For example:

- According to Hardy there were "plans that ran into pages and pages; you could paper the walls with them but they told you nothing... The planning activity was purposeless because there was not agreement in terms of what should be done."
- Smith summarized Goble's strengths as "knowing where to find resources in IBM and understanding how to work the IBM system to obtain them. He was the orchestrator of his team with a loose rein on the activity." As the project's difficulties increased, Smith argued that a more performance-driven style was called for.

Taylor's QA report further served to escalate concerns about the project, and Scott started to attend steering group meetings.

The problem of escalation to achieve conflict resolution could be considered the fourth main issue of the project. For several months, there had seemed to be very little progress in the main strand of the project. There was continuing uncertainty about the true scale of the effort required; the IAA debate was getting still fiercer, with opposing views increasingly entrenched; NU were steadily losing confidence in the program management regime IBM had established. How could these issues be resolved?

The steering group was the obvious forum for resolving key issues, but it was experiencing difficulties in exercising this role. The first problem was lack of clear information. As Kelly commented, "There were large numbers of people, nobody could argue that bodies were not actually being put to the job. But there was frustration in terms of what the output was, and the difficulty was finding out why the output was not as great as it might have been." This difficulty was compounded by the fierce but technical nature of key debates, which made it hard for steering group members to engage. And finally there was Goble's personal style, which emphasized reassurance, characterized by Kelly as "we are getting there, things are moving, trust us, etc." As the steering group's chairman, Smith was well aware that if NU executives overrode such reassurance and demanded that IBM make specific changes, they might prejudice the company's ability to make future claims for liquidated damages.

Nevertheless something had to be done. It seemed that the IAA issue was the single most fundamental one. It had become increasingly clear to

NU management that disagreements were not just between NU and IBM on this issue; there were strong differences within IBM. The small number of staff seconded from IBM's insurance business unit remained passionate advocates of IAA and its role in the project. On the other hand, Lister and the majority of IBMers in the development team had no experience of IAA prior to the project; they belonged to the software development business of IBM UK. While obviously committed to the IBM contracted approach based on IAA, they were in fact more familiar with the traditional development approaches known to NU staff. Furthermore, given the difficulties experienced in persuading IBMers to move to Norwich, more than half of those employed by IBM on the project were subcontractors – clearly without prior experience of, or commitment to, IAA. NU members of the project team were very frustrated that a few IBMers, mostly based in Brussels, were holding out for an IAA-based approach which – in their own opinion – had lost the confidence of the great majority of project staff.

Until the argument about the role and effectiveness of IAA was fully resolved, the central component of the CLASS project was more or less paralyzed. Taylor was further convinced that unless CLASS was based on IAA, it could not support NU's future business objectives. In this view, he was supported by Kelly, who consistently argued that there was no point creating a "state-of-the-art legacy system." Only an IAA-based solution could be expected to transform NU's ability to get new products to market in the way Kelly wanted. Taylor flew to Brussels to personally brief Larry Hirst on the critical status of the project. Hirst agreed that his IAA guru Mia Van Straelen should join the steering group and be increasingly available to the project.

The second attempt to resolve IAA's role in the CLASS project climaxed in a fierce debate between Van Straelen and Fogg at the steering group meeting of July 20. It was described by Scott as "the ultimate challenge of the gladiators." After an adjournment while Van Straelen, Fogg, and Lister retired to address Scott's demand for an agreed way forward, it seemed that progress had been made. But once again the issue refused to go away. Neither of the gladiators had perished.

Taylor now focused on project management issues, demanding that IBM get a more effective regime in place. At one point he even volunteered to take over the project direction himself, taking a leave of absence from NU. In September IBM brought in a consulting/audit team, headed by Jonathan Dicks. Their brief was to provide an authoritative statement of the status of the project.

Dicks's team reported at the end of October. A series of top-level meetings followed, including one between Hirst, Morgans, Scott, and Smith. A number of decisions were made:

- Dicks would formally take over as program director, succeeding Goble. It was agreed on all sides that he provided exactly the hard-driving hands-on project management style that NU was now seeking.
- The Image subproject continued to be in excellent shape, and would be carried through to completion under existing management arrangements.
- Based on recent work led by NU's Dalton-Brown, a new and effective way forward had been identified for the Client Repository/Call Center component. It would now be pursued under NU management.
- Outbound Communications represented another module to which IBM could add little value (it was largely subcontracted). It would also now come under NU management.

While the new program director's focus was clearly the contract engine module, and his ability was respected, doubts persisted in NU about the real status of IAA and its suitability for their needs. Scott took himself off to Brussels (he was by now devoting half of his time to the CLASS project) determined to make his own assessment of IAA. In order to break the deadlock he devised what became known as the "spoon test."

> It had become clear that the development of IAA was nowhere near as advanced as we (or IBM) had thought, and basically the solution was to move to more of a pilot mode. My expression was to try and get them to build me a spoon, because if their mechanized approach of producing systems could actually produce me a spoon then I believe it could be cranked up to produce the BMW I wanted. But at that stage they could not actually produce a spoon.

Meanwhile a deadline loomed. If NU wished to exercise the termination clause of the contract, it had to be done before the end of December. It was clear that the Image subproject would complete successfully by January, and major payments would be due to IBM.

Taylor was quite clear that NU should terminate the project. It was beyond dispute that IBM had missed contractual milestones for developing the new contract engine, and that they stood no chance of completing within reasonable distance of the original schedule. The contract had been carefully devised to protect NU from precisely this eventuality. Millions of pounds were at stake.

His colleagues were less sure that this represented an appropriate and sufficient course of action. Apart from concern about the inevitable damage to the relationship with IBM, they argued that they (and the Group Board) would need convincing reassurance that there was an alternative way forward for the business. Taylor and his staff devised an approach based on some reengineering of the existing Life 70 package. He drew the analogy of extending the life of a car by reboring the cylinders or putting in a reconditioned engine. Reengineering Life 70 would allow the business to be supported for a further period until IBM had proved their IAA approach, or a new contract engine package emerged from Continuum or elsewhere. IT reskilling and business process reengineering had already halved the time to launch new products. Further reengineering could halve this again.

Ultimately the decision to recommend termination of the contract fell to Scott. It was, he said, "a pretty lonely single decision. I had Roger Taylor whose view was that we should cancel. I had my business people saying we had invested so much in IBM we should negotiate with them some appropriate way forward. Not least I had to face the Group Board – and tearing up a contract with IBM is not necessarily conducive to career advancement. But I took the view that it had become too high a risk for the business to stick with this horse. I did not think the horse had the capacity to win the race."

On December 8, 1995, Scott recommended to the Group Board that the CLASS project contract be cancelled. His recommendations were accepted, and he wrote formally to Morgans on December 11. (Within the final settlement agreed, the details of which remain confidential, NU provided a small amount of funding for six months development work on IAA – basically to continue the "spoon test.") It was a traumatic moment for all concerned.

The CLASS projects: reflections of NU managers

Interviewed in the summer of 1996, the NU managers most closely involved still had clear memories of the events of the CLASS project. They were also ready to volunteer some reflections on what had happened and what might have been.

Probably most directly affected by the outcome was Roger Taylor, instrumental in the birth, life, and death of the project. Taylor was still keenly aware of the project's original promise: "NU and IBM had a mutual need within the market. We needed a new policy administration system, and they needed an insurance company to develop one with. Strategically we shared a common vision and a common goal. It should have been the perfect partnership."

All were conscious of positive outcomes from the project. The most obvious examples sprang from the introduction of imaging technology. Kelly and Smith both explained how this had enabled a radical and highly successful reorganization of NU's branch and service unit operations. It was now possible to move work to people in a very flexible way. Smith also stressed how the introduction of image had helped him to remotivate and reinvigorate the staff of the Client Services Division, giving a psychological boost to a workforce that had been under the hammer. Kelly was confident that the ongoing introduction of call center technology would enable another tremendous move forward in NU's service to clients.

Both Kelly and Smith also stressed positive outcomes of CLASS that were less obvious. In Smith's words, the challenge and momentum of CLASS, while in some ways distracting management attention, had also served as "a catalyst for many of the other things that we moved forward." Kelly gave a specific example. While CLASS had failed to achieve the hoped-for revolution in time to market for new products, it had certainly stimulated a reengineering of the process which had foreshortened previous timescales, and had raised awareness of the continuing importance of new product introduction.

When questioned about what might have been done differently, there were several references to the generation of business requirements. Taylor had hoped for a more proactive approach here by NU staff within the project. Shaw and Hardy both felt strongly that the creation of detailed requirements should have been the formal responsibility of NU, not IBM, and they should have been created before the start of the project. (Subsequent to CLASS cancellation, Shaw had sponsored an in-house project to document the requirements. It had consumed about 50 man-months of effort and was recently completed successfully.) IBM would then have had a clear start point and would surely not have underestimated the scale of the project. There was also some questioning of the role of Business Systems Division. Hardy believed that BSD had too dominant a role in the creation and management of the ITT. Shaw, on the other hand, suggested that BSD should have been more directly involved within the CLASS project team – perhaps even taking lead management of the project. Adopting the QA role had prevented BSD from making a proper contribution to the project.

Kelly drew attention to the cultural clash within the project, first in respect of the project team: "In suddenly bringing together 200 people from two different cultures – expecting them to work together, understand each other, share a single vision and view – we were probably expecting too much in behavioral terms. It was unnatural." He felt the same issue complicated and detracted from the NU/IBM management interactions: "IBM had a belief in their system, and if you like they stayed at almost a superficial level in defending it. They said, trust us, it will work. We kept saying prove it to us. Now insurance companies are notorious for being conservative, traditional, and detailed; I was not sure at the time whether we were just being awkward and bloody minded. I suppose I had more belief in what IBM were telling us because I could just see our people looking to dot every 'i' and cross every 't', build this state-of-the-art legacy system which I was against. I don't think there was a meeting of minds."

The choice of IAA as a basis for contract engine development was not regretted in general. All were conscious that the Continuum alternative was still deficient for their needs. With due acknowledgment to hindsight, Shaw believed that NU could have discovered more painlessly that there was no silver bullet solution if they had spent more time with IBM prior to contract. Ideally the spoon test should have come first. Fogg had doubts that there would ever be a silver bullet solution. As he explained, all the rapid development techniques which had captured attention in recent years assumed relatively simple systems requirements, the sort of needs which could be contained within the head of the individual. These approaches were simply not appropriate to the development of a life insurance contract administration system where "it takes me and my team weeks to sit down and think through the detailed algorithms and mathematics we need to use." NU now faced a significant period of reliance on Life 70 with concerns about functionality, responsiveness, high operating costs, and declining technical support. They were working on front-end software to create the appearance of superior client service through what Smith called the "Wizard of Oz effect – the awful mess is all behind the curtain."

Finally there were comments about the contract, which had so effectively transferred project risk to IBM. Nevertheless, were there some disadvantages resulting from the arrangements? Hardy believed that relationships were undermined to some extent within the project team, and this had been particularly unhelpful in the critical second quarter of 1995. Kelly pronounced himself a convert on this point, his early concerns about damage to relationships having been outweighed by the commercial benefit to NU. Shaw and Smith both pointed to an insidious temptation: if the contract afforded comprehensive protection, and the supplier had the confidence to step up to it, executives could easily be sufficiently reassured to turn their attention to other things.

Taylor had no doubts. NU had experienced a textbook example of risk assessment, contract negotiation, and contract management. Obviously he was disappointed that the full project could not be completed successfully, but his years in the oil exploration business had taught him to think in terms of sunk costs and drop-dead dates. Was this brand of tough commercial management part of the important learning for NU generally, as the company moved into an ever-more-demanding environment?

Reflections in time perspective

"It should have been the perfect partnership," so why did the project failed? Were there main causes that could have been identified earlier on? And what about lesser factors that led to the final outcome?

In retrospect, what could have been done differently that would have made a significant difference? And was there something about the role of the CEO and CIO of Life and Pensions that led to this outcome? How positive and significant were their contributions?

But there was also the question: What could the supplier have done differently to secure a more positive outcome? And what are the major learning points for strategic IT-based business projects?

REFERENCES

A.T. Kearney (2009). *Offshoring for long-term advantage. The 2009 A.T. Kearney global services location index.* A.T. Kearney, New York.

Agarwal, M.K., Frambach, R.T., and Stremersch, S. (2000). "Does size matter? Disentangling consumers' bundling preferences," Vrije Universiteit, Amsterdam, Faculty of Economics, Business Administration and Econometrics.

Alexander, M., and Young, D. (1996). "Strategic outsourcing," *Long Range Planning*, 29(1): 116–119.

Andriole, S. (2007). "The 7 habits of highly effective technology leaders," *Communications of the ACM*, 50(3): 67–72.

Armbrust, M., Fox, A., Griffith, R., Joseph, A.D., Katz, R., Konwinski, A., Lee, G., Patterson, Rabkin, A., Stoica, I., and M. Zaharia. (2009) "Above the clouds: a Berkeley view of cloud computing." Technical Report EECS-2009–28, EECS Department, University of California, Berkeley.

Aron, R., and Clemons, E.K. (2004). "Process complexity & productivity in off-shore outsourcing of services: evidence from cross country, longitudinal survey data," Wharton Working Paper, http://opim.wharton.upenn.edu/wise2004/sun311.pdf , *Proceedings of the Workshop on Information Systems and Economics*, http://opim.wharton.upenn.edu/wise2004.

Aron, R., and Singh, J.V. (2005). "Getting offshoring right," *Harvard Business Review*, 83(12): 135–143.

Baldia, S. (2007) "Intellectual property and knowledge process outsourcing in India," *Business & Technology Sourcing Review*, Q4, (10): 7–10; Mayer Brown Web site, http://www.mayerbrown.com/publications/article.asp?id=3975&nid=6. Last accessed February 3, 2011.

Brown-Wilson Group Inc. (2008). *The black book of outsourcing: state of the African outsourcing industry 2008.* Brown-Wilson Group Inc., Clearwater, FL.

Bruno, G., Esposito, E., Iandoli, L., and Raffa, M. (2004). The ICT service industry in North Africa and role of partnerships in Morocco. *Journal of Global Information Technology Management*, 7(3): 5–26.

Carmel, E. (1999). *Global software teams: collaborating across borders and time zones*, 1st ed. Prentice-Hall, Upper Saddle River, NJ.

Carmel, E. (2003). "The new software exporting nations: success factors," *The Electronic Journal on Information Systems in Developing Countries*, 13(4): 1–12.

Carmel, E., and Abbott, P. (2007). "Why nearshore means that distance matters," *Communications of the ACM*, 50(10): 40–46.

Chesbrough, H., and Teece, D.J. (1996). "Organizing for innovation: when is virtual virtuous?" *Harvard Business Review*, January–February: 65–73.

Chesbrough, H., Vanhaverbeke, W., and West, J. (eds.). (2006). *Open innovation: researching a new paradigm*. Oxford University Press, Oxford.

Chua, A. L., and Pan, S. L. (2008). "Knowledge transfer and organizational learning in IS offshore sourcing," *Omega*, 36: 267–281.

Coulter, L., and Fersht, P. (2010). *Service providers siloed by vertical industry are stifling innovation with clients*. HfS Research, London.

Cramm, S. (2010). "Does outsourcing destroy IT innovation?" *Harvard Business Review*, July.

Cramton, C.D., and Webber, S.S. (2005). "Relationships among geographic dispersion, team processes, and effectiveness in software development work teams," *Journal of Business Research,* 58(6): 758–765.

Crowston, K., Li, Q., Wei, K.N., Eseryel, U.Y., and Howison, J. (2007). "Self-organization of teams for free/libre open source software development," *Information and Software Technology,* 49(6): 564–575.

Cullen, S., Seddon, P., and Willcocks, L.P. (2005). "Managing outsourcing: the lifecycle imperative," *MIS Quarterly Executive,* 4(1): 229–246.

Davenport, T., Leibold, M., and Voelpel, S. (2006). *Strategic management in the innovation economy*. Wiley, New York.

Earl, M., and Feeny, D. (2000). "How to be a CEO in an information age." *Sloan Management Review*, Winter, 11–23.

Espinosa, J.A., Slaughter, S.A., Kraut, R.E., Herbsleb, J.D. (2007). "Team knowledge and coordination in geographically distributed software development," *Journal of Management Information Systems,* 24(1): 135–169.

Farrell, D. (2006). "Smarter offshoring." *Harvard Business Review*, 85–92.

Feeny, D., Lacity, M., and Willcocks, L.P. (2005). "Taking the measure of outsourcing providers," *MIT Sloan Management Review*, 46(3): 41–48.

Fersht, P. (2010). *Desperately seeking innovation in business process outsourcing: enterprises speak out*. HfS Research report, HfS Research, London.

Gartner report (December 23, 2009) "Gartner on outsourcing, 2009–2010"

Gartner Research (September 2010) "Cloud-enabled outsourcing exemplifies continued evolution in services" ID Number: G00205306.

Ghosh, P.P., and Varghese, J.C. (2004). "Globally distributed product development using a new project management framework," *International Journal of Project Management,* 22(8): 669–678.

Gooding, G. (2002). "The contribution of the CIO to business innovation." Ph.D. thesis, Oxford University, Oxford.

Hagel, J., and Seely Brown, J. (2008). *The only sustainable edge.* Harvard Business School Press, Boston.

Harris, J., and Blair, E.A. (2006) "Functional compatibility risk and consumer preference for product bundles," *Journal of the Academy of Marketing Science,* 34(1): 19–26.

Heifetz, R., and Linsky, M. (2002). *Leadership on the line.* Harvard Business School Press, Boston.

Hendry, J. (1995). "Culture, community and networks: the hidden cost of outsourcing," *European Management Journal,* 13(2): 193–200.

Hennart, J. (1988). "A transaction costs theory of equity joint ventures." *Strategic Management Journal* 9(4): 361–374.

Howe, J. (2008). *Crowdsourcing: Why the power of the crowd is driving the future of business.* New York: Crown Business.

Huber, G. P. (1991). "Organizational learning: the contributing processes and the literatures," *Organization Science,* 2(1): 88–115.

IGate Report (2004). "Six imperatives for the transition phase of an outsourcing engagement," http://www.igate.com/insights/white_papers/6-imperatives.pdf. Last accessed February 3, 2011.

Iivari, J., Hirschheim, R., and Klein, H. (2004). "Towards a distinctive body of knowledge for information systems experts: coding ISD process knowledge in two IS journals," *Information Systems Journal,* 14: 313–342.

Jalote, P., and Jain. G. (2006). "Assigning tasks in a 24-h software development model," *Journal of Systems and Software,* 79(7): 904–911.

Kakabadse, N., and Kakabadse, A. (2000). "Outsourcing: a paradigm shift," *Journal of Management Development,* 19(8): 670–728.

Kern, T., and Willcocks, L. (2000). *The relationship advantage: information technologies. Sourcing and management.* Oxford University Press, Oxford.

Koh, J. and Venkatraman N. (1991). "Joint venture formations and stock market reaction: An assessment in the information technology sector." *Academy of Management Journal,* 34: 869–892.

Kotlarsky, J., and Oshri, I. (2005). "Social ties, knowledge sharing and successful collaboration in globally distributed system development projects." *European Journal of Information Systems*, 14(1): 37–48.

Kotlarsky, J., and Oshri, I. (2008). Country attractiveness for offshoring and offshore-outsourcing: additional considerations," *Journal of Information Technology*, 23(4): 228–231.

Kotlarsky, J., Oshri, I., and van Fenema, P.C. (2008). *Knowledge processes in globally distributed contexts*. Palgrave, London.

Kotlarsky J., Oshri, I., Kumar, K., and van Hillegersberg, J. (2007). "Globally distributed component-based software development: an exploratory study of knowledge management and work division," *Journal of Information Technology*, 22(2): 161–173.

Kotlarsky, J., van Fenema, P. C., and Willcocks, L. (2008). "Developing a knowledge-based perspective on coordination: the case of global software projects," *Information and Management*, 45(2): 96–108.

Lacity, M.C., and Fox, J. (2008). "Creating global shared services: lessons from Reuters," *MIS Quarterly Executive*, 7(1): 17–32.

Lacity, M., and Willcocks, L. (2009). *Information systems and outsourcing: studies in theory and practice*. Palgrave, London.

Lacity, M.C., Willcocks, L.P., and Y. Zheng, (2010). *China's emerging outsourcing capabilities: the services challenge*, Palgrave, London.

Lee-Kelley, L., and Sankey, T. (2008). "Global virtual teams for value creation and project success: a case study," *International Journal of Project Management,* 26(1): 51–62.

Levina, N. (2006). " 'In or out' in an offshore context: the choice between captive units and third-party vendors," *Cutter Consortium: Sourcing Advisory Service Executive Update*, 7(6): 24–28.

Levina, N., and Ross, J.W. (2003). "From the vendor's perspective: exploring the value proposition in information technology outsourcing, *MIS Quarterly*, 27(3): 331–364.

Levina N., and Su, N. (2008). "Global multisourcing strategy: the emergence of a supplier portfolio in services offshoring," *Decision Sciences*, 39(3): 541–570.

Lewin, A.Y., and Peeters, C. (2006). "Offshoring work: business hype or the onset of fundamental transformation?" *Long Range Planning*, 39(3): 221–239.

Lewis, A. (2006). *Outsourcing contracts – a practical guide*, City & Financial Publishing, UK.

Liker, J., and Choi, T. (2004). "Building deep supplier relationships," *Harvard Business Review*, 82(12): 104–113.

Linder J.C., Jarvenpaa S., and Davenport, T.H. (2003). "Toward an innovation sourcing strategy," *Sloan Management Review,* 44(4): 43–49.

Mahnke, V., Wareham, J., and Bjorn-Andersen, N. (2008). "Offshore middlemen: offshore intermediation in technology sourcing," *Journal of Information Technology,* 23(1): 18–30.

Malhotra, A., and Majchrzak, A. (2005) "Virtual Workspace Technologies" *Sloan Management Review,* 46(2): 11–14.

Malhotra, A., Majchrzak, A., and Rosen, B. (2007). "Leading virtual teams," *Academy of Management Perspectives,* February: 60–70.

Mani, D., Barua, A., and Whinston, A. B. (2006). "Successfully governing business process outsourcing relationships," *MIS Quarterly Executive,* 5(1): 15–29.

McCarthy, I., and Anagnostou, A. (2003). "The impact of outsourcing on the transaction costs and boundaries of manufacturing," *International Journal of Production Economics,* 88: 61–71.

McFarlan, F.W., and Nolan, R.L. (1995). "How to manage an IT outsourcing alliance," *Sloan Management Review,* 36(2): 9–23.

Metters R. (2008) "A typology of offshoring and outsourcing in electronically transmitted services," *Journal of Operations Management,* 26(2): 198–211.

Mockus, A., and Weiss, D. M. (2001). "Globalization by chunking: a quantitative approach," *IEEE Software,* 18(2): 30–37.

NeoIT (April, 2005) "Best practices in communicating global outsourcing initiatives," Internal Report by NeoIT, http://www.neoit.com/pdfs/whitepapers/OIv3i04_0405_Best-Practices-Communication.pdf. Last accessed February 3, 2011.

Oshri I. (2011). *Offshoring strategies: evolving captive center models,* MIT Press, MA.

Oshri I., and J. Kotlarsky (2009) "The real benefits of outsourcing," a WBS white paper for Cognizant.

Oshri, I., and J. Kotlarsky (2011). *Innovation in outsourcing,* a WBS report for Cognizant.

Oshri, I., Kotlarsky, J., and Liew, C.M. (2008). "Four strategies for offshore 'Captive' Centers," *Wall Street Journal,* May 12.

Oshri, I., Kotlarsky, J., and Willcocks, L.P. (2007a). "Managing dispersed expertise in IT offshore outsourcing: lessons from TATA Consultancy Services," *MIS Quarterly Executive,* 6(2): 53–65.

Oshri I., Kotlarsky J., and Willcocks L.P. (2007b) "Global software development: exploring socialization in distributed strategic projects," *Journal of Strategic Information Systems,* 16(1): 25–49.

Oshri I., Kotlarsky J., and Willcocks L.P. (2008) "Missing links: building critical social ties for global collaborative teamwork," *Communications of the ACM*, 51(4): 76–81.

Oshri I., van Fenema, P.C., and Kotlarsky, J. (2008). "Knowledge transfer in globally distributed teams: the role of transactive memory," *Information Systems Journal*, 18(4): 593–616.

Outsourcing Institute (2011). http://www.outsourcing.com/content. asp?page=01b/articles/intelligence/oi_top_ten_survey.html. Last accessed February 3, 2011.

Overby, S. (2007). "What does it take to get IT outsourcers to innovate?" *CIO Magazine,* October 8.

Overby, S. (2010). "IT Outsourcing: three reasons why your vendor won't innovate." *CIO Magazine,* May 5.

Prahalad, C., and Ramaswamy, V. (2004). *The future of competition: co-creating unique value with customers.* Harvard Business School Press, Boston.

Puryear, R., and Detrick, C. (2006). "Are you sending your problems offshore?" *Harvard Business Online,* January.

Quinn, J.B. (1999). "Strategic outsourcing: leveraging knowledge capabilities," *Sloan Management Review*, 40(4): 9–21.

Quinn, J.B. (2000). "Outsourcing innovation: the new engine of growth," *Sloan Management Review*, 41(4): 13–28.

Quinn, J.B., and Hilmer, F.G. (1994). "Strategic outsourcing," *Sloan Management Review*, 35(4): 43–55.

Reinhardt, A., Kripalani, M., Smith, G., Bush, J., Balfour, F., and Ante, S.E. (2006). Angling to be the next Bangalore, *Business Week,* January 30.

Ross, J., and Beath, C. (2005). "Sustainable value from outsourcing: finding the sweet spot," *MIT Research Brief*, 5, Number 1A.

Rottman, J.W. (2008). "Successful knowledge transfer within offshore supplier networks: a case study exploring social capital in strategic alliances," *Journal of Information Technology*, 23: 31–43.

Rottman, J.W., and Lacity, M.C. (2006). "Proven practices for effectively offshoring IT work," *Sloan Management Review*, 47(3): 56–63.

Sarker, S., and Sahay, S. (2003). "Understanding virtual team development: an interpretive study," *Journal of the Association for Information Systems,* 4: 1–38.

Savvas, A. (2007). "Firms sceptical about outsourcing innovation." *Computer Weekly*, February 8.

Stanko, M., Bohlmann, J., and Calentone, R. (2009). "Outsourcing innovation." *MITSloan Management Review*, November.

Stewart, T. (2001). *The wealth of knowledge: intellectual capital and the twenty-first century organization*, Nicholas Brealey, London.

Su, N., and N. Levina (in press). "Global multisourcing strategy: integrating learning from manufacturing into IT service outsourcing," IEEE Transactions on Engineering Management.

Taxén, L. (2006). "An integration centric approach for the coordination of distributed software development projects," *Information and Software Technology*, 48(9): 767–780.

Tisnovsky R. (2006) 'IT Outsourcing in the Small and Medium Businesses – There is a Light at the End of the Tunnel', Everest Research Institute Report, last accessed August 10 2011, http://itonews.eu/files/f1213886412.pdf.

Vashistha, A., and Khan, I. (2008). Top 50 emerging global outsourcing cities, http://epam.com/Top-50-Emerging-Global-Outsourcing-Cities.htm. Last accessed February 3, 2011.

Vashistha, A., and M. Ravago (2010). Top 100: a study of the top outsourcing cities, http://www.globalservicesmedia.com/News/Home/Top-100:-A-Study-of-the-Top-Outsourcing-Cities/21/27/10207/GS101111518936. Last accessed February 3, 2011.

von Hippel, E. (1994). " 'Sticky information' and the locus of problem solving: implications for innovation," *Management Science*, 40(4): 429–439.

Weeks, M. (2004). "Information technology outsourcing and business innovation: an exploratory study of a conceptual framework." Ph.D. thesis, Oxford University, Oxford.

Weeks, M., and Feeny, D. (2008) "Outsourcing: from cost management to innovation and business value." *California Management Review*, 50(4): 127–147.

Wegner, D.M. 1986. Transactive memory: a contemporary analysis of the group, in *Theories of group mind*. G. Mullen, G. Goethals, eds. Springer Verlag, New York, 185–205.

Wegner, D.M. 1995. A computer network model of human transactive memory. *Social Cognition,* 13: 319–339.

Westland, J. (2008). *Global innovation management*. Palgrave, London.

Westerman G., and Curley, M. (2008). "Building IT-enabled capabilities at Intel." *MIS Quarterly Executive*, 7(1): 33–48.

Willcocks, L.P., and Craig, A. (2008). "The outsourcing enterprise: building core retained capabilities," *Logica Internal Report*.

Willcocks, L., and Craig, A. (2009). *The outsourcing enterprise: step-change: collaborating to innovate*. Logica, London.

Willcocks, L. P. and Cullen, S. (2003) *Intelligent IT outsourcing: eight building blocks for success*. Butterworth-Heinemann, Oxford.

Willcocks, L.P., and Feeny, D.F. (1998). "Core IS capabilities for exploiting information technology," *Sloan Management Review*: 9–21.

Willcocks, L., Cullen, S., and Craig, A. (2011). *The outsourcing enterprise: from cost management to collaborative innovation.* Palgrave, London.

Willcocks, L.P., Griffiths, C., and Kotlarsky, J.(2009). "Beyond BRIC. Offshoring in non-BRIC countries: Egypt – a new growth market." The LSE Outsourcing Unit report. LSE, London.

Willcocks L.P., and Lacity, M. (2006). *Global sourcing of business and IT services*, Palgrave, London.

Willcocks, L.P., and Lacity, M. (2009). *The practice of outsourcing: from IT to BPO and offshoring*, Palgrave, London.

Willcocks, L.P. and Lacity, M. (2001) *Global IT outsourcing: search for business advantage.* John Wiley & Sons, Chichester.

Willcocks, L. P., Hindle, J., Feeny, D., and Lacity, M. (2004). "IT and business process outsourcing: the knowledge potential," *Information Systems Management*, 21(3): 7–15.

Willcocks, L.P., Lacity, M., and Cullen, S. (2006). "Information technology sourcing: fifteen years of learning," Source: http://is2.lse.ac.uk/WP/PDF/wp144.pdf#search=%22Information%20Technology%20Sourcing%3A%20Fifteen%20Years%20of%20Learning%22.   Last accessed February 3, 2011.

Willcocks L.P., Oshri I., and J. Hindle (2009) "Client's propensity to buy bundled IT outsourcing services," White Paper for Accenture.

Willcocks, L. Petherbridge, P., and Olson, N. (2003). *Making IT count: strategy, delivery and infrastructure.* Butterworth, Oxford.

Name Index

Subject Index